As Certain As Death
Quotations About Taxes
(2015 Edition)

Compiled and Arranged by
Jeffery L. Yablon

Tax Analysts

taxanalysts.com

Main Switchboard:	(800) 955-3444
	(703) 533-4400
Customer Service:	(800) 955-2444
	(703) 533-4600
FAX:	(703) 533-4444

President and Publisher: Christopher Bergin
Deputy Publisher: David Brunori

Editor in Chief, News: Cara Griffith
Editor in Chief, Commentary: Jeremy Scott

Editor: Jasper Smith
Assistant Editor: Stephanie Tomlinson
Copy Chief: Betsy Sherman

Editorial Staff: Amy Kendall, Mary-Elise Sheets, Melanie Simon

Graphic Design and Production Staff: Derek Squires, Stephanie S. Wynn

© 2015 Tax Analysts. ISBN 978-0-9905381-3-4. Printed in the U.S.A.

CONTENTS

Foreword: As Certain As Death – Quotations About Taxes (2015 Edition)

By Jeffery L. Yablon

This is the 10th edition of As Certain as Death — Quotations About Taxes, the collection that I have assembled and Tax Analysts has periodically published over the last 21 years. It contains 2,051 quotations, a 584 percent increase over the 300 quotations that made up the first edition in 1994. That rate of growth exceeds even the rate of growth of the Internal Revenue Code over the same period, but not by as much as one might hope.

The collection is divided into eight somewhat arbitrary and overlapping categories. No claim of completeness is made. For a variety of reasons, many quotations were considered but not included, mostly because I place a special premium on brevity and wit. Four decades of reading the code and its associated Treasury regulations will do that to you.

Although not all of the quotes were traced back to their original sources, great effort was made to avoid mistakes. For example, circulating on the Internet and common elsewhere is a quote about taxes from Andy Rooney, the late television pundit. The quote has a hard edge that sounds like him, but it also has racist overtones that do not. Research revealed that the quote is a hoax and that Rooney did what he could to publicly affirm as much. Similarly, contrary to what many sources claim, Alexis de Tocqueville did not say or write, "The American Republic will endure until the day Congress discovers that it can bribe the public with the public's money."

The collection teaches us, among other things, that tax lawyers are not to be ignored. They are extremely smart, and they are not afraid to say so. Avoiding false modesty and implicitly referencing his own career in private practice, Professor Marty Ginsburg declares: "The tax bar is the repository of the greatest ingenuity in America, and given the chance, those people will do you in." Moreover, the tax lawyers have gotten many others to accept their self-evaluation, as is reflected in the observation of Professor Tony Amsterdam: "It is seldom given to mortal man to feel superior to a tax lawyer." To be sure, as Professor Hoffman F. Fuller writes, "A society which turns so many of its best and brightest into tax lawyers may be doing something wrong." But this misallocation of resources should surprise no one, because, as John

Maynard Keynes observes, "The avoidance of taxes is the only intellectual pursuit that still carries any reward." Alan Bennett's line must also be considered: "Of course I'm happy. I'm a tax lawyer — money's incredible." Law students should note that Bennett's line is from a work of fiction.

Perhaps surprisingly, the collection contains many song lyrics. Unsurprisingly, most are complaints about taxes, tax collectors, and the government generally. But rapper B.o.B. speaks of love: "Baby, you the whole package plus you pay your taxes." One has to admire both the nerve it takes to rhyme "package" with "taxes," and the clear-minded practicality of choosing a romantic partner who obeys the strictures of the tax laws.

The central message, however, is that people often disagree about taxes. Most of these disagreements are fundamentally political, such as whether there should be progressivity in income or estate taxation. "Taxes should be proportioned to what may be annually spared by the individual," says Thomas Jefferson, while J.R. McCulloch tells us, "The moment you abandon . . . the cardinal principle of exacting from all individuals the same proportion of their income or their property, you are at sea without rudder or compass, and there is no amount of injustice or folly you may not commit."

Sometimes, however, the disagreement is not about rates or progressivity, but about what should be taxed and why. Agreeing with many others quoted herein, John Marshall Harlan writes, "There is no tax which, in its essence, is more just and equitable than an income tax," and Williams Jennings Bryan declares, "The income tax is a just law. It simply intends to put the burdens of government justly upon the backs of the people." But Plato says, "Where there is an income tax, the just man will pay more and the unjust less on the same income." The smart Athenian tax lawyers of 24 centuries ago must have made a real impression on him.

* * *

This collection is a labor of love that required an extraordinary amount of time. In the late 1970s, I started a file called "Tax Quotes" into which I tossed every pithy quotation about taxes that I happened upon. The file grew and grew. Once I decided to publish, I realized that finding the quotes was the easy part. More difficult was arranging them within useful categories and in an order that created an interesting progression, a clever juxtaposition, or a bit of humor. Another difficulty was what to do when the author denied having said the words. One of

Leona Helmsley's employees swore that she said, "Only little people pay taxes," but Helmsley denied it. She was alive and litigious when the line became famous, so I included it, but parenthetically added the word "attributed."

By 1994 I was ready. With trepidation, I called Chris Bergin, who was then the editor of *Tax Notes,* and described the collection. He asked only one question: "Is it funny?" I replied that some parts were funny. He immediately said he was sending a messenger to pick it up. The next day Chris called to say that he would publish it. To quote from the Casablanca screenplay, it was "the beginning of a beautiful friendship."

Readers have always been invited to send additional quotes about taxes. Many have done so, most notably law professors who offer clever lines about taxes that they themselves wrote. Of course, I cannot complain of their immodesty, because I have immodestly included a number of my own quotes.

Occasionally someone will ask which of the quotations is my favorite. I always cite George Bernard Shaw: "A government which robs Peter to pay Paul can depend upon the support of Paul." But as good as that line is, I find that my 35-plus years of practicing tax law in Washington has made me appreciate more a quotation from Lily Tomlin that is not in the collection because it is not specific to taxes, although it clearly applies to the topic: "No matter how cynical you get, you can never keep up."

* * *

Many people helped create this book by finding quotations or otherwise providing moral and logistical support. Thanks to Raquel Alexander, Connie Angle, Adam Apatoff, Ron Argintar, Dick Arndt, Chris Bergin, Cory Bingaman, Brian Blum, Bill Brockner, Eileen Brownell, Paul L. Caron, Michael Cartusciello, Vladimir Checkik, Jim Chudy, Sheldon S. Cohen, Guy Collier, Stan Crock, Terry Cuff, Sean G. D'Arcy, Julie A. Divola, Jeff Eisenach, Peter L. Faber, Pete Freeman, Marty Ginsberg, Jeff Gottlieb, Eric M. Green, Marty Greif, Ellen Harrison, Friedrich E.F. Hay, Gordon D. Henderson, Nell Hennessy, Cynthia Holcomb Hall, John F. Iekel, J. Mark Iwry, Rob James, Mike Jelormine, Calvin H. Johnson, Wayne S. Kaplan, John Kaufmann, Bill Lehrfeld, Eric R. LoPresti, Kirk F. Maldonado, Larry McCutchen, Robert E. McKenzie, Sue Mills, Dean Morley, Tom Morton, Michael O'Connor, Phil Parisi, Marina Park, Sheldon D. Pollack, Alex Ratnofsky, James Q. Riordan, Bob Robbins, Jody Robinson, Jack Ross, Marc P. Seidler, Karen Sheely, Allan Sloan, Jasper Smith, Dale L. Sorden, Lynn Soukup (whose name should appear on this list at least twice), Meredith Stevenson Fath, Michael A. Talbert, Pat Thomas, Martin B. Tittle, Stan Veliotis, Jeff Vesely, John T. Wadsworth, Tim Watkins, Mark Weinberg, Bob Wells, Jerry S. Williford, Lydia E. Wilson, and Steve Zisser.

Special thanks to the redoubtable Cory Bingaman, who provided outstanding administrative assistance and skillfully created and manipulated the computerized database. He always gets the job done — a Marine for all seasons.

And very special thanks to Jean L. Yablon — sine quo non.

Interested readers are invited to send additional quotes for possible inclusion in a future edition to Jeffery L. Yablon, c/o Pillsbury Winthrop Shaw Pittman LLP, 1200 17th Street NW, Washington, DC 20036-3006 or via e-mail to jeffery.yablon@pillsburylaw.com.

Taxes Generally

We have long had death and taxes as the two standards of inevitability. But there are those who believe that death is the preferable of the two.

— Erwin N. Griswold

Taxes Generally

As certain as death and taxes.

— Daniel DeFoe

Tis impossible to be sure of any thing but Death and Taxes.
— Christopher Bullock

Death and Taxes, they are certain.

— Edward Ward

Death and taxes are inevitable.

— Thomas Chandler Haliburton

Our Constitution is in actual operation; everything appears to promise that it will last; but nothing in this world is certain but death and taxes.

— Benjamin Franklin

We have long had death and taxes as the two standards of inevitability. But there are those who believe that death is the preferable of the two. "At least," as one man said, "there's one advantage about death; it doesn't get worse every time Congress meets."

— Erwin N. Griswold

Another difference between death and taxes is that death is frequently painless.

— Anonymous

Death and taxes and childbirth. There's never any convenient time for any of them.

— Margaret Mitchell
(*Gone With the Wind*)

Death and taxes may be inevitable, but they shouldn't be related.

— J.C. Watts Jr.

Taxes: Of life's two certainties, the only one for which you can get an automatic extension.

— Anonymous

[T]axation, in reality, is life. If you know the position a person takes on taxes, you can tell their whole philosophy. The tax code, once you get to know it, embodies all the essence of life: greed, politics, power, goodness, charity.

— Sheldon S. Cohen

As a society, we will never be free of taxes — that is unless we all want to be bathing down by the river, catching our own dinner, and freezing to death in the dark.

— Christopher Bergin

Taxes matter. They matter to business and life decisions alike. They matter to the rich and to the poor. They are, or at least they should be, incorporated into nearly every financial decision made. Discussing tax policy without acknowledging this fundamental reality is bizarre. Actually asserting the opposite is willful ignorance.

— Clifford S. Asness

Taxation . . . makes us all part owners of each others' wages just as the stock market allows us to share ownership of each others' physical capital. Society gains tax revenue when anyone makes more income; it loses tax revenue when anyone loses income. As a result, income taxes lead to some diversification of our human capital risks by forcing us to share them with others.

— Jonathan Lipow

[The Internal Revenue Code is] about 10 times the size of the Bible — and unlike the Bible, contains no good news.

— Don Nickles

Only God knows where we got our tax system.

— Sam Gibbons

[L]iving a life where you pay your taxes, are kind to your neighbors, create a good home — that's the ultimate spiritual life.

— Dov Yona Korn

Taxation, for example, is eternally lively; it concerns nine-tenths of us more directly than either smallpox or golf, and has just as much drama in it; moreover, it has been mellowed and made gay by as many gaudy, preposterous theories.

— H.L. Mencken

One great advantage in America is, that there is nobody to over-shadow men of moderate property; no swaggering, shining, tax-eating wretches to set examples of extravagance, pride and insolence to your sons and daughters, who are brought up in the habit of seeing men estimated, not according to the show that they make, not according to their supposed wealth, not according to what is called *birth*, but according to the real intrinsic merit of the party: this is a wonderful advantage.

— William Cobbett

Taxes must matter, or else why would we spend so much time on them?

— David Cay Johnston

America's tax laws are similar to the writings of Karl Marx and the writings of Sigmund Freud in that many of the people who loudly proclaim opinions about these documents have never read a word of them.

— Jeffery L. Yablon

[Tax law jurisprudence is] a field beset with invisible boomerangs.

— Robert H. Jackson

If a client asks in any but an extreme case whether, in your opinion, his sale will result in capital gain, your answer should probably be, "I don't know, and no one else in town can tell you."

— James L. Wood

Blessed are the young, for they shall inherit the national debt.

— Herbert Hoover

Philosophy teaches a man that he can't take it with him; taxes teach him he can't leave it behind either.

— Mignon McLaughlin

He who builds a better mousetrap these days runs into material shortages, patent-infringement suits, work stoppages, collusive bidding, discount discrimination — and taxes.

— H. E. Martz

No taxes can be devised which are not more or less inconvenient and unpleasant.

— George Washington

Our founding fathers never intended a larger-than-life government manipulating our very economy via the tax code.

— Michele Bachman

Every year, the night before he paid his taxes, my father had a ritual of watching the news. We figured it made him feel better to know that others were suffering.

— Narrator, *The Wonder Years* television series

Earth gets its price for what Earth gives us;
The beggar is taxed for a corner to die in.

— James Russell Lowell

You must pay taxes. But there's no law that says you gotta leave a tip.

— Morgan Stanley
(advertisement)

Very few nations or individuals regard themselves as liable to pay too little tax.

— Christopher Hitchens

Pothinus: Is it possible that Caesar, the conqueror of the world, has time to occupy himself with such a trifle as our taxes?

Caesar: My friend, taxes are the chief business of a conqueror of the world.

— George Bernard Shaw
(*Caesar and Cleopatra*)

War is the parent of armies; from these proceed debts and taxes; and armies, and debts, and taxes are the known instruments for bringing the many under the domination of the few.

— James Madison

More taxes were raised [by England] per capita in the war against Napoleon than in the war against Hitler.

— Andrew Lambert

Yes, if you support our troops, you have to support the work of the Internal Revenue Service.

— E.J. Dionne Jr.

War costs money. So far, we have hardly even begun to pay for it. We have devoted only 15 percent of our national income to national defense. As will appear in my Budget Message tomorrow, our war program for the coming fiscal year will cost . . . more than half of the estimated annual national income. That means taxes and bonds and bonds and taxes.

— Franklin D. Roosevelt

The term "tax humor" is no doubt an oxymoron to many people; to the more cynical, it is an apt description of the entire tax code.

— John F. Iekel

Tax issues are fun. Getting to love them may take a bit of effort, but the same is true for Beethoven's string quartets, and think of how much pleasure they give if one does make the effort.

— Peter L. Faber

A fine is a tax for doing something wrong. A tax is a fine for doing something right.

— Anonymous

Taxes are a penalty on progress.

— James R. Cook

We are told that this is an odious and unpopular tax. I never knew a tax that was not odious and unpopular with the people who paid it.

— John Sherman

You know we all hate paying taxes, but the truth of the matter is without our tax money, many politicians wouldn't be able to afford prostitutes.

— Jimmy Kimmel

I have always paid income tax. I object only when it reaches a stage when I am threatened with having nothing left for my old age — which is due to start next Tuesday or Wednesday

— Noel Coward

A "tax" is an enforced contribution to provide for the support of government; a "penalty," as the word is here used, is an exaction imposed by statute as punishment for an unlawful act. The two words are not interchangeable one for the other. No mere exercise of the art of lexicography can alter the essential nature of an act or a thing, and if an exaction be clearly a penalty, it cannot be converted into a tax by the simple expedient of calling it such.

— George Sutherland

A citizen can hardly distinguish between a tax and a fine, except that the fine is generally much lighter.

— G.K. Chesterton

A punishment for a crime, such as a fine, is not the same as a tax on a course of conduct, though both involve directions to officials to inflict the same money loss. What differentiates these ideas is that the first involves, as the second does not, an offence or breach of duty in the form of a violation of a rule set up to guide the conduct of ordinary citizens. It is true that this generally clear distinction may in certain circumstances be blurred. Taxes may be imposed not for revenue purposes but to discourage the activities taxed, though the law gives no express indications that these are to be abandoned as it does when it "makes them criminal." Conversely the fines payable for some criminal offence may, because of the depreciation of money, become so small that they are cheerfully paid.

— H.L.A. Hart

The reward of energy, enterprise and thrift — is taxes.

— William Feather

[Genie Emerging from Lamp]: Actually, it's just two wishes, after taxes.

— Tom Thaves
("Frank and Ernest")

The mounting burden of taxation not only undermines individual incentives to increased work and earnings, but in a score of ways discourages capital accumulation and distorts, unbalances, and shrinks production.

— Henry Hazlitt

Raising taxes encourages taxpayers to shift, hide and underreport income . . . . Higher taxes reduce the incentives to work, produce, invest and save, thereby dampening overall economic activity and job creation.

— Kurt Hauser

People don't work to pay taxes; they work and invest for the after-tax return.

— Arthur B. Laffer

Taxation is a way of containing the rat race.

— Richard Layard

First of all, I am going to show her one of our tax returns. Once she sees how much money we have, I have a hunch we are gonna look a whole lot whiter.

— Scene from *Desperate Housewives* television series

I don't know if I can live on my income or not — the government won't let me try it.

— Bob Thaves
("Frank & Ernest")

What is one really trying to do in the investment world? Not pay the least taxes, although that may be a factor to be considered in achieving the end. Means and end should not be confused, however, and the end is to come away with the largest after-tax rate of compound.

— Warren Buffett

The TaxSlayer Bowl is an annual college football bowl game played at EverBank Field in Jacksonville, Florida. Originally named the Gator Bowl, it has been held continuously since 1946, making it the sixth oldest college bowl, as well as the first one ever televised nationally. TaxSlayer.com became the title sponsor in 2011 and the bowl took its current name in 2014 after a new contract.

— Wikipedia

Academicians and politicians have finally come to understand that it's the after-tax rate of return that determines people's behavior.

— Arthur B. Laffer

[C]apital migrates away from regimes in which it is treated harshly, and toward regimes in which it is free to be invested profitably and safely. In this regard, the capital controlled by our richest citizens is especially tax-intolerant.

— David Ranson

The government deficit is the difference between the amount of money the government spends and the amount it has the nerve to collect.

— Sam Ewing

Though many have tried, nobody can defy the iron law of budget gravity. It states: Deficits = Spending − Taxes

— Martin A. Sullivan

The budget should be balanced not by more taxes, but by reduction of follies.

— Herbert Hoover

Our view is that taxpayer dollars should be spent wisely or not at all.

— George W. Bush

It is not the heavily taxed realm which executes great deeds but the moderately taxed one.

— Old Asian Proverb

The general feeling about the income-tax appears to have been that it is all right this time, but it mustn't happen again. I was looking through a volume of Punch, for the year 1882, the other day, and I came across a picture of a gloomy-looking individual paying his tax.

"I can just do it this time," he is saying, "but I wish you would tell Her Majesty that she mustn't look on me as a source of income in the future."

— P.G. Wodehouse

Neither will it be that a people over-laid with taxes should ever become valiant . . . . No people over-charged with tribute is fit for empire.

— Francis Bacon

Now the truth of the matter is that there are a lot of things people don't understand. Take the Einstein theory. Take taxes. Take love. Do you understand them? Neither do I. But they exist. They happen.

— Dalton Trumbo
(*The Remarkable Andrew* screenplay)

Unquestionably, there is progress. The average American now pays out almost as much in taxes alone as he formerly got in wages.

— H.L. Mencken

It is perfectly normal for [new] college graduates to have [political temper tantrums], particularly if they graduate during an election year. As time goes by, though, the tantrums will lessen in intensity and frequency, and they tend to stop entirely once the graduate begins to pay taxes.

— Simon Rich

Alexander Hamilton started the U.S. Treasury with nothing, and that was the closest our country has ever been to being even.

— Will Rogers

If you get up early, work late, and pay your taxes, you will get ahead — if you strike oil.

— J. Paul Getty

As of mid-2005, if you search the word "tax" on Google, you get about 127 million hits. If you search the word "love," you get about 149 million hits. This is comforting, but not overwhelmingly so.

— Jeffery L. Yablon

A person doesn't know how much he has to be thankful for until he has to pay taxes on it.

— Ann Landers
(quoting an anonymous source)

My father has a great expression: "The capital-gains tax has created more millionaires than any other government policy." The capital-gains tax tends to make investors hold longer. That is almost always the right decision.

— Chris Davis

Capital punishment: The income tax.

— Jeff Hayes

The best things in life are free, but sooner or later the government will find a way to tax them.

— Anonymous

This country doesn't need any weird new tax ideas seeping in from abroad. We have already got enough weird taxes of our own. In this country, there are already taxes in some states on fountain soda, tattoos and blueberries. Taxes on jogging, getting one's soul patch trimmed and playing the ukulele in public cannot be far off.

— Joe Queenan

As a people the Jews have always been small in number but gigantic in their impact on the course of civilization. Setting aside the religious aspect of Jewish history, their economic and political story has been one continuous struggle after another against outrageous taxation.

— Charles Adams

FISCI IVDAICI CALVMNIA SVBLATA ("The abusive tax on Jews and suspected Jews has been abolished")
— Announcement Stamped on Coins Issued by Roman Emperor Nerva

A tax can be a means for raising revenue, or a device for regulating conduct, or both.

— Felix Frankfurter

When it comes to meeting its funding requirements, a government has four basic choices as to what it can tax: income, wages, consumption or wealth.

— Michael J. Graetz

The justification for consumption taxes rests on their built-in incentives to save and invest. By exempting investment from taxation, consumption taxes encourage investment and discourages spending.
— Robert E. Hall and Alvin Rabushka

Students come in thinking [tax law] is about numbers and calculations and it's going to be dry and boring. Then they realize it's about money, greed and power, and they really get into it.

— Evelyn Brody

Basic tax, as everyone knows, is the only genuinely funny subject in law school.

— Martin D. Ginsburg

Many challenges await aspiring tax lawyers: Find a job. Repay student loans. Balance work life and personal life. Become accustomed to keeping track of time in six-minute increments. Adapt to the professional work environment. Prove your worth to colleagues and clients. Learn as much substantive tax law as possible. Keep up with changes to the tax law. And figure out how to translate substantive knowledge into useful legal advice.

— Heather M. Field

[Psychiatrist to tax accountant]: We both treat the same neurosis: what to declare and what to hide.

— Patrice Leconte and Jerome Tonnerre
(*Intimate Strangers*)

Those men would deserve the gratitude of ages, who should discover a mode of government that contained the greatest sum of individual happiness, with the least national expense.

— Giacinto Dragonetti

You are fortunate to live here. If I were your President, I would levy a tax on you for living in San Francisco!

— Mikhail Gorbachev

Pay Taxes — Build Rwanda — Be Proud.

— Billboard in Rwanda

Like mothers, taxes are often misunderstood, but seldom forgotten.

— Lord Bramwell

The models of motherhood we had did not serve us in the lives we led . . . . We were often the first female members of our families to stay in hotel rooms alone, to raise children alone, to face tax problems alone.

— Erica Jong

I have worked with investors for 60 years and I have yet to see anyone — not even when capital gains rates were 39.9 percent in 1976-77 — shy away from a sensible investment because of the tax rate on the potential gain.

— Warren Buffett

The way taxes are, you might as well marry for love.

— Joe E. Lewis

A fool and his money are soon parted. It takes creative tax laws for the rest.

— Bob Thaves
("Frank & Ernest")

We don't seem to be able to check crime, so why not legalize it and then tax it out of business?

— Will Rogers

You'd be surprised at the frivolous things people spend their money on. Taxes, for example.

— Nuveen Investments
(advertisement)

Loophole: To liberals, any provision of the tax code that fails to claim money earned, inherited, saved, or otherwise pocketed by known taxpayers.

— *The Conservative's Dictionary*

Supply-siders never tire of proclaiming that taxes are the root of all evil, but reasonable people do get tired of explaining, over and over again, that they aren't.

— Paul Krugman

What Mae West said about sex is true about taxes. All tax cuts are good tax cuts; even bad tax cuts are good tax cuts.

— Grover Norquist

[Sex is] the last important human activity not subject to taxation.

— Russell Baker

Enjoy better sex! — Legalize and Tax Marijuana.

— Change the Climate, Inc.

You have to be oblivious to common sense to believe that taxing people who do work and paying people who don't work results in more people working. That's just not the way the world works.

— Arthur B. Laffer

As taxpayers, we have quietly accepted the fact that our taxes will be spent to pay big bucks for all sorts of ugly, twisted metal to be displayed in front of or inside government buildings, in the name of "art" — art that was obviously never meant to give the public any enjoyment and often represented a thumbing of the artist's nose at the public.

— Thomas Sowell

I'm putting all my money in taxes — it's the only thing sure to go up.

— Anonymous

Baseball is a skilled game. It's America's game — it, and high taxes.

— Will Rogers

Lower income taxes do not, by themselves, create investment; lower taxes on investment create more investment. Federal spending for consumption does not create as much investment as does targeted federal spending and incentives for investment. The differences are real.

— Peter R. Fisher

Investors get advice that leaves them hurt, from performance that is below benchmark and the high fees and taxes on the pittance that is left.

— Laurence Siegel

If you sell your soul to the Devil, do you need a receipt for tax purposes?

— Mark Russell

. . . I am never sure if tithing should be calculated before or after tax.

— Dan Ariely

I must be the only person in America that every time — I pay the maximum tax rates — every time I sign that tax form, I smile. I thank God I live in a country that gave me a chance to make the money I do.

— Bill Clinton

I'm proud to be paying taxes in the United States. The only thing is — I could be just as proud for half the money.

— Arthur Godfrey

If you drive a car, I'll tax the street.
If you try to sit, I'll tax your seat.
If you get too cold, I'll tax the heat.
If you take a walk, I'll tax your feet.
Taxman!
Well, I'm the taxman. Yeah, I'm the taxman.

— The Beatles
("Taxman")

I feel so good come payday
I think of all the things I'm gonna buy when I pick up my pay
Don't you know but then they hand me that little brown envelope
I peep inside Lord I lose all hope
Cause from those total wages earned down to that net amount
   that's due
I feel the painful sense of loss between the two.

— Jerry Leiber and Billy Edd Wheeler
("After Taxes")

How can I keep my arm around my woman
With Uncle Sam's hands in my pants?
If I can't pay the fiddler
How the hell am I gonna dance?
Don't mind kickin' in my fair share
I might even back up and say yes
But the big man plays, while the little man pays
So the hell with the IRS.

— Johnny Paycheck
("Me and the IRS")

The farmer is the man, the farmer is the man
Lives on his credit until Fall
Well, his pants are wearing thin
His condition, it's a sin
'Cause the taxes on the farmer feeds us all
— Traditional American Song
("Taxes on the Farmer Feeds Us All" — Adapted by Ry Cooder)

Evolution, revolution, gun control, sound of soul
Shooting rockets to the moon
Kids growing up too soon
Politicians say more taxes will solve everything
And the band played on . . .
Eve of destruction, tax deduction . . . .
— Norman Whitfield and Barrett Strong
("Ball of Confusion")

Down to the Banana Republics
Down to the tropical sun
Go the expatriated Americans
Hopin' to find some fun
Some of them go for the sailing
Brought by the lure of the sea
Tryin' to find what is ailing
Living in the land of the free
Some of them are running to lovers
Leaving no forward address
Some of them are running tons of ganja
Some are running from the IRS.

— Jimmy Buffett
("Banana Republics")

I pay the Fed tax and the FICA tax before I cash my check
And then the sales tax and this and that tax get most of what's left
They're taxing me to death and it's my money
They say the wheel tax and the property tax and are going
    up again
I don't like that I'm gonna fight that every way I can
They spend it like it's theirs, they've got to understand

It's my money, it belongs to me
It's mine, I made it
It's as simple as it can be
Enough's enough how much more do you need
It's my money

> — Aaron Sain and Frank Highland
> ("It's My Money")

The tax man's taken all my dough
And left me in this stately home
Lazing on a sunny afternoon
And I can't even sail my yacht
He's taken everything I've got
All I got's this sunny afternoon.

> — Ray Davies
> ("Sunny Afternoon")

I know everybody's income and what everybody earns;
And I carefully compare it with the income-tax returns;
But to benefit humanity, however much I plan,
Yet everybody says I'm such a disagreeable man!
And I can't think why!

> — William S. Gilbert and Arthur S. Sullivan
> ("Princess Ida")

My father always said that there's no free ride
You've got to make a sacrifice
With so many Prophets on the Lord's side
Even your soul has got a price
But talk is cheap it takes money to buy your freedom
And the tax man's knockin' at your door.

> — Jimmy Buffett, Roger Guth, and Jay Oliver
> ("Carnival World")

I'm squared up with the USA.
You see those bombers in the sky.
Rockefeller helped to build them.
So did I.
I paid my income tax today.

— Irving Berlin
("I Paid My Income Tax Today")

Hang ups, let downs
Bad breaks, set backs
Natural fact is, honey
That I can't pay my taxes

— Marvin Gaye
("Inner City Blues (Make Me Wanna Holler)")

I know the game it's old and lame
You're holdin' a flame for my name and my fame
Livin' like Givens schemin' on Tyson
But she got lucky cause he was a nice one
But I ain't nice and I don't play that
If it ain't tax I don't pay that

— Kool Moe Dee
("They Want Money")

It's fun to charter an accountant,
And sail the wide accountan-cy.
To find, explore the funds offshore,
And skirt the shoals of bankruptcy.
It can be manly in insurance. We'll up your premium
    semi-annually.
It's all tax-deductible,
We're fairly incorruptible.
We're sailing on the wide accountan-cy.

— Monty Python
("Accountancy Shanty")

I mean sure there's some bills and taxes I'm still evading
But I blew 6 million on myself and I feel amazing

— Drake
("The Ride")

This country's taxes must be fixed
And I know what to do with it
If you think you're paying too much now
Just wait 'til I get through with it.

— Harry Ruby and Bert Kalmer
("These Are The Laws of My Administration"
from the Marx Brothers movie *Duck Soup*)

Cut the tax, Jack, and please don't spend no
more, no more, no more, no more.
Cut the tax, Jack, and please don't spend no more.
Woo Politician, politician don't treat us so mean.
You're the biggest spenders that we've ever seen.
Pretty soon we'll be out of dough, and you'll
have to pack your things and go.
Cut the tax, Jack, and please don't spend no
more, no more, no more, no more.
Cut the tax, Jack, and please don't spend no more.
Now voter, listen voter hear what we say,
They have to cut spending, ain't no other way.
If they spend all our money that just ain't okay.
Remember if you say so,
They'll have to pack their things and go
(That's right). Hit the road, Jack, and don't you
spend no more. Don't you come tax no more.

[To be sung to the tune of "Hit the Road, Jack"]

— National Taxpayers Union

I hate taxes
Taxes gonna break my back I swear
Don't you know I paid a lot more than my share
You know I've thinkin' about movin' somewhere else
But I can't because I love America too much
Especially California
Yeah I guess I'm gonna have to pay these taxes
If I'm gonna live here.

— Robert Cray
("1040 Blues")

I don't know why they think they've got to squeeze us
But I'll tell you just exactly where I stand
I believe if ten percent is good enough for Jesus
Well it oughta be enough for Uncle Sam.

— Ray Stevens
("If Ten Percent Is Good Enough For Jesus
(It Oughta Be Enough For Uncle Sam)")

Another vacant building is a tax shelter and nothing more
Cemented doors and windows keeping out the poor
What purpose does it serve to keep these buildings empty
Destroying our community to protect abandoned property
Functioning as financial loopholes instead of the housing they
    could make
Because those owning empty buildings claim a generous
    government tax break

— Aus-Rotten
("Tax Shelter")

Like rain, tax
After lightning the thunder cracks
(It's inevitable)
Sooner or later it had to come true
Like rain, tax
Weeds grow up through the pavement cracks
(It's inevitable)
You see what I want
What I want is you

— Terry Britten and Charlie Dore
("Rain, Tax (It's Inevitable)")

Beautiful girls all over the world
I could be chasing but my time would be wasted
They got nothin' on you baby
Nothin' on you baby . . .
Baby you the whole package plus you pay your taxes

— B.o.B.
("Nothin' on You")

You work hard, you make money
There ain't no one in the world who can stop you
You work hard, you went hungry
Now the taxman is out to get you
You worked hard
And slaved and slaved for years
Break your back sweat a lot
Well, it's just not fair
He hates you, he loves money
And he'll steal your shit and think that it's funny
Like the Beatles he ain't human.

— Rick Nielsen
("Taxman, Mr. Thief")

Skip a rope skip a rope . . .
Cheat on your taxes don't be a fool
Now what was that they said about the golden rule
Never mind the rule just play to win
And hate your neighbor for the shade of his skin
Skip a rope skip a rope . . .

— Jack Moran and Glenn D. Tubb
("Skip a Rope")

Some folks are born silver spoons in hand,
Lord, don't they help themselves, oh.
But when the taxman comes to the door,
Lord, The house looks like a rummage sale, yes.

— John Fogerty
("Fortunate Son")

Never forget
There's life after death and taxes
Forgiveness comes
And all of the rest
Is what passes away
Death and decay can't touch us now

— Matthew Arnold Thiessen
("Life After Death And Taxes (Failure II)")

I'm not looking for compensation
I want some justice
Tell you what they want from me
Blood, death and taxes

— Agnostic Front
("Blood, Death And Taxes")

Taxes are strong-armed robbery the collectors of taxes funnel the majority of funds to police and intuitions counter productive to spiritual advancement.

Well taxes are stealing and I get the feeling that . . .
They take what they want to whenever they want to
And our needs they always come last.

They lie, they cheat, they steal from you and me.
They lie, they cheat, they steal from you and me.

— Corporate Avenger
("Taxes Are Stealing")

You can pay Uncle Sam with overtime
Is that all you get for your money?

— Billy Joel
("Movin' Out")

You have many contacts
Among the lumberjacks
To get you facts
When someone attacks your imagination
But nobody has any respect
Anyway they already expect you
To just give a check
To tax-deductible charity organizations . . . .

— Bob Dylan
("Ballad of a Thin Man")

Away for the weekend
I've gotta play some one-night stands
Six for the tax man, and one for the band

— John Entwistle
("Success Story")

Don't stress,
Relax,
Let life roll off
Your backs
Except for death and paying taxes,
Everything in life is only for now!
— Robert Lopez, Jeff Marx, and Jeff Whitty
("For Now" from "Avenue Q — The Musical")

When you were a child
You were treated kind
But you were never brought up right.
You were also spoiled with a thousand toys
But you still cried all night.
Your mother who neglected you
Owes a million dollars tax.
And your father's still perfecting ways of making ceiling wax.
— Mick Jagger and Keith Richards
("19th Nervous Breakdown")

I love America, but I can't spend the whole year here. I can't afford the taxes.

— Mick Jagger

The whole business thing is predicated a lot on the tax laws. It's why we [the Rolling Stones] rehearse in Canada and not in the U.S. A lot of our astute moves have been basically keeping up with tax laws, where to go, where not to put it. Whether to sit on it or not. We left England because we'd be paying ninety-eight cents on the dollar. We left, and they lost out. No taxes at all.

— Keith Richards

I decided not to become a tax exile, so I stayed in Britain, but they kept putting the tax up, so I'd do any old thing every now and then to pay the tax, that was my tax exile money. I realised that's not a socialist country, it's a communist country without a dictator, so I left and I was never going to come back. Maggie Thatcher came in and put the taxes back down and in the end, you know, you don't mind paying tax. What am I going to do? Not pay tax and drive around in a Rolls Royce, with cripples begging on the street like you see in some countries?

— Michael Caine

The glittering hotpants, sequined jumpsuits and platform heels that Abba wore at the peak of their fame were designed not just for the four band members to stand out — but also for tax efficiency . . . . the band's style was influenced in part by laws that allowed the cost of outfits to be deducted against tax — so long as the costumes were so outrageous they could not possibly be worn on the street.

> — The Guardian (U.K.) online

Whoever hopes a faultless tax to see, hopes what ne'er was, is not, and ne'er shall be.

> — Alexander Pope

Unnecessary taxation is unjust taxation.

> — Abram Stevens Hewitt

Collecting more taxes than is absolutely necessary is legalized robbery.

> — Calvin Coolidge

[Paying taxes is] a glorious privilege.

> — Woodrow Wilson

Why is it inflationary if the people keep their own money, and spend it the way they want to, [but] not inflationary if the government takes it and spends it the way it wants to?

> — Ronald Reagan

See, when the GOVERNMENT spends money, it creates jobs; whereas when the money is left in the hands of TAXPAYERS God only knows what they do with it. Bake it into pies, probably. Anything to avoid creating jobs.

> — Dave Barry

All taxation is an evil, but heavy taxes, indiscriminately levied on everything . . . are one of the greatest curses that can afflict a people.

> — Brooks Adams

Tax reform is ultimately a decision about values.

> — Bill Bradley

I am sure that during the Roman or some other empire there must have been tax experts who "assisted" the newly conquered territories in reforming their tax systems.

— Vito Tanzi

We have come to love income tax laws so much that we have chosen to have a lot of them. There are (1) the basic federal income tax, (2) the federal corporate alternative minimum tax, (3) the federal individual alternative minimum tax, (4) the federal computation of earnings and profits for dividends payable to shareholders other than 20% corporate owners, (5) the federal computation of earnings and profits for distributions to corporate shareholders that own 20% or more of the distributing corporation's stock, (6) state income taxes, departing in various ways from the federal rules, (7) state minimum taxes, departing in various ways from the federal rules, and (8) city income and minimum taxes, departing in various ways from both the federal and the state rules. The resulting loss of efficiency in our economy, and cost of private sector compliance are staggering.

— Gordon D. Henderson

The taxpayer — that's someone who works for the federal government but doesn't have to take a civil service examination.

— Ronald Reagan

Old Mack was fast as a bullet, mean as a hornet, as sure as income tax. He could do anything, find anything. You didn't order him to find a coon, you declared how many you wanted and what colors they should be, and he got them for you.

— Janisse Ray

Cheerios can lower cholesterol 4% in 6 weeks. To appreciate that number, give the IRS an extra 4%.

— Advertisement for breakfast cereal

Every time this country . . . has cut tax rates across the board, revenues went up and the economy grew.

— Jack Kemp

The math of the late 1980s was simple. Any company that exchanged its equity for debt was immediately worth more, courtesy of the U.S. tax code. And *every* company was thought to be ripe for such a maneuver.

— Roger Lowenstein

Taxes are paid in the sweat of every man who labors. If those taxes are excessive, they are reflected in idle factories, tax-sold farms and in hordes of hungry people, tramping the streets and seeking jobs in vain.

— Franklin D. Roosevelt

All taxation, however disguised, is a loss per se . . . it is the duty, and the sacred duty, of Government to take only from the people what is necessary to the proper discharge of the public service; and that taxation in any other mode is simply in one shape or another, *legalized robbery*.

— Richard Cartwright

We understandably hesitate to talk about law in explicitly moral terms. But tax has unavoidable moral and political dimensions.

— Edward J. McCaffery

Tax 'em, my boy, tax 'em.

— Felix Frankfurter
(Apocryphal comment to William O. Douglas concerning the wealthy)

My friends, don't you believe that our taxes are too high, too complicated, and utterly unfair?

— Ronald Reagan

If you believe your life is largely the result of your own discipline and decisions, you're going to feel very differently about taxes, regulations and redistribution than if you believe your life is largely the sum of your genes and your environment — factors irretrievably beyond your control.

— Daniel Akst

Everyone who has anything to do with the tax code agrees it's just an unbelievable mess.

— Paul H. O'Neill

Our tax laws are a series of extemporized responses to immediate pressures with no long-term objectives.

— Randolph E. Paul

[The federal income tax system is] a disgrace to the human race.

— Jimmy Carter

The U.S. income tax turns 100 this year [2013]. And for the first time, despite my long affection for it, I'm thinking that it may be time to begin retiring it.

— Christopher Bergin

We must care for each other more, and tax each other less.

— Bill Archer

If income inequality is the main economic problem, it could be solved tomorrow, through confiscation and redistribution. If the main problem is the unequal generation of social capital in institutions such as families, schools and communities, the solutions get more difficult. One task can be accomplished by a tax collector; the other is the work of a civilization.

— Michael Gerson

Taxation is transactional and not cuneiform.

— Irving Loeb Goldberg

The hardest thing in the world to understand is the Income Tax.

— Albert Einstein
(attributed)

Count the day won when, turning on its axis,
This earth imposes no additional taxes.

— Franklin P. Adams

It's not what you make, it's what you keep.

— Anonymous

To the extent that you're lowering the [tax] rate on savings, you're essentially placing it on consumption.

— Alan Greenspan

Indoors or out, no one relaxes
In March, that month of wind and taxes,
The wind will presently disappear,
The taxes last us all the year.

— Ogden Nash

The taxing authority is an uninvited party to all contracts.
— Myron S. Scholes, Mark A. Wolfson, Merle M. Erickson,
Edward L. Maydew, and Terry J. Shevlin

If taxation is to be successful as a revenue producer in times of depression as well as in times of business prosperity, it must have a broad base as a foundation.

— John Nance Garner

Political liberty, the peace of a nation, and science itself are gifts for which Fate demands a heavy tax in blood!

— Honoré De Balzac

Censure is the tax a man pays to the public for being eminent.

— Jonathan Swift

Fear is the tax that conscience pays to guilt.

— Howard Aiken

Inflation is a form of tax, a tax that we all collectively must pay.
— Henry Hazlitt

We pay that tax [*i.e.*, tipping in restaurants] knowing it to be unjust and an extortion; yet we go away with a pain at the heart if we think we have been stingy with the poor fellows.

— Mark Twain

Black tax: The higher prices that black people have to pay for
      (1) goods — often due to lack of large grocery stores, mass
      market discounters
      (2) insurance, mortgages, loans
      due to their ethnicity
[Used in a sentence:] *Buffy and Biff can get a lower rate on a home mortgage than Rasheed and LaShawna due to the black tax.*

— Urban Dictionary

Change of fashion is the tax levied by the industry of the poor on the vanity of the rich.

— Sébastien-Roch Nicolas De Chamfort

And anyone is free to condemn me to death
If he leaves it to nature to carry out the sentence.
I shall will to the common stock of air my breath
And pay a death tax of fairly polite repentance.

— Robert Frost

Once — just once — I'd like to be fixed up with a guy who earns in a year what I pay in taxes.

— Anonymous Female Lawyer

Friends and neighbors complain that taxes are indeed very heavy, and if those laid on by the government were the only ones we had to pay, we might the more easily discharge them; but we have many others, and much more grievous to some of us. We are taxed twice as much by our idleness, three times as much by our pride, and four times as much by our folly.

— Benjamin Franklin

No one can become rich by the efforts of only their toil, but only by the discovery of some method of taxing the labor of others.

— John Ruskin

[A]fter the outbreak of the Civil War, Congress realized the war's escalating cost could not be financed solely through debt, and it enacted legislation creating the first U.S. income tax and, to administer it, a new federal agency that we now know as the IRS. The wartime legislation also included an excise tax on alcohol at the hefty rate of $2 per gallon. The tax was not enough to kill citizens' thirst for distilled liquor, but it made alcohol too costly to burn. Kerosene replaced alcohol as the main fuel for lamps.

— Martin A. Sullivan

Every society makes choices as to the tax systems that not only raise the necessary revenues to support government expenditures, but within that choice are inherent reflections of societal values. Not only does a society choose a tax system but the tax system becomes one of the basic institutions that in itself shapes and molds the society.

— Karen M. Yeager

[A] budget is not just a catalog of programs and taxes. It reflects a society's priorities and values.

— Robert J. Samuelson

By this time fashion had condemned the beard in every other country in Europe, and with a voice more potent than popes or emperors, had banished it from civilized society. But this only made the Russians cling more fondly to their ancient ornament, as a mark to distinguish them from foreigners, whom they hated. Peter [the Great], however, resolved that they should be shaven . . . . Wiser, too, than the popes and bishops of a former age, he did not threaten them with eternal damnation, but made them pay in hard cash the penalty of their disobedience. For many years, a very considerable revenue was collected from this source . . . . Those who were refractory, and refused to pay the tax, were thrown into prison.

— Charles Mackay

Men in America were so conditioned that they felt differently about taxes and about prices. The former was an involuntary taking; the latter a voluntary giving . . . . No one observed the obvious fact that in terms of total income of an individual it made no difference whether his money went for prices or taxes.

— Thurman W. Arnold

Give us day by day our Real Taxed Substantial Money bought Bread; deliver from the Holy Ghost whatever cannot be Taxed; for all its debts & Taxes between Caesar & us & one another.

— William Blake

[I will consult with others before raising taxes, unless the revenue is needed] for ransoming our person, for making our eldest son a knight, and for once marrying our eldest daughter.

— King John of England

When a new source of taxation is found it never means, in practice, that an old source is abandoned. It merely means that the politicians have two ways of milking the taxpayer where they had only one before.

— H.L. Mencken

The government taxes you when you bring home a paycheck. It taxes you when you make a phone call. It taxes you when you turn on a light. It taxes you when you sell a stock. It taxes you when you fill your car with gas. It taxes you when you ride a plane. It taxes you when you get married. Then it taxes you when you die. This is a taxual insanity and it must end.

— J.C. Watts Jr.

[W]hat are the inevitable consequences of being too fond of glory: — Taxes upon every article which enters the mouth, or covers the back, or is placed under foot . . . taxes on everything on earth and the waters under the earth.

— Sidney Smith

You wake up in the morning and have your first cup of coffee, you pay a sales tax. You go to your garage; you start your car; you pay an automobile tax. You drive to work; you pay a gas tax. You go to work; you pay an income tax. You turn on the lights; you pay an electricity tax. You flush the toilet; you pay a water tax. You fly somewhere; you pay an airport tax. You stay overnight; you pay a hotel occupancy tax. You call home; you pay a telephone tax. You finally get home; you pay a property tax. You turn on the TV; you pay a cable tax. Even when you die, you pay a death tax. You are taxed from the moment you wake up in the morning until the moment you go to bed at night. You're taxed from your cradle to your grave . . . .

— Frank Luntz

The Eiffel Tower is the Empire State Building after taxes.

— Anonymous

Abracadabra, thus we learn
The more you create, the less you earn.
The less you earn, the more you're given,
The less you lead, the more you're driven,
The more destroyed, the more they feed,
The more you pay, the more they need,
The more you earn, the less you keep,
And now I lay me down to sleep.
I pray the Lord my soul to take,
If the tax-collector hasn't got it before I wake.

— Ogden Nash

The schoolboy whips his taxed top; the beardless youth manages his taxed horse with a taxed bridle.

— Sydney Smith

Wealth has always gravitated towards those that take risk with other people's money, but especially so when taxes are low.

— Bill Gross

Thinking is one thing no one has ever been able to tax.

— Charles F. Kettering

Bookstore pickup line: Have you seen *Tax Tips for Billionaires*?

— David Letterman

A good new chairman of the Federal Reserve Bank is worth a $10 billion tax cut.

— Paul H. Douglas

Taxes cause the most bad business decisions.

— James R. Cook

Tax hatred is what holds the Republican Party together.

— Bill Schneider

Many conservatives would have us believe that there is nothing worse than higher taxes. This is nonsense.

— Bruce Bartlett

Men who prefer any load of infamy, however great, to any pressure of taxation, however light.

— Sydney Smith

Taxes go against the very foundation of free enterprise! That's why it's called "free"!

— Quark
(Character in *Star Trek* television series)

We believe that it is our patriotic duty, as well as our personal interest, to divert more of the income we currently spend on taxes into personal savings.

— Mission Statement of the American
Shareholder Association

The principle is this — that you ought not in a free country to lay a tax on the expression of political opinion — a tax on the diffusion of that information on public affairs which the spirit of our constitution makes the interest and concern of every subject in the State. Still more, you should not, by means of that tax, create such an artificial necessity for capital that you secure the monopoly of thought upon the subjects that most interest the public at large to a handful of wealthy and irresponsible oligarchs.

— Edward George Bulwer-Lytton

Income taxes punish the very things we want more of: productive work, risk-taking and success. We can't say this enough: A tax on income is the price you pay for working; a tax on profits, the price you pay for success; and a tax on capital gains, the price you pay for taking risks that work out.

— Steve Forbes

We have a system that increasingly taxes work and subsidizes non-work.

— Milton Friedman

The logic is this: When the government taxes something, people use less of it. Right now our system taxes income from work, so people are discouraged from working. This is particularly true of men nearing retirement age at the peak of their careers, and women in dual-income households, who face above average marginal tax rates. If we could replace income taxes with levies on consumption, or shopping, then we would not discourage work, and we would have more savings, more work, and less consumption.

— Diana Furchtgott-Roth

Economic theory indeed supports the view that high tax rates can actually spur, rather than hinder, work effort.

— Jeffrey Sachs

If you want more of something, subsidize it; if you want less, tax it.
— Old Economic Adage

Taxing profits is tantamount to taxing success.
— Ludwig von Mises

We always get more of anything we tax less. So if you reduce the tax on sin, you'd probably get more sin.

— John Snow

[W]e should first tax things that we like the least, or dislike the most, as a society, before we tax human labor, and necessities . . . through a sales tax . . . . So we should tax securities speculation first, before we tax labor. If you go to a store and buy $1,000 worth of products, you pay a sales tax. You buy $1 million worth of derivatives, you pay no sales tax!
— Ralph Nader

Everyone hates taxes, but the government needs to fund its operations, and some taxes can actually do some good in the process.
— N. Gregory Mankiw

Through taxation, the government shares in some of the investor's risk.
— Stephen Horan

Everybody pays taxes! Even businessmen, who rob and cheat and steal from people everyday, even they have to pay taxes.
— William Rose and Tania Rose
(*It's a Mad Mad Mad Mad World* screenplay)

People who complain about taxes can be divided into two classes: men and women.
— Anonymous

Tax pollution — not people.
— Gerry E. Studds

All taxes are a drag on economic growth. It's only a question of degree.
— Alan Greenspan

We contend that for a nation to try to tax itself into prosperity is like a man standing in a bucket trying to lift himself up by its handle.
— Winston Churchill

No nation ever taxed itself into prosperity.
— Rush Limbaugh

Substance controls over form, except where form controls over substance.

— Sheldon I. Banoff

Taxation under every form presents but a choice of evils.

— David Ricardo

Taxation of earnings from labor is on a par with forced labor.

— Robert Nozick

We must place limits upon every form of compulsory taxation, until we are strong enough to destroy it finally and completely; and to transform it into a system of voluntary giving. Under that voluntary system alone can a nation live in peace and friendship and work together happily and profitably for common ends.

— Auberon Herbert

In a fully free society, taxation — or, to be exact, payment for government services — would be *voluntary*. Since the proper services of a government — the police, the armed forces, the law courts — are demonstrably needed by individual citizens and affect their interests directly, the citizens would (and should) be willing to pay for such services, as they pay for insurance.

— Ayn Rand

The sum total of the Gross National Product is several trillion dollars, of which one third is sent to the government in the form of taxes for the express purpose of being wasted.

— Dave Barry

There's nothing like self-interest to motivate behavior. When people ask me what are ways to pick out tax-efficient [mutual] funds, the first thing I say is, "Find out whether the manager has his or her own taxable dollars in the fund."

— Susan Belder

Was it Bonaparte who said that he found vices very good patriots? — "he got five millions from the love of brandy, and he should be glad to know which of the virtues would pay him as much." Tobacco and opium have broad backs, and will cheerfully carry the load of armies.

— Ralph Waldo Emerson

I shall never use profanity except in discussing house rent and taxes.

— Mark Twain

Woo-Hoo! I put a dollar under my pillow, and the tax fairy left me two quarters!

— Dave Coverly
("Speed Bump")

Politicians never accuse you of "greed" for wanting other people's money — only for wanting to keep your own money.

— Joseph Sobran

When men once get the habit of helping themselves to the property of others, they are not easily cured of it.

— *The New York Times*

Among the many other questions raised by the nebulous concept of "greed" is why it is a term applied almost exclusively to those who want to earn more money or to keep what they have already earned — never to those wanting to take other people's money in taxes or to those wishing to live on the largess dispensed from such taxation. No amount of taxation is ever described . . . as "greed" on the part of government or the clientele of government.

— Thomas Sowell

At their core, taxpayer rights are human rights. They are about our inherent humanity.

— Nina E. Olson

[T]he tax system should not be treated as wholly divorced from morality.

— Terence Floyd Cuff

Why tribute? why should we pay tribute? If
Caesar can hide the sun from us with a
Blanket, or put the moon in his pocket,
We will pay him tribute for light; else, sir,
No more tribute.

— William Shakespeare
(*Cymbeline*)

The U.S. tax code is now four times longer than the combined works of William Shakespeare — 3.8 million words long. In fact, if Romeo and Juliet were alive today and tried to do a joint return, they'd probably kill themselves again.

— Jay Leno

William Shakespeare was a "ruthless businessman" and tax dodger, researchers have claimed. Although he wrote plays that championed the rights of the poor and the needy, archived documents show the playwright was actually a wealthy landowner repeatedly dragged before the courts and fined for illegally stockpiling food and threatened with jail for evading taxes.

— *Daily Mail*

Taxes grow without rain.

— Old Jewish Proverb

According to biologists, billions of years ago the first sea creature wiggled onto the beach. This was a pivotal moment in life's long march from amorphous sea snot into the highest form of mammalian beings — hedge-fund managers. Many people see that as an improvement, but I'm not judgmental. What we don't know is why the first sea creatures were so anxious to leave their ocean habitats. My guess is that it had something to do with taxes.

— Scott Adams

The thing generally raised on city land is taxes.
— Charles Dudley Warner

A lottery is a tax on people who are bad at math.
— Anonymous

It's understandable if you don't think the subject [of taxes] is sexy. But my guess is that if anyone other than the government was taking money from you, you'd want to know what they were up to.

— Christopher Bergin

The marvel of all history is the patience with which men and women submit to burdens unnecessarily laid upon them by their governments.

— William E. Borah

If a thousand men were not to pay their tax-bills this year, that would not be a violent and bloody measure, as it would be to pay them, and enable the State to commit violence and shed innocent blood. This is, in fact, the definition of a peaceable revolution, if any such is possible.

— Henry David Thoreau

I want to find out who this FICA guy is and how come he's taking so much of my money.

— Nick Kypreos

Last time I looked at a check, I said to myself, "Who the hell is FICA? And when I meet him, I'm going to punch him in the face. Oh my God, FICA is killing me."

— Shaquille O'Neil

All the Congress, all the accountants and tax lawyers, all the judges, and a convention of wizards all cannot tell for sure what the income tax law says.

— Walter B. Wriston

[P]eople don't complain about taxes because they are selfish or stingy. They complain because they simply don't believe they're getting their money's worth.

— Zell Miller

No matter what the objective of the spending program may be, government expenditures always constitute economic costs that are borne by taxpayers, lenders, or inflation victims.

— Hans F. Sennholz

There is a school which holds that critics of taxation levels merely want to opt out of the social contract, that they don't want to pay their "fair share" to help the least well off. No, what critics of taxation want is accountability.

— Daniel Henninger

We now in the United States have more security guards for the rich than we have police services for the poor districts. If you're looking for personal security, far better to move to the suburbs than to pay taxes in New York.

— John Kenneth Galbraith

Taxes are not levied for the benefit of the taxed.

— Robert A. Heinlein

Joseph had to travel with Mary to Bethlehem to pay the census tax decreed by Caesar Augustus. Many people traveled to Bethlehem to pay the tax, so when they arrived, the inn was full and they stayed in the manger. Taxation was the reason Jesus wound up being born in a manger

— Jay Starkman

Render therefore unto Caesar the things which are Caesar's; and unto God the things that are God's.

— *New Testament*

[At the time of Jesus] Jews everywhere long for the coming of a messiah . . . [because] Rome will be defeated and their lives will be free of taxation and want.

— Bill O'Reilly

When Jesus tells his audience to "render to Caesar" his point is not that they should pay their taxes like dutiful Roman citizens; his point is that they should be rendering their *selves* to God. When it comes to what people owe God, Jesus is saying, we are all in the very highest tax bracket.

— David T. Ball

When I was young, I was taught the story of Jesus and the taxman. The point was that Jesus was good to everyone; so much so that he could even eat with the taxman. The story tells a lot about being good, but it also tells a lot about historical perceptions of the tax collector.

— Christopher Bergin

[T]ax collectors and prostitutes are making their way into the Kingdom of God before you.

— *New Testament*

Our tax code is perhaps the second most remarkable book in Western civilization. Of only one other book can it be said, with equal conviction, that great minds have devoted countless hours to the scrutiny and learned exegesis of every passage; that differing interpretations of the text have given rise to some of humanity's most epic struggles; and that, while millions mine it for valuable insights and inspiration, those who claim to live by the book and follow its precepts probably far outnumber those who actually do so.

— J. Mark Iwry

Introduce a wise and efficient system of taxation, and life and energy will pervade the country. Without such a system, it will sink into general and fatal paralysis.

— *The Atlantic* Magazine

Taxes, after all, are dues that we pay for the privileges of membership in an organized society.

— Franklin D. Roosevelt

Can I write off last year's taxes as a bad investment?

— Character in *Wall Street Journal* cartoon

Inflation is taxation without legislation.

— Milton Friedman

If inflation is high enough, effective tax rates on capital can rise above 100%.

— Michael T. Darda

Because of the income tax, a penny saved is more than a penny earned.

— Jeffery L. Yablon

Any tax is a discouragement and therefore a regulation so far as it goes.

— Oliver Wendell Holmes Jr.

Taxes are what we pay for civilized society .... A penalty on the other hand is intended altogether to prevent the thing punished.

— Oliver Wendell Holmes Jr.

If Justice Holmes was correct that "[t]axes are what we pay for civilized society," then the question in this case is how much civilization the taxpayers will be required to purchase.

— Homer Thornberry

Although Mr. Justice Holmes said: "Taxes are what we pay for civilized society," too many citizens want the civilization at a discount.

— Henry E. Morgenthau Jr.

Taxation is the price which civilized communities pay for the opportunity of remaining civilized.

— Albert Bushnell Hart

We agree with Oliver Wendell Holmes Jr. that taxes are the price we pay for civilization. Liberals should not ignore the consequences of taxation for economic growth and family well-being, of course, but we cannot accept the anti-tax fundamentalism of so many contemporary conservatives. If the public does not believe that tax increases are buying more civilization, however, it will resist them.

— William Galston

Crime had to be committed before liability for the imposition [of disputed levy on illegal liquor] arose. Taxes are not so conditioned.

— Pierce Butler

A sales tax is a tax on the freedom of purchase.

— Felix Frankfurter

The sales tax seems to be more politically acceptable than the income tax.

— Raymond C. Scheppach

A use tax is a tax on the enjoyment of that which was purchased.

— Felix Frankfurter

There are some taxes that are good for our economy, because they discourage harmful activities.

— David M. Roodman

The gas tax is no longer a user fee, as it was intended to be. As we have seen so often in government, higher taxes do not result in better outcomes.

— Akash Chougule

An old tax is a good tax.

— Old Folk Saying

Borrowing imposes a hidden burden upon taxpayers in the short run and an explicit burden in the long run, while taxes impose an explicit short-run burden and a more hidden burden in the long run.

— Richard K. Vedder and
Lowell E. Gallaway

There is no abstract justice in any system of taxation.

— Owen J. Roberts

The law of taxation is more concerned with the substance of economic opportunity than with classifying legal concepts, and tagging them with names and labels.

— Benjamin N. Cardozo

Virtually all persons or objects in this country . . . may have tax problems. Every day the economy generates thousands of sales, loans, gifts, purchases, leases, wills and the like, which suggests the possibility of tax problems for somebody. Our economy is tax relevant in almost every detail.

— Potter Stewart

Put not your trust in money, but put your money in trust.

— Oliver Wendell Holmes Sr.

Though tax records are generally looked upon as a nuisance, the day may come when historians will realize that tax records tell the real story behind civilized life. How people were taxed, who was taxed, and what was taxed tell more about a society than anything else. Tax habits could be to civilization what sex habits are to personality. They are basic clues to the way a society behaves.

— Charles Adams

Martins: [on the Ferris wheel] Have you ever seen any of your victims?

Harry Lime: You know, I never feel comfortable on these sort of things. Victims? Don't be melodramatic. [gestures to people far below] Tell me. Would you really feel any pity if one of those dots stopped moving forever? If I offered you twenty thousand pounds for every dot that stopped, would you really, old man, tell me to keep my money, or would you calculate how many dots you could afford to spare? Free of income tax, old man. Free of income tax — the only way you can save money nowadays.

— Graham Greene
(Scene from *The Third Man* screenplay)

Moral turpitude is not a touchstone of taxability.

— Frank Murphy

And Samuel told all the words of the Lord unto the people that asked of him a king. And he said, This will be the manner of the king that shall reign over you: . . . he will take the tenth of your seed, and of your vineyards, and give to his officers, and to his servants. And he will take your menservants, and your maidservants, and your goodliest young men, and your asses, and put them to his work. He will take the tenth of your sheep: and ye shall be his servants. And ye shall cry out in that day because of your king which ye shall have chosen you; and the Lord will not hear you in that day.

— *Old Testament*

He [the King] will place a tax on the air you breathe and on the bread you eat; he will give you a legislation which is as legitimate as it is unjust and instead of reasons, he'll give you laws. These will grow in the course of time, until you no longer exist for yourselves but for others.

> — Franz Grillparzer
> (*Libussa*)

. . . For imposing Taxes on us without our Consent. . . .

> — The Declaration of Independence

Over-taxation cost England her colonies of North America.

> — Edmund Burke

Taxes rise with inflation, however caused or to whatever extent, whether temporary or permanent; and depression, be it ever so great, and whether caused by imaginary difficulties or by war or famine, lessens the demand for contribution in a corresponding ratio.

> — Nathan Clifford

Almost all taxes on production fall finally on the consumer.

> — David Ricardo

When King Philip of France expelled the Jews in 1306, the reason given was that they charged excessively high interest rates. However, he did not cancel the debts owed to Jews, but instead set about collecting them for his own treasury. To his disappointment, the king discovered that the money collected in this way was less than the taxes that Jews had been paying.

> —Thomas Sowell

I heard a very warm Debate between two Professors, about the most commodious and effectual ways and means of raising Money without grieving the Subject. The first affirmed the justest Method would be to lay a certain Tax upon Vices and Folly, and the Sum fixed upon every Man, to be rated after the fairest manner by a Jury of his Neighbours. The second was of an Opinion directly contrary, to tax those Qualities of Body and Mind for which Men chiefly value themselves, the Rate to be more or less according to the Degrees of excelling, the Decision whereof should be left entirely to their own Breast. The highest Tax was upon Men, who are the greatest Favourites of the other Sex, and the Assessments according to the Number and Natures of the Favours they have received; for which they are allowed to be their own Vouchers. Wit, Valour, and Politeness were likewise proposed to be largely Taxed, and collected in the same manner, by every Persons giving his own Word for the Quantum of what he possessed. . . . The Women were proposed to be taxed according to their Beauty and skill in Dressing, wherein they had the same Privilege with the Men, to be determined by their own Judgment.

— Jonathan Swift

Natural rights, so called, are as much subject to taxation as rights of less importance.

— Benjamin N. Cardozo

The tax which will be paid for education is not more than the thousand part of what will be paid if we leave the people in ignorance.

— Thomas Jefferson

The ideologists of taxation are constantly attributing their own preferences to some higher disinterested wisdom.

— Louis Eisenstein

There is no end, of course, to people promoting the use of the tax code to support nice-sounding things. That's why we have the tax code we do.

— Holman W. Jenkins Jr.

Failure to use tax money to finance things not liked by the taxpaying public is routinely called "censorship."

— Thomas Sowell

My meaningless office job: they pay me for my body and mind, but my heart gets no paycheck and my soul pays the taxes.

— Carrie Latet

For there to be relief, there has to be an affliction, an afflicted party, somebody who administers the relief, and an act in which you are relieved of the affliction. The reliever is the hero, and anybody who tries to stop them is the bad guy intent on keeping the affliction going. So, add "tax" to "relief" and you get a metaphor that taxation is an affliction, and anybody against relieving this affliction is a villain.

— Bonnie Azab Powell

Taxation is eminently practical, and is in fact brought to every man's door.

— Rufus W. Peckham

Trade being a sensitive plant, a direct tax upon it to some extent at least deters trade even if its effect is not precisely calculable.

— Felix Frankfurter

The payment of taxes gives a right to protection.

— James M. Wayne

[Tax] liability is one of the notorious incidents of social life.

— Oliver Wendell Holmes Jr.

Visibility enables individuals and businesses to know the true cost of transactions. It also enables them to see what their total tax liability is and to which level of government it is being paid. When a tax is not visible, it can be easily retained or raised with little, if any, awareness among taxpayers about how the tax affects them.

— Tax Division of the American Institute of Certified Public Accountants

The idea that jobs, businesses and wealth follow low tax rates is widely accepted.

— Stephen Moore

Those who can do a good trade don't wrangle over taxes.
— Old Chinese Proverb

China has no income tax, no unemployment and not a single soldier outside its borders
— Zhou Enlai

In my own case the words of such an act as the Income Tax, for example, merely dance before my eyes in a meaningless procession; cross-reference to cross-reference, exception upon exception — couched in abstract terms that offer no handle to seize hold of — leave in my mind only a confused sense of some vitally important, but successfully concealed, purport, which it is my duty to extract, but which is within my power, if at all, only after the most inordinate expenditure of time.
— Learned Hand

Taxation without comprehension is as inimical to democracy as taxation without representation.
— Lawrence A. Zelenak

[T]o tax and to please, no more than to love and to be wise, is not given to men.
— Edmund Burke

Since the purpose of the tax code is to raise revenue, it has as its core mission the objective of making people poorer. The central question is: who?
— Douglas Holtz-Eakin

Has [the tyrant] not also another object which is that [the people] may be impoverished by payment of taxes, and thus compelled to devote themselves to their daily wants and therefore less likely to conspire against him?
— Plato

Taxation is, in fact, the most difficult function of government and that against which their citizens are most apt to be refractory.
— Thomas Jefferson

There are those who seem to have nothing else to do but to suggest modes of taxation to men in office.

— Robert Peel

Peter [the Great] in 1708 created a service of revenue officers, men whose duty it was to devise new means of taxing the people. Called by the foreign name "fiscals," they were commanded "to sit and make income for the Sovereign Lord." ... There was a tax on births, on marriages, on funerals and on the registration of wills. There was a tax on wheat and tallow. Horses were taxed, and horse hides and horse collars. There was a hat tax and a tax on the wearing of leather boots. The beard tax was systemized and enforced, and a tax on mustaches was added. Ten percent was collected from all cab fares. Houses in Moscow were taxed, and beehives throughout Russia. There was a bed tax, a bath tax, an inn tax, a tax on kitchen chimneys and on the firewood that burned in them. Nuts, melons, cucumbers, were taxed. There was even a tax on drinking water.

— Robert K. Massie

The income tax created more criminals than any other single act of government.

— Barry M. Goldwater

If the Nation is living within its income, its credit is good. If, in some crises, it lives beyond its income for a year or two, it can usually borrow temporarily at reasonable rates. But if, like a spendthrift, it throws discretion to the winds, and is willing to make no sacrifice at all in spending; if it extends its taxing to the limit of the people's power to pay and continues to pile up deficits, then it is on the road to bankruptcy.

— Franklin D. Roosevelt

And it came to pass in those days, that there went out a decree from Caesar Augustus that all the world should be taxed.

— *New Testament*

Of course [the Orthodox Jewish dietary laws] are inconvenient at times, but not nearly as inconvenient as paying the federal income tax.

— Herman Wouk

There is no such thing as a good tax.
— Winston Churchill

It was as true . . . as taxes is. And nothing's truer than them.
— Charles Dickens

Taxation must affect the distribution of income, whether we will it so or not.
— Henry C. Simons

Taxation is paying your dues, paying your membership fee in America.
— George Lakoff

We pay taxes not because we get benefits from the state, but because it is as much our duty to support the state as to support ourselves or our family; because, in short, the state is an integral part of us.
— Edwin R.A. Seligman

I like to pay taxes. With them I buy civilization.
— Oliver Wendell Holmes Jr.

If this is the price we pay for our society, shouldn't we be getting a little more civilization or a lot lower price?
— Thomas G. Donlan

Holmes got it precisely wrong. In fact, I would argue that the level of taxation and of government regulation is a measure of our failure to civilize our society.
— Edward H. Crane

[T]axes have become the price we pay to support people who deny our civilization.
— Malcolm Wallop

The institution of taxation is not a civilized but a barbaric method to fund anything . . . it amounts to . . . a gross violation of human liberty.
— Tibor R. Machan

I like to pay taxes. It makes me feel less guilty.
— Anonymous Member of a
Two-Income Couple

I am thankful for the taxes I pay because it means that I'm employed.
— Nancie J. Carmody

[E]very real American is proud to carry his share of any burden . . . .
I simply do not believe for one second that anyone privileged to live in
this country wants someone else to pay his fair and just share of the cost
of his Government.
— Dwight D. Eisenhower

Do you know what the taxes are on five million dollars? Six million
dollars.
— Marianne and Cormac Wibberley
(*National Treasure: Book of Secrets* screenplay)

[The tax code] is a monstrosity and there's only one thing to do with
it. Scrap it, kill it, drive a stake through its heart, bury it and hope it
never rises again to terrorize the American people.
— Steve Forbes

I think our tax system is not worthy of an advanced society.
— Paul H. O'Neill

The physical power to get the money does not seem to me a test of
the right to tax. Might does not make right even in taxation.
— Robert H. Jackson

The incidence of taxation depends upon the substance of a transaction.
— Hugo L. Black

Taxes are the lifeblood of government and no taxpayer should be
permitted to escape the payment of his just share of the burden of
contributing thereto.
— Arthur T. Vanderbilt

1. Tax Luxuries.
2. Tax Inheritances.
3. Tax Large Incomes.
4. Tax Monopolies.
5. Tax the Privileged Corporation.
6. A Tariff for Revenue.
7. Reform the Civil Service.
8. Punish Corrupt Officers.
9. Punish Vote Buying.
10. Punish Employers who Coerce their Employees in Elections.

This is a popular platform of ten lines. We recommend it to the politicians in place of long-winded resolutions.

— Joseph Pulitzer

Man is not like other animals in the ways that are really significant: animals have instincts, we have taxes.

— Erving Goffman

Bats have no bankers and they do not drink and cannot be arrested and pay no tax and, in general, bats have it made.

— John Berryman

When we played, World Series checks meant something. Now all they do is screw up your taxes.

— Don Drysdale

The invention of the teenager was a mistake. Once you identify a period of life in which people get to stay out late but don't have to pay taxes — naturally, no one wants to live any other way.

— Judith Martin
(writing as "Miss Manners")

There's nothing wrong with the younger generation that becoming taxpayers won't cure.

— Dan Bennett

[Since 1975] American tax laws have changed to reflect a citizenry that has generally become more individualistic, less honest, more sophisticated, less honorable, more worshipful of wealth, and less caring about the opinions of others.

— Jeffery L. Yablon

The expenses of government, having for their object the interest of all, should be borne by everyone, and the more a man enjoys the advantages of society, the more he ought to hold himself honored in contributing to those expenses.

— Anne Robert Jacques Turgot

Any intelligent thinking on taxes eventually reaches the ultimate purpose of life on this planet as each of us conceives it.

— Louis Eisenstein

Those figures are after tax, but before spin.

— *The Wall Street Journal*
("Pepper . . . and Salt")

[I]n most situations, the changes that taxes induce are symptoms of economic waste or, using economic jargon, inefficiency. In the absence of taxes, people and businesses react to prices that approximately reflect the true social costs and benefits of what they buy and sell, and taxes can turn prices from being pretty good signals of social cost and benefit into very bad ones.

— Joel Slemrod

Driving your car is associated with various adverse side effects, which economists call externalities. These include traffic congestion, accidents, local pollution and global climate change. If the tax on gasoline were higher, people would alter their behavior to drive less. They would be more likely to take public transportation, use car pools or live closer to work. The incentives they face when deciding how much to drive would more closely match the true social costs and benefits.

— N. Gregory Mankiw

This tax [on soda] is charged to the industry that profits off of drinks that promote diabetes and obesity, diseases that disproportionally affect people with limited incomes and communities of color.
— Berkeley vs. Big Soda Website

Taxes send messages, and in several ways. They affect the costs and returns to different kinds of activity, thereby influencing patterns of use of capital and labor. They also make statements about the relative desirability of different types of activity and patterns of conduct. Conduct that carries a low tax induces people to emulate that conduct. Conduct that carries a high tax discourages such conduct.
— Edward J. McCaffery and Richard E. Wagner

Tax subsidies cause Americans to overinvest in oversized homes.
— Robert J. Samuelson

[I]n one sense the tax structure is art — a subsuming of the infinite muddle of human activity under a single rubric, as though it had a single purpose and could be ordered by a mind heaving the line of a single vision.
— John Casey

I thought at first that the power of taxation [given in the new Federal Constitution] might have been limited. A little reflection soon convinced me it ought not to be.
— Thomas Jefferson

It would be a hard government that should tax its people one-tenth part of their income.
— Benjamin Franklin

We shall now embark on a voyage through the various sections of the Income Tax Regulations which are enough to boggle the mind of an English-speaking U.S. Citizen.
— William A. Goffe

Our tax code is so long it makes *War and Peace* seem breezy.
— Steven LaTourette

The tax law is six times longer than *War and Peace* and not nearly as easy to read.

— Michael J. Graetz

He [fellow U.S. Sen. Russell B. Long] knows the Tax Code as thoroughly as the Pope knows the Lord's Prayer.

— William Proxmire

Don't tax you, don't tax me;
Tax the fellow behind the tree.

— Russell B. Long

Don't tax you. Don't tax me.
Tax the companies across the sea.

— Dan Rostenkowski

When it comes to finances, remember that there are no withholding taxes on the wages of sin.

— Mae West

The wages of sin are death, but by the time taxes are taken out, it's just sort of a tired feeling.

— Paula Poundstone

Cursed war and racking tax
Have left us scarcely raiment to our backs.

— Sir Walter Scott

Misera contribuens plebs.
(The poor taxpaying people.)

— Law of the Hungarian Diet of 1751,
Article 37

Peace and prosperity are inversely proportional to the level of taxation.

— John Pugsley

Work and earn; pay taxes and die.

— Old German Proverb

[W]e have a paradoxical situation where the least heavily taxed are the most resentful. But perhaps this is less of a paradox than it seems. People who are accustomed to a large disposable income will be inclined to think that they can find better uses for the money than the government can.

— Christopher Hitchens

More Americans pay taxes than vote.

— J. Robert Kerrey

The Legislative Process

We shall tax and tax, spend and spend, and elect and elect.

— Harry L. Hopkins
(attributed)

The Legislative Process

The story is always the same [in Congress]: Higher rates are imposed and at the same time loopholes are carefully framed which permit the wealthy to get out from under the higher taxes.

— Hubert H. Humphrey

Raising revenue through tax reform is better than simply raising rates, which Democrats insist upon with near religious fervor. It is more economically efficient because it eliminates credits, carve-outs and deductions that grossly misallocate capital. And it is more fair because it is the rich who can afford not only the sharp lawyers and accountants who exploit loopholes but the lobbyists who create them in the first place.

— Charles Krauthammer

Once again the lesson is that high tax rates fail to raise the revenue that liberals claim, not least because liberal politicians follow their tax increases by passing out favors to the rich and powerful.

— *The Wall Street Journal*

The tax system today is not promoting prosperity based on individual enterprise and thriftiness. It is instead working, as all socialist redistribution schemes do, to enrich and benefit those who have access to the levers of power. In America that is the political donor class.

— David Cay Johnston

Unfortunately, bad tax policy is sometimes good politics.

— Daniel J. Mitchell

The U.S. tax code is the most political law in the world.

— Jonathan Blattmachr

That one's tax policy views are wholly divorced from one's political views is a petty conceit.

— Kip Dellinger

[American tax laws] are constantly changing as our elected representatives seek new ways to ensure that whatever tax advice we receive is incorrect.

— Dave Barry

It currently requires the same majority to raise taxes as it does to declare National Banana Peel Week. That is wrong. Raising taxes should require a high enough threshold that elected officials do it only when there is a clear and compelling reason.

— Mike Huckabee

The tax subsidies tumble into the law without supporting studies, being propelled instead by clichés, debating points, and scraps of data and tables that are passed off as serious evidence. A tax system that is so vulnerable to this injection of extraneous, costly, and ill-considered expenditure programs is in a precarious state from the standpoint of . . . providing adequate revenues and maintaining tax equity.

— Stanley S. Surrey

There is an ancient belief that the gods love the obscure and hate the obvious. Without benefit of divinity, modern men of similar persuasion draft provisions of the Internal Revenue Code. Section 341 is their triumph.

— Martin D. Ginsburg

[Twenty-one years after noting to the Senate Finance Committee that section 341 contains a single sentence that is longer than the entire Gettysburg Address:] [T]he senators expressed horror about this, but, needless to say, the sentence is still there and the senators in question are not.

— Peter L. Faber

Is there a method to resolve the current problem of the tax system? Perhaps as a first step, Congress can pass its own ethical rules that will require each representative and senator to prepare and file his own tax return without any professional help or guidance and under penalty of being dismissed from Congress, certify his compliance to his respective ethic committees.

— Denis A. Kleinfeld

It might help if Americans called welfare programs — current benefits for select populations, paid for by current taxes — by their proper name, rather than by the soothing (and misleading) labels of "entitlements" and "social insurance." That way, we might ask ourselves who deserves welfare and why.

— Robert J. Samuelson

Legislative changes in tax policy usually begin as marginal adjustments to the existing tax structure . . . . The tax code offers a variety of easily grasped levers. In this sense, it is an incrementalist paradise, susceptible and seductive to political tinkerers. As a result, most changes in tax bills consist of simple adjustments in existing tax provisions.

— John F. Witte

The problem is not just that the law is overly complex. The problem is also that we change it all the time.

— Gordon D. Henderson

One of the problems with trying to have a rational discussion about taxes is that so many people want to believe what's convenient rather than what's accurate. Believing, after all, requires so much less effort than thinking.

— Allan Sloan

A low tax burden is essential to maintain America's global competitiveness. But tax cuts need to be funded by permanent outlay reductions.

— Alan Greenspan

If you want to be a low-tax person, you want to be in favor of low taxes; you also need to have the associated spending cuts that make that feasible. If you want to be a high-spending person because you think government programs are valuable, then you also have to accept the tax implications.

— Ben Bernanke

Complex laws spawn many inadvertent errors as well as opportunities for intentional noncompliance. Complex laws also contribute to taxpayer confusion and real or perceived unfairness in the tax system. Studies have shown that taxpayers are less likely to be compliant if they perceive the tax system to be inequitable.

— George K. Yin

The most fundamental maxim of tax reform is that, holding revenue and distribution constant, we should broaden the base and lower the rates. Politics is always pushing the tax system in the other direction, as taxpayers come in to make arguments about special circumstances that ostensibly call for more favorable treatment. Although these arguments often sound appealing, the long-run effect of special rules is to make the system more complicated, less efficient, and less fair.

— Daniel N. Shaviro

The most damaging thing you can do to any businessman in America is to keep him in doubt, and to keep him guessing, on what our tax policy is.

— Lyndon B. Johnson

[S]ome uncertainty [in the tax laws] may be useful in discouraging taxpayers from venturing too close to the edge, and thereby going over the edge, of established principles.

— Don Lubick

[T]here are dangers in having the tax laws up in the air all the time.

— Martin Neil Baily

This idea that you start with a clean slate and end up with a beautiful, logical tax system just isn't democracy.

— John L. Knapp

[T]he features of a sales tax that make it so economically attractive are the same features that make it politically unfeasible.

— Martin A. Sullivan

[N]othing guarantees more applause and more support than the call to abolish the IRS.

— Frank Luntz

Underfunding the Internal Revenue Service in itself has an element of tax relief.

— Terence Floyd Cuff

Late one night, just blocks from the Capitol, a mugger jumped into the path of a well-dressed fellow and stuck a gun in his ribs. "Give me your money," the thief demanded. "Are you kidding?" the man said. "I'm a U.S. congressman." "In that case," the mugger growled, cocking his weapon, "give me my money."

— *Playboy* Magazine

Politicians certainly must be considered the most formidable barrier to fundamental tax reform.

— David A. Hartman

The tax expert has power that no one else does, which is to say to the candidate and the political advisers that "you can't do that," or to say if you go ahead and do that, then it would be an economic catastrophe and you will be laughed at.

— Kevin Hassett

Tax reform, as distinct from tax reduction, inevitably involves curtailing some entrenched tax benefits.

— Edward P. Lazear and James M. Poterba

No matter how much badly designed tax policies stand as evidence that getting it "right" is difficult, when good policies are enacted and revisions well timed, they remind us that political honesty, tenacity, and integrity can help create a better, more efficient, and equitable system.

— Gene Steuerle

If we don't do something to simplify the tax system, we're going to end up with a national police force of internal revenue agents.

— Leon Panetta

When Congress talks about simplification, taxpayers may well be reminded of Emerson's comments regarding an acquaintance, "[t]he louder he talked of his honor, the faster we counted our spoons."

— Michael J. Graetz

Whenever politicians talk about streamlining or harmonizing taxes, clutch your wallets and pocketbooks — it's going to cost you money.

— Steve Forbes

Congress can raise taxes because it can persuade a sizable fraction of the populace that somebody else will pay.

— Milton Friedman

The Congress is a circus. To the music of braying donkeys, each elephant is led in circles by the tail of another. While they have the peoples' attention, the clowns write the tax laws.

— Jim Boren

The smart money bets against tax reform — always and everywhere. But every once in a while — usually a long while — the smart money is wrong.

— Joseph J. Thorndike

If there is ever going to be fundamental tax reform [in the United States], it will occur in the second term of a popular president.

— Martin A. Sullivan

Reform proposals to eliminate tax preferences and broaden the tax base run contrary to the incentives and interests established by the political institutions within which policymakers act, and hence are unlikely to succeed.

— Sheldon D. Pollack

Tax simplification is everyone's favorite orphan. All of us involved in the tax system — Congress, the executive branch, practitioners and taxpayers — proclaim our affection for this child of our dreams, but few are willing to adopt her as our own.

— Fred Goldberg

The question is: What can we, as citizens, do to reform our tax system? As you know, under our three-branch system of government, the tax laws are created by: Satan. But he works through the Congress, so that's where we must focus our efforts.

— Dave Barry

[S]ome in our [Republican] party miss no opportunity to roundly and loudly condemn affirmative action that helped a few thousand black kids get an education, but you hardly hear a whimper when it's affirmative action for lobbyists who load our federal tax code with preferences for special interests.

— Colin Powell

Our party has been accused of fooling the public by calling tax increases "revenue enhancement." Not so. No one was fooled.

— Dan Quayle

[The phaseouts of personal exemptions and itemized deductions] are just complicated, backhanded rate increases for cowardly politicians who are afraid to raise the rate outright.

— Martin A. Sullivan

Thus the triple whammy: first, high [tax] rates reduce investment and growth; second, they encourage baroque loophole-seeking, which further exacerbates the unequal treatment of different kinds of income; third, the system gets ever more burdensome, shifting 6 billion person-hours yearly out of the productive economy and into the parasite economy of accountants and lobbyists.

— James P. Pinkerton

Tax provisions favoring one activity over another or providing targeted tax benefits to a limited number of taxpayers creates complexity and instability, impose large compliance costs, and can lead to an inefficient use of resources. A rational system would favor a broad tax base, providing special tax treatment only where it can be persuasively demonstrated that the effect of a deduction, exclusion, or credit justifies higher taxes paid by all taxpayers.

— Report of the President's Advisory Panel on
Federal Tax Reform (2005)

The United States is a low-tax country, but we are not a low-income-tax country. Our income tax takes a share of our economic output similar to other nations. The big difference is that we are the only OECD country without a national level tax on sales of goods and services. Reforming the income tax will do nothing to change this fundamental economic disadvantage.

— Michael J. Graetz

The United States will get a value added tax when conservatives realize that it is regressive, and liberals realize that it is a money machine.

— Lawrence Summers
(attributed)

Policymakers have long understood that the less visible — or "salient," to use the economist's term of art — a tax is, the easier it is to raise. Which is why Milton Friedman, looking for ways the federal government could collect more money during World War II, recommended the creation of income tax withholding (an innovation he was not proud of). It's also why "value-added taxes" act like steroids when it comes to bulking up government.

— Eric Felten

The most important ways in which I think the Internet will affect the big issue is that it will make it more difficult for government to collect taxes.

— Milton Friedman

[T]axes should not be hidden by being collected in bits and pieces over the course of a year as the taxpayer goes shopping, as either sales or value-added taxes.

— Stephen J. Entin

[Taxes] ought to be raised in such a way, that the public might not only pay them, but at the same time, *feel* them. This would teach them to think a little better in what way their money goes.

— John Smilie

The first 9 pages of the Internal Revenue Code define income; the remaining 1,100 pages spin the web of exceptions and preferences.

— Warren G. Magnuson

The most earnest student can falter and reel in the ghost-world of [*The Talmud's* discussion of the laws pertaining to] the Temple: the orders of priests and Levites, the different sacrifices, the varying purity rules for wine, bread, fish, water, metal, glass, wood, clay, leather, textiles; the times and immersions of purification — a network of laws fully as involved and as searching as the U.S. Internal Revenue Code.

— Herman Wouk

If the Lord loveth a cheerful giver, how he must hate the taxpayer!

— John Andrew Holmes

Our income tax system has been destroyed by complexity — a complexity caused largely by well-meaning efforts to achieve theoretical purity, eliminate every real and imagined "abuse," and address nontax policy objectives.

— Fred T. Goldberg Jr.

When government uses subsidies to moralize, as with tax preferences for bonds that can be used to finance this but not that, government is speaking. It is expressing opinions about what is and is not wholesome. And once government starts venting such opinions, how does it stop?

— George Will

. . . I was brought up to believe that Scotch whisky would need a tax preference to survive in competition with Kentucky bourbon . . . .
— Hugo L. Black

Since the content of tax policy is both complex and uninteresting to most readers, the press prefers to write about corruption and lobbying. The ideal story reports on a political campaign contribution to a member of the tax committee who has gotten a special interest amendment adopted for the contributor.
— Thomas J. Reese

Killing the corporate income tax would improve the efficiency and competitiveness of U.S. business; eliminate incentives to relocate overseas or to engage in mind-boggling shelter transactions; cut down a major source of accountants' compensation and a temptation to look the other way; eliminate disincentives to pay dividends and foster more efficient corporations, sensibly valued. Who can argue with that?
— Edward J. McCaffery

The corporate income tax is one of the best examples in American political history of the law of unintended consequences. It was originally intended as a means to tax the rich, but it quickly became one of the prime means by which the rich have avoided taxes.
— John Steele Gordon

Over the years, a parade of lobbyists has rigged the tax code to benefit particular companies and industries. Those with accountants or lawyers to work the system can end up paying no taxes at all. But all the rest are hit with one of the highest corporate tax rates in the world. It makes no sense. It has to change.
— Barack Obama

Beware politicians who say they only want to tax the rich. Sooner or later their tax schemes will soak the middle class because that's where the real money is.
— *The Wall Street Journal*

One of the fundamental lessons of economics is that the burden of a tax is not necessarily borne by the person who sends a check to the government.

— N. Gregory Mankiw

Bear in mind that the higher [capital gains] tax is principally directed toward individual investors. Not foundations or pension funds. It will be the individual who takes the hit.

— Chuck Schwab

The first neat thing they teach you about taxes in economics school is that it does not matter if a tax is imposed on a buyer or a seller. It all comes out in the wash . . . . For some reason (probably our mistrustful human nature), this most basic of economic lessons always gets lost on politicians and lobbyists.

— Martin A. Sullivan

Shareholders need to recognize that discussions about the corporate tax rate are about them.

— Safra A. Catz

No matter what anyone may say about making the rich and the corporations pay taxes, in the end they come out of the people who toil.

— Calvin Coolidge

Taxes are a changing product of earnest efforts to have others pay them.

— Louis Eisenstein

There may be liberty and justice for all, but there are tax breaks only for some.

— Martin A. Sullivan

It's admirable when people back their charitable impulses up with donations. But the tax code shouldn't allow the wealthy the kind of loopholes that let them, essentially, force other taxpayers to underwrite donations to their pet causes.

— Scott Klinger

I'm telling you right now, if these tax breaks are not reinstated into the budget, film production in this town [New York City] is going to collapse, and television is going to collapse and it's all going to go to California.

— Alec Baldwin

If they'd lower the taxes and get rid of the smog and clean up the traffic mess, I really believe I'd settle here [in California] until the next earthquake.

— Groucho Marx

The less people know about how sausages and laws are made, the better they'll sleep at night.

— Otto von Bismarck

[A]ny business that doesn't seek a tax subsidy is foolish because the rate of return is far higher than that business could get in the market.

— Martin Lobel

No one who has witnessed tax lobbyists' perennial infestation of Capitol Hill can ever again confuse the making of tax laws with the making of sausages: at least when you make sausages, you know the pigs won't be coming back.

— J. Mark Iwry

Lobbyists are professional optimists, especially when it comes to tax reform. They have a vested interest in promoting the idea that reform might happen, even when everyone knows it won't.

— Joseph J. Thorndike

From the citizens' point of view, the function of tax legislation is to decide who shall pay how much to finance government spending. But from Congress's point of view, tax legislation has an additional and very important function: It is a way to raise campaign funds. . . . So long as a tax bill is under consideration, with many billions of dollars at stake, lobbyists are actively pressing for the introduction or retention of special provisions to benefit their clients. And so long as lobbyists are active, thousand-dollar-a-plate dinners and similar devices will tap them for campaign funds.

[But] this process had come to a dead end. As it were, the tax space was overcrowded with loopholes. There was no room to add any more. . . . [The Tax Reform Act of 1986] was an ingenious solution to the potential collapse of tax reform as a source of campaign funds. [It] disappoints almost all the lobbyists in one fell swoop, but it also wipes the slate clean, thereby providing space for the tax reform cycle to start over again. . . . The members of Congress look forward to being re-elected and the lobbyists to being retained — so this tactic promises future benefits to both groups.

— Milton Friedman

The more progressive the tax system's marginal rates, the easier it is for politicians and their fellow travelers to extort money from those seeking special favors or protection from adverse legislation or regulation.

— Kip Dellinger

When plunder is organized by law for the profit of those who make the law, all the plundered classes try somehow to enter — by peaceful or revolutionary means — into the making of laws.

— Claude-Frederic Bastiat

We've got the hardest working people in the world. We've got the best tax policy in the world. I mean, we've got a lot going for us.

— George W. Bush

In a reversal of "No taxation without representation," women were required to pay federal income tax seven years before they won the right to vote.

— Loch Adamson

In case you didn't know, ethanol is made by mixing corn with your tax dollars.

— Paul A. Gigot

[M]ost people don't understand that regulatory laws can have the same effect as taxes.

— Gary S. Becker and Richard A. Posner

Excessive spending has no partisan affiliation. Regardless of the party in power, special interests always favor more spending, because they can earmark the benefits for themselves and diffuse the costs of excessive taxes or debt on the general citizenry.

— John O. McGinnis and Michael B. Rappaport

The powerful behavioral effects of taxation (more a tribute to the power of markets because all taxes do is change prices) have seduced politicians into thinking the tax code is an omnibus instrument for social good. It is not.

— Douglas Holtz-Eakin

Business has made it quite clear that the tax credit is the form in which it prefers to receive subsidies.

— Charles H. Percy

There's a lot of evidence you can sell people on tax increases if they think it's an investment.

— Bill Clinton

For me it's a little difficult to give tax relief to people that don't pay income taxes.

— Tom DeLay

Tax cuts are for tax*payers*.

— Phil Gramm

Tax sanctimony gets in the way of tax reform. In a progressive rate structure, the rich almost always get bigger tax cuts, because their rates are higher to begin with. So their cuts sound unfair. The more progressive a tax structure, the more unfair its dismantlement appears.

— Amity Shlaes

Tax cuts chronically fare poorly in opinion polls but do quite well at the ballot box.

— Fred Barnes

Never trust a member [of the U.S. House of Representatives] who quotes the Bible, the Internal Revenue Code or the Rules of the House.

— Eugene McCarthy

Complexity does not enter the tax code so much out of malevolence as through misguided reform efforts and excessive demands made on tax laws as the vehicle for implementing public policy.

— Sheldon D. Pollack

It is beyond serious question that a tax does not cease to be valid merely because it regulates, discourages, or even definitely deters the activities taxed . . . . The principle applies even though the revenue obtained is obviously negligible . . . or the revenue purpose of the tax may be secondary . . . .

— Tom C. Clark

Tax systems can have multiple goals. For example, in addition to the common goal of raising revenue for the government, goals can also include redistributing income, stabilizing the economy, and achieving various other social and economic objectives through the use of preferences. Generally speaking, the greater the number of goals, the more complex is the tax system.

— General Accounting Office

Tax policies geared toward "social engineering" will invariably have unintended consequences . . . .

— Steve Kirkpatrick

The analysis of tax policy and tax legislation can be "highly conjectural" and consequently more art than science.

— Joint Economic Committee

It is impossible to simplify the tax code without at the same time affecting the fairness of the tax code.

— William G. Gale

Tax revolutions are few and far between. Taxes are so important to the economy that major changes in tax law are best achieved incrementally, giving notice well in advance and avoiding potentially large disruptions from big surprises.

— Robert H. Nelson

[A]lmost every time we pass a tax bill, we make the code more complex, increase the burden on the taxpayer, and make it harder to enforce.

— Trent Lott

Our tax system is so screwed up that even if we could agree on a better one, there is no way to get there from here.

— Jeffery L. Yablon

[W]ithout increased spending discipline, even the best tax reforms are doomed to be undone.

— Michael J. Boskin

I think if we go back to basics and say the tax code is only to raise revenue and social welfare ought to be somewhere else, we would have a much better system.

— Martin Lobel

[T]he tax code is littered with relics of failed attempts at social engineering. Every one of them leaves more tax for someone else to pay.

— Thomas G. Donlan

I don't think the tax code should be a substitute for the appropriations process in making social change.

— Charles B. Rangel

[T]aking a government spending program and converting it into a tax preference does absolutely nothing to make the government truly smaller, even it is shrinks officially reported taxes and spending.

— Daniel N. Shaviro

The tax system should be designed to impose and to collect taxes, not to administer social programs.

— Donald C. Alexander

It would have made more sense to do Obamacare the way we did in Massachusetts, which would be to just give people money to offset the cost of their health insurance. That was politically infeasible and so instead it was done through the tax code.

— Jonathan Gruber

Real [tax] simplification has eluded us because we have failed to address head-on the public's addiction to tax incentives as a means of providing social services and funding government programs. Unless we deal with that problem, real simplification is impossible.

— Thomas F. Field

Enact Fundamental Tax Reform: Adopt a simple and fair single-rate tax system by scrapping the internal revenue code and replacing it with one that is no longer than 4,543 words — the length of the original Constitution.

— Agenda Item Number Four of Tea Party's Contract From America

The political function of the [individual and corporate] income taxes, which is served by their being complex, is to provide a means whereby the members of Congress who have anything whatsoever to do with taxation can raise campaign funds. That is what supports the army of lobbyists in Washington who are seeking to produce changes in the income tax, to introduce special privileges or exemptions for their clients, or to have what they regard as special burdens on their clients removed. A [flat tax] would [thwart those objectives] since the structure of the tax is so simple and straightforward.

— Milton Friedman

I'm called by my faith tradition to speak truth to power when I see injustice being done. And a flat tax is an injustice.

— Jason Coulter

Lawmakers have hit upon some ingenious ways to keep milking the cash cow. Rather than making certain changes in tax law permanent, they enact them for one- or two-year periods, after which the provisions expire. As the expiration date nears, special interests begin to lobby for an extension and invariably cough up more campaign funds.

— Donald L. Barlett and James B. Steele

[P]eople have suggested that using computer software really masks for individuals the complexity of the individual tax system.

— Mary Schmitt

In the tax law, complexity stems from rapacity taking cover in obscurity.

— J. Mark Iwry

The purse of the people is the real seat of sensibility. Let it be drawn upon largely, and they will then listen to truths which could not excite them through any other organ.

— Thomas Jefferson

If Patrick Henry thought that taxation without representation was bad, he should see how bad it is with representation.

— *The Old Farmer's Almanac*

We put those payroll contributions there so as to give the contributors a legal, moral, and political right to collect their pensions and their unemployment benefits. With those taxes in there, no damn politician can ever scrap my social security program.

— Franklin D. Roosevelt
(attributed)

I'm not for increasing taxes to increase spending on anything no matter how meritorious it is. It's a bad precedent.

— Phil Gramm

One way to reduce taxes is to hold elections every year because there never seem to be tax increases in an election year.

— Anonymous

At some level, of course, every election is about taxes. The level of taxation determines the size of government the country can afford, and size of government goes a long way toward determining the role government plays in the economy and the society.

— Gerald F. Seib

My opponent won't rule out raising taxes, but I will. Congress will push me to raise taxes, and I'll say no, and they'll push, and I'll say no, and they'll push and I'll say, "Read my lips: *no new taxes*."

— George H.W. Bush

Conservative governments which increase taxation lose elections.

— Margaret Thatcher

Not over my dead body will they raise your taxes.

— George W. Bush

During the [California gubernatorial] campaign it looked almost as if we could put our fiscal house in order without resorting to new taxes. We did not know just how bad the situation was then. Now we have had access to, and a chance to read, the fine print. As a result, we have, as you know, submitted a revenue bill of nearly one billion dollars in increased taxes.

— Ronald Reagan

Campaign tax plans should come with a disclaimer: "All policies appearing in this proposal are fictitious. Any resemblance to real-world tax policies is purely coincidental."

— Joseph J. Thorndike

Trouble is, a promise to maintain fiscal discipline doesn't make anyone stand up and cheer. Tax cuts, on the other hand, make millions stand up and cheer and hundreds of thousands so happy they'll write millions of dollars in checks to fund a re-election campaign.

— Bob Kerrey

No party ever won the White House (or Congress) by balancing the federal budget, nor did anyone ever lose a national election by producing huge deficits.

— William Greider

Tax cuts are never as popular with politicians in good times as are tax increases in bad times.

— Arthur B. Laffer

We don't have a trillion-dollar debt because we haven't taxed enough; we have a trillion-dollar debt because we spend too much.

— Ronald Reagan

The politicians say "we" can't afford a tax cut. Maybe we can't afford the politicians.

— Steve Forbes

We don't have a revenue problem. We have a spending problem. We could raise taxes by billions but they would only further drive up spending by billions of dollars.

— Arnold Schwarzenegger

The reality is that for the last quarter century, Congress and the presidents have betrayed us by concocting tax laws that are insincere, unfair, and convoluted. We're just learning that when it comes to taxes, Washington speaks with an accomplished forked tongue.

— Martin L. Gross

It used to be that the sole purpose of the tax code was to raise the necessary funds to run government. But in today's world the tax mandate has many more facets. These include income redistribution, encouraging favored industries, and discouraging unfavorable behavior.

To make matters worse there are millions and millions of taxpayers who are highly motivated to reduce their tax liabilities. And, as those taxpayers finagle and connive to find ways around the tax code, government responds by propagating new rules, new interpretations of the code, and new taxes in a never-ending chase. In the process, we create ever-more arcane tax codes that do a poor job of achieving any of their mandates.

— Arthur B. Laffer

Consider the United States Constitution. The Constitution is open-ended, generalized and telescopic in character. What has it spawned? Pervasive ambiguity and unending litigation.

Contrast the extreme counter-model of law, the Internal Revenue Code and its festooned vines of regulations. Code and regulations are particularized, elaborated and microscopic in character. What have they spawned? Pervasive ambiguity and unending litigation.

— Bayless Manning

People often criticize the language of the [tax] code as impenetrable, but it is meant to be — and usually is — both remarkably precise and consistent.

— Charles I. Kingson

Just because the Tax Code allows an action doesn't necessarily make it a good idea.

— Jane C. Nober

There is a constant cry and a natural desire for a "simple" income tax law. America can have a simple income tax law anytime it wants it. It would not be especially difficult to draft .... The trouble is you wouldn't want that law. You wouldn't stand for it. Americans would not tolerate any "simple" income tax law. Why? The reason is simple. Any "simple" income tax law would take a "meat axe" approach. It would be outrageously discriminatory. It would be grossly inequitable and unfair to a lot of people.

— Laurens Williams

[V]irtually every major accounting firm is an aggressive adversary of tax simplification.

— Stephen Moore

In every free country the power of laying taxes is considered a legislative power over the property and persons of the citizens.

— Salmon P. Chase

Getting a narrow tax break into the tax code is hard enough; getting it out can be even harder.

— Jackie Calmes

They [the people] prescribe no limits to the exercise of this right [taxation], resting confidently on the interest of the legislator, and on the influence of the constituents over their representative, to guard them against its abuse.

— John Marshall

Since the 1980s, it seems as if every journalist writing on tax policy is out to win a Pulitzer Prize by exposing some Watergate-type scandal of corruption and greed lurking behind the provisions of the tax code.

— Sheldon D. Pollack

Our taxes reflect a continuing struggle among contending interests for the privilege of paying the least.

— Louis Eisenstein

An irrepressible conflict has been raging for a thousand years between the strong and the weak, [with] the former always trying to keep the chief tax burdens upon the latter.

— Cordell Hull

Taxation, like water flowing downstream, some day will seek its level and cover those who have and those who have not, and the very people upon whom you are attempting to place the burden of taxation will shift the proper share to the people whom you are attempting to make believe you are relieving from taxation.

— Edward Cooper

The great correction of excessive taxation is its oppression on the constituent, which causes a reaction to reduce it.

— Levi Woodbury

The power to make distinctions exists with full vigor in the field of taxation.

— Stanley F. Reed

Any substantial tax reform would involve substantial redistributions of tax burdens and substantial changes in asset values, and you need some "lubrication" [*i.e.*, transition rules].

— Robert Reischauer

Tax complexity itself is a kind of tax.

— Max Baucus

The tax code has just grown so complex and so ugly, like an unkempt hedge or lawn that never gets mowed.

— Alan Blinder

The tax code is like daytime television — almost anything done to it would improve it.

— George Will

The complexity of our [tax] code in the main is not there because of some mischief. Most of it is there in the effort to do more perfect justice.

— Russell B. Long

Dear Mr. President: I am writing to express my concerns with your definition of tax reform. . . . I am very concerned that, under the guise of tax reform, you intend to increase revenues to pay for more spending. . . . The country cannot afford the kind of "tax reform" you are promoting.

— Charles Grassley

I trust that the Congress will give its immediate consideration to the problem of future taxation. Simplification of the income and profits taxes has become an immediate necessity.

— Woodrow Wilson

Senator, I was at one of those hearings in 2008, and one of my more colorful colleagues sat down next to me and said, "You know, I've been coming to these hearings on tax reform for 20 years, and none of us is getting any prettier."

— Jonathan Talisman

The greatest tax simplification would be to have the law remain settled for several years so we could all catch up.

— Sheldon S. Cohen

[T]wo things are abundantly clear. One, tax simplification is desperately needed. Two, any effort is likely to be an unmitigated disaster.

— Jonathan Clements

The long avoidance of a wealth tax has been one of the great triumphs of the American upper classes.

— Richard Todd

Of course the truth is that the congresspersons are too busy raising campaign money to read the laws they pass. The laws are written by staff tax nerds who can put pretty much any wording they want in there. I bet that if you actually read the entire vastness of the U.S. Tax Code, you'd find at least one sex scene ("'Yes, yes, YES!' moaned Vanessa as Lance, his taut body moist with moisture, again and again depreciated her adjusted gross rate of annualized fiscal debenture").

— Dave Barry

Distinctions which originated under a feudal economy when land dominated social relations are peculiarly irrelevant in the application of tax measures now so largely directed toward intangible wealth.

— Felix Frankfurter

[Tax expenditures are] those revenue losses attributable to provisions of the Federal tax laws which allow a special exclusion, exemption or deduction from gross income or which provide a special credit, preferential rate of tax or a deferral of tax liability.

— Congressional Budget and
Impoundment Control Act of 1974

Americans like to use taxes to encourage some activities and to discourage others, and as a way to grant favors and subsidies without directly appropriating money. As every politician knows, tax expenditures are a much easier sell than functionally equivalent spending programs.

— Joseph J. Thorndike

As long as the minority party [i.e., the Republicans] insists on thinking that targeted tax cuts are tax reductions, instead of what they really are, which are spending hikes, then there is no possibility of rational discourse.

— Edward D. Kleinbard

When was the last time you saw an article pointing out the hypocrisy of a politician calling for tax cuts and cuts in expenditures? As long as the media fail in their responsibility, we will have an increasing number of people seduced by false promises that by cutting taxes and appropriated funds we can cut the deficit.

— Martin Lobel

Precisely because appropriations and tax breaks can achieve identical objectives, the government can easily substitute one for the other.

— Elena Kagan

I know that people have sat in the office of the secretary of the Treasury and said, "You know, we can't get this through as a spending item; let's sneak it in the tax code and we'll do exactly the same thing." I've sat there in meetings where they've done that.

— Gene Steuerle

We need to regard enacting tax expenditures as analogous to engaging in incest. Both can seem like good ideas at the moment. But history has taught us that both are very bad ideas.

— Jeffery L. Yablon

There is nothing in the Constitution which requires a state to adopt the best possible system of taxation.

— Harlan F. Stone

Fundamental [tax] reform almost always runs the risk of making things worse.

— Dan Rostenkowski

[P]oliticians don't like to talk about taxes, except to use them the way a matador uses a red cape.

— Jill Lepore

When the people are weary of any one sort of Tax, presently some Projector propounds another, and gets himself Audience, by affirming he can propound a way how all the Publick Charge may be born without the way that is.

— William Petty

TARIFF, n. A scale of taxes on imports, designed to protect the domestic producer against the greed of his consumer.

— Ambrose Bierce

The tariff, then nearly synonymous with federal taxes, was a prime cause of the Civil War.

— *American Heritage* Magazine

Systems of taxation need not achieve the ideal. But the fact that the Constitution does not demand pure reason and is satisfied by practical reason does not justify unreason.

— Felix Frankfurter

[A tax loophole is] something that benefits the other guy. If it benefits you, it is tax reform.

— Russell B. Long

I've found that the making of tax policy is like politics and much of life; if you expect ingratitude, you are rarely disappointed.

— Tom Downey

Lobbyists know that a 0 percent tax rate on capital income is not, in fact, the lowest possible rate. There can be negative tax rates. There can be subsidies. There can be allowances for depreciation. Lobbyists are adaptive creatures.

— Joel Achenbach

When [politicians] start naming tax laws after themselves, we are definitely not on the road to simplicity. It crosses some kind of line.

— Christopher Bergin

Taxation . . . in most communities is a long way off from a logical and coherent theory.

— Oliver Wendell Holmes Jr.

[W]e tax generosity within families — even as we encourage people to deduct gifts to strangers.

— Allan Reynolds

Contrary to what some people claim, the tax laws have a lot of respect for logic. They use it so sparingly.

— Jeffery L. Yablon

[The U.S. Tax Code is a] rotting mess of a carcass.

— Ron Wyden

Although it often seems as though the drafters of tax statutes delight in taxing people on the basis of what their advisers are likely to miss, Congress has not explicitly adopted this as policy.

— Lee A. Sheppard

Representation is the ordinary guaranty of fairness in taxation.

— Robert H. Jackson

Nothing has contributed more to retarding the emergence of a democratic context in places like Venezuela, Nigeria, Saudi Arabia, and Iran than the curse of oil. As long as the monarchs and dictators who run these oil states can get rich by drilling their natural resources — as opposed to drilling the natural talents and energy of their people — they can stay in office forever . . . . They never have to tax their people, so the relationship between ruler and ruled is highly distorted. *Without taxation, there is no representation.*

— Thomas L. Friedman

In the Arab world, oil has been another negative factor. Of the sixteen Arab countries, nine are oil rich, and all but three of them have quite small indigenous populations. Their oil revenues and small populations have allowed most of these countries to exempt their citizens from paying taxes. That is one more strike against democracy: a citizenry that pays no taxes lacks the moral authority to demand representation.

— M. Shahid Alam

Oil-rich rulers have no need to levy taxes and therefore no need to satisfy elected representatives. (In the Arab world, the converse of a familiar dictum is true: No representation without taxation.)

— Bernard Lewis

If oil is discovered in a country before democratic institutions are in place, the probability of that country becoming democratic is very low. In countries where the state does not rely on the taxation of its citizens for its revenues, it doesn't have to listen to what its citizens want to do with that money. So instead of building roads or schools or doing things that taxpayers would demand of them, they use their money in ways that threaten the security of other countries, and, ultimately, their own.

— Michael McFaul

In a country advancing in wealth, whose increasing revenue gives it the power of ridding itself from time to time of the most inconvenient portions of its taxation, I conceive that the increase of revenues should rather be disposed of by taking off taxes, than by liquidating debt, as long as any very objectionable imposts remain.

— John Stuart Mill

Taxes are the killing fields for Democrats.

— Grover Norquist

Democrats were put on earth to raise taxes; Republicans were put here to stop them.

— Anonymous Republican Congressional
Staff Member

The genius of our ruling class is that it has kept a majority of the people from ever questioning the inequity of a system where most people drudge along, paying heavy taxes for which they get nothing in return.

— Gore Vidal

In every community those who feel the burdens of taxation are naturally prone to relieve themselves from it if they can . . . . One class struggles to throw the burden off its shoulders. If they succeed, of course, it must fall upon others. They also, in their turn, labor to get rid of it, and finally the load falls upon those who will not, or cannot, make a successful effort for relief.

— James C. Carter

The soundest principles of republicanism do sanction some relation between representation and taxation . . . . The two ought to be connected . . . . This was the principle of the revolution.

— John Marshall

A desire for equality among taxpayers is to be attributed to Congress, rather than the reverse.

— Stanley F. Reed

[S]cratch the surface in a "business-unfriendly" state and you'll find a low property tax and high voter demand for services.

— Julia Homer

The method of raising revenue ought not to impede the transaction of business; it ought to encourage it.

— Calvin Coolidge

You [senators] and the American people don't have a clue about how the IRS does its job, and that's just the way they like it.

— Shelley Davis

If you ask me what single law I would pass to gain the greatest amount of tax simplification with fairness, I would say, without hesitation, campaign financing reforms. That would be a giant step forward. It's not that problems of complexity are not understood. Complexity is the result of a failure of will to do anything about it.

— Jerome Kurtz

The Internal Revenue Code is the most persuasive brief ever written for campaign finance reform.

— J. Mark Iwry

[M]aking tax law based on personal anecdote is never a good idea.

— Alan Murray

Lasting tax reform will not come without lasting political reform.

— John F. Witte

Tax reform is a lot like cleaning out your garage. Just because you cleaned it last week, do you really expect that it will never need cleaning again?

— Joseph J. Thorndike

In the last twenty years, revenue needs have come to exceed the demands that legislatures feel it expedient to make upon accumulated wealth or property with fixed location within the state. The states therefore have turned to taxing activities connected with the movement of commerce, such as exchange and consumption.

— Robert H. Jackson

Objects and means of taxation were not in the years past sought for with the same avidity as at present [*i.e.*, 1904]. The demand for revenue was not so great.

— David J. Brewer

If the history of taxation teaches any one lesson, it is that all social and moral advance is the result of a slow process and that while fiscal systems are continually modified by the working out of ethical ideals, these ideals themselves depend for their realization upon the economic forces which are continually transforming the face of human society.

— Edwin R.A. Seligman

Sound principles will not justify our taxing the industry of our fellow citizens to accumulate treasure for wars to happen we know not when, and which might not perhaps happen but from the temptations offered by that treasure.

— Thomas Jefferson

Our modern income tax experience began with the Revenue Act of 1913. The World War soon brought high rates.

— Robert H. Jackson

Customarily, sound finance resumed with peace. What's new is that, starting about 1919, the taxing and inflating has kept right on going even after the shooting stopped.

— James Grant

Taxes are never popular, but they are never more popular than during wars.
— Steven A. Bank, Kirk J. Stark, and Joseph J. Thorndike

The tax law often favors cohabitation to marriage, institutional to family child-care, and indebtedness to parsimony. Is this good social policy?
— Richard K. Vedder and Lowell E. Gallaway

I can't make a damn thing out of this tax problem. I listen to one side and they seem right — and then I talk to the other side and they seem just as right, and here I am where I started. God, what a job!
— Warren G. Harding

I guess you will have to go to jail. If that is the result of not understanding the Income Tax Law I will meet you there. We shall have a merry, merry time for all our friends will be there. It will be an intellectual center, for no one understands the Income Tax Law except persons who have not sufficient intelligence to understand the questions that arise under it.
— Elihu Root

The income tax laws do not profess to embody perfect economic theory.
— Oliver Wendell Holmes Jr.

I know of no power, indeed, of which a free people ought to be more jealous, than of that of levying taxes and duties.
— Joseph Story

If any behavior needs to be reined in, it should be the propensity of people to use the political system to take other people's money.
— Jeffrey A. Singer

I have long said, "I never met a tax cut I didn't like" — though I would go on to say that I like some better than others.
— Milton Friedman

Conservatism should be all about context. For example, from a proper conservative point of view, it's insane to have a universal rule about taxes. If you need revenue, then taxes are an instrument to provide the revenue you need. They've turned it into this ideology where you never have tax increases. That goes against the whole grain of what conservatism is supposed to be about.

— David Brooks

Not all tax cuts are created equal .... [T]hose accompanied by spending restraint would be more effective than those which are not.

— Ben Bernanke

Tax reduction thus sets off a process that can bring gains for everyone, gains won by marshalling resources that would otherwise stand idle — workers without jobs and farm and factory capacity without markets. Yet many taxpayers seemed prepared to deny the nation the fruits of tax reduction because they question the financial soundness of reducing taxes when the federal budget is already in deficit. Let me make clear why, in today's economy, fiscal prudence and responsibility call for tax reduction even if it temporarily enlarged the federal deficit — why reducing taxes is the best way open to us to increase revenues.

— John F. Kennedy

If tax cuts are phased in over time, people will defer economic activity to take advantage of the lower future tax rates, which only makes the economy worse right now.

— Kenneth Blackwell and Arthur B. Laffer

The best way to restrain the politicians' impulse to spend and to expand government's reach is to keep the surplus modest. That means lowering taxes.

— R. Emmett Tyrrell

The purpose of a tax cut is to leave more money where it belongs: in the hands of the working men and working women who earned it in the first place.

— Robert Dole

[Responding to Chancellor of the Exchequer Gladstone's question as to the practical uses of electricity:] Why, sir, there is every probability that you will soon be able to tax it!

— Michael Faraday

This year is not much different from other years. The Ways and Means Committee worked up its draft of the 1997 tax bill in secret and revealed it on June 9 and 10. The bill passed the House less than a month later. No hearings were held on the actual bill. It was funny (if that is the proper word) to watch the chief of staff of the Joint Tax Committee on June 12 describe the bill to the members. He was speaking at a rapid pace, so fast that most of the members could not possibly have understood him. I, as a tax expert, had a very tough time in following his rapid explanation. He answered questions very narrowly, and there was a vote. A few good lobbyists got advanced word and were able to change a few things, but most of us only watched in awe, or disbelief, that this was the way to make a law.

— Sheldon S. Cohen

We shall tax and tax, and spend and spend, and elect and elect.

— Harry L. Hopkins
(attributed)

Liberals have practiced "tax and tax, spend and spend, elect and elect" but conservatives have perfected "borrow and borrow, spend and spend, elect and elect."

— George Will

The fiscal policy habitually associated with social-democratic political orientation is tax-and-spend. Considering the true nature of taxation, what passed as supply-side fiscal policy in the past 30 years boils down to spend-and-tax. In the bigger picture there is little or no functional difference between them. The spend level in these patterns drives the tax level either way. Self-styled supply-side economics in the 1980s and then again earlier in this century was simply old-style fiscal stimulus, Keynesian policy delivered on the tax side. It implied no significant possibility of lower taxes over time.

— Joseph Isenbergh

Republicans say tax cuts, tax cuts, tax cuts. Democrats say spend, new programs, more money. You can't spend enough for the Democratic base, or cut enough for the Republican.

— Peggy Noonan

[T]here are always numerous desirable things that government officials can offer to provide to voters who want them — either free of charge or at reduced, government-subsidized prices — even when these voters do not want these increments enough to sacrifice their own money to pay for them. Ultimately, of course, the public ends up paying as taxpayers for things that they would not have chosen to pay for as consumers.

— Thomas Sowell

The tendency of taxation is to create a class of persons who do not labor, to take from those who do labor the produce of that labor, and to give it to those who do not labor.

— William Cobbett

Lower taxes that force cutbacks and reforms in spending programs often produce a double benefit. Besides the direct benefit from lower marginal tax rates on income, dividends, or investments, there are indirect benefits from the forced reductions in inefficient spending programs. This might be an overly generous welfare system or programs that benefit constituents of powerful members of Congress.

— Gary S. Becker, Edward P. Lazear, and Kevin M. Murphy

New taxes are so unpopular that most "social" handout schemes are originally enacted without enough increased taxation to pay for them. The result is chronic government deficits, paid for by the issuance of additional paper money.

— Henry Hazlitt

The stamping of paper is an operation so much easier than the laying of taxes, that a government, in the practice of paper emissions, would rarely fail in any such emergency to indulge itself too far.

— Alexander Hamilton

An abstention for long periods from the use of taxation to cover all expenditures necessarily weakens what may be called "tax morale." The willingness consciously to impose a tax burden upon oneself declines, and the ultimate restoration of governmental finances to a normal basis becomes correspondingly more difficult.

— Carl Shoup

A government which robs Peter to pay Paul can always depend on the support of Paul.

— George Bernard Shaw

A liberal is someone who feels a great debt to his fellow man, which debt he proposes to pay off with your money.

— G. Gordon Liddy

I wish I had a dollar for every time a wealthy liberal has declared he thinks he should pay more taxes. . . . If wealthy liberals want to pay more . . . I'm all for it. But don't hold your breath, because when liberals say they want higher taxes, they mean on you.

— Stephen Moore

Like most of the neighborhood, she was a fighting liberal, fighting to have her money taken from her.

— John Updike

I cannot undertake to lay my finger on that article of the Constitution which granted a right to Congress of expending, on objects of benevolence, the money of their constituents . . . .

— James Madison

[A] democratic government is the only one in which those who vote for a tax can escape the obligation to pay it.

— Alexis de Tocqueville

Hypocrisy . . . raises its head every time the subject of tax simplification comes up.

— Lee A. Sheppard

To extinguish a Debt which exists and to avoid contracting more are ideas almost always favored by public feeling and opinion; but to pay Taxes for the one or the other purpose, which are the only means of avoiding the evil, is always more or less unpopular. These contradictions are in human nature.

— Alexander Hamilton

The only way you can do that [decrease taxes, balance the budget, and increase military spending] is with mirrors, and that's what it would take.

— John B. Anderson

What an increase of rent is to the farmers, an increase of taxation is to the public . . . so long as it is confined within moderate limits, it acts as a powerful stimulus to industry and economy, and most commonly occasions the production of more wealth than it abstracts.

— J.R. McCulloch

There is a prevailing maxim among some reasoners, *That every new tax creates a new ability in the subject to bear it, and that each increase of public burdens increases proportionably the industry of the people.*

— David Hume

The appropriation of public money always is perfectly lovely until someone is asked to pay the bill.

— Calvin Coolidge

Don't be bamboozled. When big spenders call for "deficit reduction," they mean raising your taxes.

— Betsy McCaughey

Why should the federal government tax the consumption of red wine, while it does not tax cola drinks, particularly in light of empirical evidence that suggests that moderate wine drinking is actually beneficial?

— Richard K. Vedder and Lowell E. Gallaway

All taxes discourage something. Why not discourage bad things like pollution rather than good things like working or investment?
— Lawrence Summers

If the government pays people not to work and taxes people who do work, is it really so difficult to see why employment is so low?
— Arthur B. Laffer

The best legislator is the one who votes for all appropriations and against all taxes.
— Walter P. Brownlow
(attributed)

In my opinion, I don't know who takes a tax vote, in their right mind, just before an election. But that's just me.
— Dianne Feinstein

Taxing less and spending more . . . it's fun in the short run, but it's a recipe for disaster.
— Bill Clinton

The design of a tax system, including the extent to which it confers avoidance power, reflects the values of its designers. Tax systems, after all, do not follow the laws of nature. The design of a tax system is not ordained by anything even remotely analogous to the law of gravity. Unlike the falling of a pebble released from a hand, a particular tax system is not the inevitable result of forces which humans can understand, perhaps control and sometimes escape from, but cannot alter. Rather, tax systems are products of human creation. They exist because they serve human objectives, reflecting the values of their designers. A tax system's design can reveal much about those values.
— Alice G. Abreu

Although it makes exceptions and backslides, the U.S. welcomes most imports and taxes them lightly because that's the policy that's best for most Americans.
— Thomas G. Donlan

If the rich are so powerful, why are they taxed so heavily?
— Robert J. Samuelson

The financial policy of the welfare state requires that there be no way for the owners of wealth to protect themselves.
— Alan Greenspan

Are the Republicans in Congress more Machiavellian than we tend to give them credit for? Can it be that their objective is to so burden every taxpayer that they — of every income bracket — will rise up and revolt and demand a new tax system?
— Denis A. Kleinfeld

If your goal is to get rid of the income tax, creating a variety of unnecessary complexities is a strategic advantage. It gives people a reason to move to another tax system.
— William G. Gale

The failure of tax replacement campaigns is attributable to many factors, not least the functional success of our current tax regime; for all its problems, the income tax has always managed to pay the bills, and regimes change only when they must.
— Joseph J. Thorndike

[A] reformed [tax] system might be unworkable or not function as intended.
— Pam Olson

Taxation is neither a penalty imposed on the taxpayer nor a liability which he assumes by contract. It is but a way of apportioning the cost of government among those who in some measure are privileged to enjoy its benefits and must bear its burdens. Since no citizen enjoys immunity from the burden, its retroactive imposition does not necessarily infringe due process.
— Harlan F. Stone

Tax legislation is not a promise, and a taxpayer has no vested right in the Internal Revenue Code.
— Harry Blackmun

That most delicious of all privileges — spending other people's money.

— John Randolph

Taxing is an easy business. Any projector can contrive new impositions; any bungler can add to the old; but is it altogether wise to have no other bounds to your impositions than the patience of those who are to bear them?

— Edmund Burke

It's not a new tax; it's simply collecting an existing tax. I don't regard it as a tax increase. It's only a tax increase to the person who is paying it.

— Paul Francis

Q. I understand that Congress is considering a so-called "flat" tax system. How would this work?
A. If Congress were to pass a "flat" tax, you'd simply pay a fixed percentage of your income, and you wouldn't have to fill out any complicated forms, and there would be no loopholes for politically connected groups, and normal people would actually understand the tax laws, and giant talking broccoli stalks would come around and mow your lawn for free, because Congress is NOT going to pass a flat tax, you pathetic fool.

— Dave Barry

We have created a tax monster. I don't know anybody who defends our current tax system — anybody. We have used taxes inappropriately to achieve political, ideological, and social goals.

— David Cay Johnston

The federal income tax is a complete mess. It's not efficient. It's not fair. It's not simple. It's not comprehensible. It fosters tax avoidance and cheating. It costs billions of dollars to administer. It costs taxpayers billions of dollars in time spent filling out tax forms and other forms of compliance. It costs the economy billions of dollars in lost output of goods and services from investments being made for tax rather than for economic purposes. It involves tens of thousands of lawyers and lobbyists getting tax benefits for their clients instead of performing productive work. It can't find ten serious economists to defend it. It is not worth saving.

— Robert E. Hall and Alvin Rabushka

[W]e have to get a hold of the tax system and remake it so that at the very least we can remove the sense of agitated grievance that marks our daily economic life . . . .

— Peggy Noonan

Government

Government is emphatically a machine: to the discontented a "taxing machine," to the contented a "machine for securing property."

— Thomas Carlyle

Government

The repose of nations cannot be secure without arms, armies cannot be maintained without pay, nor can the pay be produced except by taxes.

— Tacitus

Taxation is the legitimate support of government.

— Louis Adolphe Thiers

The revenue of the state is the state.

— Edmund Burke

Without taxes, society has no common destiny, and collective action is impossible.

— Thomas Piketty

Public works are not accomplished by the miraculous power of a magic wand. They are paid for by funds taken away from the citizens.

— Ludwig von Mises

They [the Government] have no money except what they take in taxes from men like you and me.

— Graham Greene
(*Our Man in Havana* screenplay)

The point to remember is that what the government gives it must first take away.

— John Strider Coleman

The government has nothing to give to anybody that it doesn't first take from someone else.

— Henry Hazlitt

The removal of large numbers of people from the tax rolls makes the political system more unstable. Individuals and households that pay no income taxes have a diminished stake in limited government.

— Phil Gramm

A stable democracy requires skin in the game. If you aren't contributing, you are free-riding off others, and you have an incentive to demand more of government because it's free to you.

— Scott Hodge

For people who pay no income tax, general government is practically a free good. They embrace higher taxes and more government spending, because someone else seems to be paying for it.

— Stephen J. Entin

About half of Americans who file tax returns pay almost all the income taxes; the top quarter of filers pay 86% of the taxes; 10% pay two-thirds of the taxes. A mere 1% of Americans earning income pay 38% of the tax revenues . . . .

— Thomas G. Donlan

You cannot legislate the poor into freedom by legislating the wealthy out of freedom. What one person receives without working for, another person must work for without receiving. The government cannot give to anybody anything that the government does not first take from somebody else. When half of the people get the idea that they do not have to work because the other half is going to take care of them, and when the other half gets the idea that it does no good to work because somebody else is going to get what they work for, that my dear friend, is about the end of any nation. You cannot multiply wealth by dividing it.

— Adrian Rogers

In general, the art of government consists of taking as much money as possible from one class of citizens to give to the other.

— Voltaire

Every time you cut [government] programs, you take away a person who has a vested interest in high taxes and you put him on the tax rolls and make him a taxpayer. A farmer on subsidies is part welfare bum, whereas a free-market farmer is a small businessman with a gun.

— Grover Norquist

A survey says that American workers work the first three hours every day just to pay their taxes. So that's why we can't get anything done in the morning: We're government workers.

— Jay Leno

The same government that requires a taxpaying citizen to document every statement on his tax return decrees that questioning a welfare applicant demeans and humiliates him.

— Ronald Reagan

[I want to change the poor from] tax eaters to tax payers.

— Lyndon B. Johnson

When you listen to tax-cut rhetoric, remember that giving one class of taxpayer a "break" requires — now or down the line — that an equivalent burden be imposed on other parties. In other words, if I get a break, someone else pays. Government can't deliver a free lunch to the country as a whole. It can however, determine who pays for lunch.

— Warren Buffett

The tax code . . . should not be a tool of industrial policy.

— Dave Camp

The government is mainly an expensive organization to regulate evildoers, and tax those who behave; government does little for fairly respectable people except annoy them.

— Edgar W. Howe

Serious arguments about taxes are never just about taxes. They are about government's proper size and purposes.

— George Will

The tax system touches more people in this country than any other part of the government or our laws. The loss of confidence in its integrity is the loss of confidence in the government itself.

— B. John Williams

If, from the more wretched parts of the old world, we look at those which are in an advanced stage of improvement, we still find the greedy hand of government thrusting itself into every corner and crevice of industry, and grasping the spoil of the multitude. Invention is continually exercised, to furnish new pretenses for revenues and taxation. It watches prosperity as its prey and permits none to escape without tribute.

— Thomas Paine

[A]ll governments must have a regard not only for what the people are *able* to bear, but what they are *willing* to pay, and the *manner* in which they are willing to pay, without being provoked to a rebellion.

— Henry Fox

Poor people! How much disillusionment is in store for them! It would have been so simple and so just to ease their burden by decreasing their taxes; they want to achieve this through the plentiful bounty of the state and they cannot see that the whole mechanism consists in taking away ten to give back eight, not to mention the true freedom that will be destroyed in the operation.

— Claude-Frederic Bastiat

The real cost of government is measured by what government spends, not by the receipts labeled taxes. The goods and services it buys are not available for other use.

— Milton Friedman

The real tax over any significant period is the level of government spending in relation to national output. The higher public spending as a percentage of GDP, the higher the real tax. That amount must in time be transferred from private to public hands — be it now or later. The current tax, for its part, is the amount actually paid to a government in any given period, and is almost never equal to the real tax.

— Joseph Isenbergh

[P]eople don't generally feel tax cuts. They feel tax hikes.
— Barack Obama

Government expands to absorb revenue and then some.
— Tom Wicker

New Hampshire has always been cheap, mean, rural, small-minded, and reactionary. It's one of the few states in the nation with neither a sales tax nor an income tax. Social services are totally inadequate there, it ranks at the bottom in state aid to education — the state is literally shaped like a dunce cap — and its medical assistance program is virtually nonexistent. Expecting aid for the poor there is like looking for an egg under a basilisk .... The state encourages skinflints, cheapskates, shutwallets, and pinched little joykillers who move there as a tax refuge to save money.
— Alexander Theroux

It is a good thing that we do not get as much government as we pay for.
— Will Rogers

One thing is true of all governments — their most reliable records are tax records.
— Alan Moore
(*V for Vendetta* graphic novel and screenplay)

The state has grown used to treating its taxpayers as a farmer treats his cows, keeping them in a field to be milked.
— James Dale Davidson and Lord William Rees-Mogg

Milk the cow, but do not pull off the udder.
— Old Greek Proverb

[A] happy society is one in which government is rolling in revenues not because of high tax rates but because its citizens report a lot of income.
— Holman W. Jenkins Jr.

[T]ax reform consists of more than changes in those items that are called taxes. The real cost of government — the total tax burden — equals what government spends plus the cost to the public of complying with government mandates and regulations and of calculating, paying and taking measures to avoid taxes. Currently, this burden, at federal, state and local levels combined, exceeds half of national income: 40 percent in direct spending, and more than 10 percent in indirect costs. Anything that reduces that real cost — lower government spending, elimination of costly regulations on individuals or businesses, simplification of explicit taxes — is a tax reform.

— Milton Friedman

For a legislator these are relatively easy votes. You pick out the thing the majority of people don't do [*e.g.*, gambling, watching nude pole dancing] and slap a tax on it.

— Billy Hamilton

Tax reform is taking the taxes off things that have been taxed in the past and putting taxes on things that haven't been taxed before.

— Art Buchwald

Somewhere, in a fantasy land populated by economists and governed by benevolent technocrats from safe districts, there exists an ideal tax code. It provides a stable, reliable platform for savings and investment, and it generates enough revenue to run the government without distorting decisions by individuals and businesses.

That's not the country we live in, and that's not the tax code we have.

— Richard Rubin

The trouble with comprehensive tax reform is that it would be a vast project that would plunge the country into two years of furious, all-consuming debate. In that time, nothing else would get done.

— David Frum

[M]odern taxation or tax making in its most characteristic aspect is a group contest in which powerful interests vigorously endeavor to rid themselves of present or proposed tax burdens. It is, first of all, a hard game in which he who trusts wholly to economics, reason, and justice, will in the end retire beaten and disillusioned.

— T.S. Adams

The history of taxation from the earliest ages has been the history of the attempts of one class to make other classes pay the expenses, or an undue share of the expenses, of the Government. Aristocrats have always been trying to shift the taxes on to the people, and the people on to the aristocrats; the landed interests on to the commercial and the commercial on to the landed.

— E.L. Godkin

[I am vetoing this because it is] not a tax bill but a tax relief bill providing relief not for the needy but for the greedy.

— Franklin D. Roosevelt

It should be the policy of governments . . . never to lay such taxes as will inevitably fall on capital; since by so doing, they impair the funds for the maintenance of labor, and thereby diminish the future production of the country.

— David Ricardo

When a man has accumulated a sum of money within the law, that is to say, in the legally correct way, the people no longer have any right to share in the earnings resulting from the accumulation.

— John D. Rockefeller

Money made by money should be taxed at the same rate as money made by men.

— George McGovern

Logic and taxation are not always the best of friends.

— James C. McReynolds

Lobbyists act to promote tax changes that benefit their clients, to oppose tax changes that harm their clients, to challenge tax changes that help their clients' competitors, and to advocate tax changes that harm their client's competitors. All this activity is directed toward Congress.

— Franklin L. Green

A sound tax system . . . [is] a system that the public views as correct and is willing to support, allowing it to remain stable without constant churning and tinkering by government.

— Lawrence A. Hunter and Stephen J. Entin

Do senators introduce tax bills because the tax system is a mess, or is the tax system a mess because senators introduce tax bills?

— Martin A. Sullivan

Congress's decisions with respect to tax policy do not always fit a neat and logical pattern. Sometimes they are even influenced by less-than-objective forces.

— Stephen Reinhardt

They [the Republicans] want your vote, but they don't want you to know their plan. And that's because all they have to offer is the same prescriptions they've had for the last 30 years.

Have a surplus? Try a tax cut.

Deficit too high — try another.

Feel a cold coming on? Take two tax cuts, roll back some regulations, and call us in the morning.

— Barack Obama

It took 25 years in the tax business for your correspondent to understand that the phrase "tax policy" means the government forgoing tax it really ought to be collecting.

— Lee A. Sheppard

They [the members of Congress] have established a system remarkable for its complexity and vexatiousness. They have rendered taxation as mischievous and depressing as a perverted ingenuity could make it.

— *The New York Times*

[T]he tax code is the single greatest source of lobbying activity in Washington.

— Dick Armey

Tax lobbying often offers corporations a higher return on investment than any other form of capital deployment.

— S. Douglas Hopkins

The income tax is a highly effective tool for raising revenue for the federal government. It also happens to be ideally suited for use by individual lawmakers in distributing economic benefits to their constituents. That nonpartisan, *instrumental* use of the income tax takes the form of enacting special rules, regulations, and statutory amendments to the tax code that shelter favored groups and taxpayers from the burden of the impost. It is now practically expected that lawmakers will pursue special tax provisions that benefit organized interest groups, industries, economic sectors, and wealthy individuals located in their home districts and states. They do not always succeed, but they constantly try.

— Sheldon D. Pollack

It is logically impossible for the tax law to attain stable equilibrium so long as Congress keeps responding to special interests' demands to "level the playing field." In this area, there is no such thing as a "level playing field:" tax topography is in the eye of the beholder.

— J. Mark Iwry

Those who have been in Washington for more than a few days know that the more complicated a tax scheme is, the more likely it is to benefit some special interest whose subsidy can't be justified.

— Martin Lobel

Tax complexity doesn't occur just because of big money special interests. It occurs because of the tax provisions that benefit each one of us. We are the special interests. And until we acknowledge that, tax reform discussions will deteriorate into shouting matches and finger pointing about cutting "their" special tax breaks and not "ours."

— Nina E. Olson

The tax on capital gains directly affects investment decisions, the mobility and flow of risk capital . . . the ease or difficulty experienced by new ventures in obtaining capital and thereby the strength and potential for growth in the economy.

— John F. Kennedy

I don't think that cutting the capital gains tax contributed one iota to our economy. There is nothing that I have seen anywhere in my entire experience of some decades that suggests to me it increased our savings rate by one iota or increased our investment rate by one iota, and I am told that there's a lot of academic research that would tend to support that, but leaving the academic research aside, that's my experience.

— Robert E. Rubin

When I chaired the appropriations committee, I saw the poor. And when I chaired the tax committee, I saw the rich.

— Gordy Voss

What at first was plunder assumed the softer name of revenue.

— Thomas Paine

A great civilization is not conquered from without until it has destroyed itself from within. The essential cause of Rome's decline lay in her people, her morals, her class struggle, her failing trade, her bureaucratic despotism, her stifling taxes, her consuming wars.

— William Durant

To earn money to finance his many scientific experiments, [Antoine-Laurent Lavoisier] had become a member of a privileged private association of state-protected tax collectors. There is probably no time in history when having such a position would inspire your fellow citizens to invite you into their homes for a nice hot cup of gingerbread cappuccino, but when the French Revolution came, it proved an especially onerous credential. In 1794, Lavoisier was arrested with the rest of the association and quickly sentenced to death. Ever the dedicated scientist, he requested time to complete some of his research so that it would be available to posterity. To that the presiding judge famously replied, "The republic has no need of scientists." The father of modern chemistry was promptly beheaded, his body tossed into a mass grave.

— Leonard Mlodinow

There is no art which one government sooner learns from another than that of draining money from the pockets of the people.

— Adam Smith

Dictators have learned from each other to stamp out any buds of independent civil society by means of tax laws and supposedly neutral regulation.

— Fred Hiatt

No country ever takes notice of the revenue laws of another.

— Lord Mansfield

The revenue rule is a longstanding common law doctrine providing that courts of one sovereign will not enforce final tax judgments or unadjudicated tax claims of other sovereigns.

— Robert A. Katzman

We should not interfere in any other country's decision about how to structure its own tax system when that system does not serve as an obstacle to enforcing our own tax laws.

— Paul H. O'Neill

So inscrutable is the arrangement of causes and consequences in this world that a two-penny duty on tea, unjustly imposed in a sequestered part of it, changes the condition of all its inhabitants.

— Thomas Jefferson

History shows that even one unjust or anomalous tax can create immense political unrest and ill-feelings.

— Christopher Hitchens

The art of taxation consists in so plucking the goose as to obtain the largest possible amount of feathers with the least possible amount of hissing.

— Jean-Baptiste Colbert
(attributed)

Duties on commodities are the ones least felt by the people, because no formal request is made for them. They can be so wisely managed that the people will be almost unaware that they pay them.

— Charles Louis de Secondat,
baron de la Brede et de Montesquieu

Q. Are we EVER going to have a federal tax system that regular people can understand?

A. Our top political leaders have all voiced strong support for this idea.

Q. So you're saying it will never happen?

A. Right.

— Dave Barry

I make a fortune from criticizing the policy of the government, and then hand it over to the government in taxes to keep it going.

— George Bernard Shaw

We don't do tax policy in this country anymore, we do tax politics.

— Christopher Bergin

My position is this — I repeat it — I will maintain it to my last hour, — taxation and representation are inseparable — this position is founded on the laws of nature; it is more, it is itself an eternal law of nature, for whatever is a man's own, is absolutely his own; no man hath a right to take it from him without his consent, either expressed by himself or representative; whoever attempts to do it attempts an injury; whoever does it commits a robbery; he throws down and destroys the distinction between liberty and slavery.

— Lord Camden

No taxation without representation.

— Anonymous
(Slogan first used in Ireland during 1750s)

Taxation without representation is tyranny.

— James Otis
(attributed)

The American colonies, all know, were greatly opposed to taxation without representation. They were also, a less celebrated quality, equally opposed to taxation with representation.

— John Kenneth Galbraith

Taxation Without Representation
> — Banner on District of Columbia
> License Plates

Taxation and representation are inseparably united. God hath joined them; no British Parliament can put them asunder.
> — Lord Camden

Taxation without representation is one thing, but taxation for no reason is quite another.
> — Paul Phillips

Our forefathers made one mistake. What they should have fought for was representation without taxation.
> — Fletcher Knebel

If Thomas Jefferson thought taxation without representation was bad, he should see how it is with representation.
> — Rush Limbaugh

Taxation *with* representation ain't so hot either.
> — Gerald Barzan

Have you ever wondered if taxation without representation was cheaper?
> — Anonymous

"No taxation without representation" was a political demand; "No representation without taxation" is a political reality.
> — Samuel Huntington

Taxation without representation is tyranny. Tax lawyers provide representation. Tax lawyers avoid tyranny. Tax lawyers are an absolutely critical part of our national government process. The taxpayers' right to representation is a fundamental right. Tax professionals make the system and the government work. Tax law is an honorable profession. We need to keep it an honorable profession.
> — Terence Floyd Cuff

When did "No taxation without representation" devolve into a battle cry for the right of the very rich to retain professional tax counsel?
— J. Mark Iwry

You don't want the tax law pointy heads running the world.
— Fred T. Goldberg Jr.

Liberty produces excessive taxes; the effect of excessive taxes is slavery.
— Charles Louis de Secondat,
baron de la Brede et de Montesquieu

[John Galt:] "You want me to be Economic Dictator?"
[Mr. Thompson:] "Yes!"
"And you'll obey any order I give?"
"Implicitly!"
"Then start by abolishing all income taxes."
"Oh no!" screamed Mr. Thompson, leaping to his feet. "We couldn't do that . . . . How would we pay government employees?"
"Fire your government employees."
"Oh no!"

— Ayn Rand
(*Atlas Shrugged*)

Our tax system sucks the substance and spirit of entrepreneurs and workers alike, filters that substance through Washington, then sends it back through countless federal programs that instruct us in minute detail about how to use the government's beneficence.
— Roger Pilon

The politicians don't just want your money. They want your soul. They want you to be worn down by taxes until you are dependent and helpless.
— James Dale Davidson

Nothing is so well calculated to produce a death-like torpor in the country as an extended system of taxation and a great national debt.
— William Cobbett

There can be no taxation without legislation.
— Sheldon S. Cohen

Republicans believe every day is the Fourth of July, but Democrats believe every day is April 15.
— Ronald Reagan

America is a land of taxation that was founded to avoid taxation.
— Laurence J. Peter

All the taxes paid over a lifetime by the average American are spent by the government in less than a second.
— Jim Fiebig

[T]he federal government has [at one time or another] imposed more than 50 kinds of taxes. These include, for example, taxes on incomes, estates, gifts, capital stock, excess profits, admissions, club dues, documents, playing cards, safe deposit boxes, circulation of bank notes, cotton futures, tobacco, snuff and cigarettes, oleomargarine, filled cheese, firearms, and liquor, as well as taxes on the manufacture of many articles, including tires, tubes, toilet preparations, automobiles, radios, refrigerators, matches, electrical energy, gasoline, and lubricating oil, on the transportation of oil by pipeline, and on telegraph, telephone, radio, and cable messages.
— Michael J. Graetz

Retirement tax, income tax, property tax, excise tax, sales tax, beer tax, tobacco tax, cable tax, telephone tax, gasoline tax, hotel tax, surtaxes, taxes on taxes, and don't forget when you die, inheritance tax. But also how about tolls, user fees, service charges, licenses, transfers. And some experts around the country are saying we don't need tax reform.
— James Traficant

Little else is requisite to carry a state to the highest degree of opulence from the lowest barbarism but peace, easy taxes, and a tolerable administration of justice: all the rest being brought about by the natural course of things.
— Adam Smith

[A] prince should show himself a patron of merit, and should honor those who excel in every art. He ought accordingly to encourage his subjects by enabling them to pursue their callings, whether mercantile, agricultural, or any other, in security, so that this man shall not be deterred from beautifying his possessions from the apprehension that they may be taken from him, or that other refrain from opening a trade through fear of taxes.

— Niccolò Machiavelli

Why are the people starving? Because the rulers eat up the money in taxes.

— Lao Tzu

A government which lays taxes on the people not required by urgent public necessity and sound public policy is not a protector of liberty, but an instrument of tyranny. It condemns the citizen to servitude.

— Calvin Coolidge

[A] reduction in taxes would have the same stimulative effect as an increase in spending, yet it would avoid the long-term adverse effect of increasing the role of government in the economy.

— Milton Friedman

It is impossible to manage all of the permutations of people's economic aspirations and lives through a complex tax code. It is impossible to try to second-guess the market. It is impossible, from a managerial standpoint, for the federal government to do the things it is trying to do today.

— Frederick W. Smith

Only the staunchest defender of the big government status quo could claim that a tax cut of any size is a selfish action.

— Newt Gingrich

A wise and frugal Government, which shall restrain men from injuring one another, which shall leave them otherwise free to regulate their own pursuits of industry and improvement, and shall not take from the mouth of labor the bread it has earned. This is the sum of good government, and this is necessary to close the circle of our felicities.

— Thomas Jefferson

Tax competition for jobs between states is nothing new. Within America's 50-state free-trade zone, lawmakers have long known that changes in their state tax codes affect their competitiveness with neighbors. Unfortunately, when it comes to tax competition, most states get it wrong.

— Curtis S. Dubay and Scott A. Hodge

We're in competition with other cities around the world for entrepreneurs and the best and the brightest; it's not the time to be raising taxes [in New York City].

— Michael Bloomberg

Tax competition is to be celebrated, not persecuted. It forces politicians to be more responsible, pushing tax rates down and allowing people to enjoy more of the money they earn. It is good for taxpayers and good for the global economy.

— Dan Mitchell

Indeed, to the extent tax competition between jurisdictions holds down the increase in the growth of governments, citizens of all countries experience more job opportunities and higher standards of living.

— Richard W. Rahn

Britain has deliberately turned itself into a tax haven for foreign investors and bankers, into which vast sums of both legitimate money and hot money flow to escape taxation and securities regulation.

— Lee. A. Sheppard

Taxes are a nation's Rorschach test. In taxes you discover how a nation wants to be known to others. The burden of taxation may say that a nation more than anything wants to produce (say, Malaysia), or taxes may say that what a nation most wants is to be thought of as fair (Belgium).

— Daniel Henninger

If the concern is with whether a country's tax regime induces economic activity to shift, then all tax competition is necessarily harmful. The only way to prevent tax-induced changes of investment location would be for all countries to adopt the same tax system and the same tax rates.

— Terry Dwyer

Indeed, the dramatic flow of international capital to the lowest tax environment is one of the strongest and most reliable findings in the history of economic science.

— Kevin Hassett

It is not the island [of Jersey] that has made itself more and more attractive, it is the relatively high tax structures of the main industrial countries that have made them relatively unattractive.

— Colin Power

Tax competition [among nations] is a positive force in the global economy. It forces politicians to be more responsible, pushing tax rates down and allowing people to enjoy more of the money they earn.

— Daniel J. Mitchell

But let's get real. Raising income taxes in a world in which people and capital are ultra-mobile is a dangerous game for any state.

— Allan Sloan

[T]he time has come for the world to wake up and do something about the fact that tax avoidance, tax competition, and tax havens cause poverty.

— John Christensen

Giving money and power to government is like giving whiskey and car keys to teenage boys.

— P.J. O'Rourke

Taxation is the main relationship that people have with their government.

— Lee A. Sheppard

Since so many millions of people get married every year, it stands to reason that there must be some practical benefit to the tradition. A thorough investigation into the matter reveals the following results: You pay less in taxes.

— George Carlin

When two-thirds of married couples are required to pay higher income taxes solely because they have married, the American public rightly loses respect for the law.

— Michael J. Graetz

[The lottery is a] painless tax, paid only by the willing.

— Thomas Jefferson

We can applaud the state lottery as a public subsidy of intelligence, for it yields public income that is calculated to lighten the tax burden of us prudent abstainers at the expense of the benighted masses of wishful thinkers. It differs morally from the private casino or underground numbers game in that its beneficiaries are all of us in the prudent sector of the general public, rather than a greedy few private operators on or over the edge of the law.

— W.V. Quine

Many liberal persons defend levies like the tobacco tax on the curious grounds that tobacco is not a necessity — that poor people may or can avoid the burden by not consuming the commodity .... [I]t seems a little absurd to go around arguing that poor people could or ought to do without tobacco, especially if it is taxed, in the face of the facts that they simply do not do anything of the kind, that the commodity was selected for taxation because they are not expected to do so, and that the government would not get much revenue if they did .... [T]axes like the tobacco taxes are the most effective means available for draining government revenues out from the very bottom of the income scale. The usual textbook discussions on these points hardly deserve less lampooning than their implied definition of luxuries (and semiluxuries!) as commodities which poor people ought to do without and won't.

— Henry C. Simons

Perhaps the lesson to be drawn from the historical experience is that prohibiting nonviolent activities and substances that people are going to insist on doing or using anyway will never stamp them out. But if they are legalized, controlled, and taxed, society may be able to keep them within acceptable bounds while raising significant government revenue exclusively on the backs of those who insist on engaging in the behavior. That's about as close to a win-win situation as one is going to find in the public policy arena.

— Bruce Bartlett

In economics school . . . I was taught that the federal excise tax on cigarettes is a "sin tax." Now that I think about it, that was not really much of an explanation. The septuagenarian instructor provided no economic justification for taxing sins. Nor did he offer any definition of sin. At the time, all of us in the class knowingly nodded our heads at the notion of sin and the need to tax it. It was not a very scientific idea, but it appealed to our baser instincts.

— Martin A. Sullivan

There is an inherent hypocrisy in increasing taxes on consumers to discourage smoking, while simultaneously relying on that revenue to fund the increasing cost of children's healthcare.

— Lorillard Tobacco Company
(advertisement)

The only sin taxes of any significance that have survived for any length of time are the two we know and love: taxes on booze and smokes.

— Joseph J. Thorndike

Taxing fattening foods has its advocates, but they tend to overlook the fact that consumers can overeat otherwise healthy foods, and that taxes are regressive because they raise the food budget of poor individuals who do not overeat. It would be desirable, but infeasible, to tax just overconsumption of food.

— Tomas J. Philipson and Richard A. Posner

The great myth of modern American politics is that the middle class is groaning under the burden of huge taxes deployed to support the undeserving poor. In fact, what the welfare state really does is to take from the well-off (a little) and give to the poor (also a little, but because they are so poor it matters a lot). Families in the middle are not much affected either way.

— Paul Krugman

A "decay in the social contract" is detectable; there is a growing feeling, particularly among middle-income taxpayers, that they are not getting back, from society and government, their money's worth for taxes paid.

— IRS Strategic Plan
(May 1984)

We do sympathize with the urge to level playing fields by squeezing the squeezable. It has been demonstrated beyond cavil that you can't get blood out of a stone or even a turnip. So it's an absurd and futile exercise to try to raise taxes on folks who are perennially shy of taxable income. The middle class, though, is fair game: All the noble field leveler need do is find a new statutory way to shake the hard-earned coins out of their piggybanks.

— Alan Abelson

There is just one thing I can promise you about the outer space program: Your tax dollar will go farther.

— Wernher von Braun

One of the reasons some of the advocates of ever-larger government and more government intrusiveness get nervous about discussions of the actual cost of government is that they fear if the American people had a discussion about what government costs, the true cost of taxes, that they might not want as much government as they are presently getting.

— Grover Norquist

But of course, cutting taxes doesn't shrink government, at least not by itself. Spending is a better barometer of government activism than taxing, and tax cuts without spending cuts can actually *increase* the size and intrusiveness of the state.

— Joseph J. Thorndike

When your money is taken by a thief, you get nothing in return. When your money is taken through taxes to support needless bureaucrats, precisely the same situation exists. We are lucky, indeed, if the needless bureaucrats are mere easy-going loafers. They are more likely today to be energetic reformers busily discouraging and disrupting production.

— Henry Hazlitt

Essentially, no politician wants to be identified with making people recognize the cost of government. Neither party wants to be known as having increased taxes or having cut expenditures.

— Gene Steuerle

Your federal government needs your money so that it can perform vital services for you that you would not think up yourself in a million years.

— Dave Barry

If a people tie the hands of their government, it cannot serve them; if they do not, it uses its hands to pick their pockets and squeeze their throats.

— Charles Issawi

It is the settled policy of the Government, pursued from the beginning and practiced by all parties and Administrations, to raise the bulk of our revenue from taxes upon foreign productions entering the United States for sale and consumption, and avoiding, for the most part, every form of direct taxation, except in time of war.

— William McKinley Jr.

[America's] commitment to wartime fiscal sacrifice has always been uneasy — and more than a little ambiguous. In some wars, political leaders have asked Americans to accept new taxes as the price of freedom and security. But in others, they have tried to delay, deny, and obscure the trade-off between guns and butter. And even when Americans have embraced the call for sacrifice, their elected representatives have often made room for self-indulgence, easing burdens for some constituents while raising them for others.

— Steven A. Bank, Kirk J. Stark, and Joseph J. Thorndike

War involves in its progress such a train of unforeseen and unsupposed circumstances that no human wisdom can calculate the end. It has but one thing certain, and that is to increase taxes.

— Thomas Paine

Politicians like to talk about their plans for revamping the country's tax system, but important tax reform usually happens when it must, not when it should. War has been the most important catalyst for long-term, structural change in the nation's fiscal system. Indeed, the history of America's tax system can be written largely as a history of America's wars.

— Steven A. Bank, Kirk J. Stark, and Joseph J. Thorndike

[O]ne of the most fatal mistakes that governments have made in all countries has been the failure to impose fearlessly and promptly upon the existing generation a fair burden of the cost of war.

— William G. McAdoo

The war is over — the part you see in the picture papers. But the tax collector will continue his part with relentless fury. Cavalry charges are not the only ones in a real war.

— Finley Peter Dunne

Why does a slight tax increase cost you two hundred dollars and a substantial tax cut save you thirty cents?

— Peg Bracken

Every man, to be sure, is desirous of pushing off from himself the burden of any tax, which is imposed, and of laying it upon others.

— David Hume

Every election is a sort of advance auction sale of stolen goods.
— H. L. Mencken

The corruption of democracies proceeds directly from the fact that one class imposes the taxes and another class pays them. The constitutional principle, "No taxation without representation," is utterly set at nought.
— W.R. Inge

He has, acting personally and through his subordinates, endeavored to obtain from the IRS, in violation of the constitutional rights of citizens, confidential information contained in income tax returns, for purposes not authorized by law, and to cause income tax audits or other income tax investigations to be initiated or conducted in a discriminatory manner.
— Articles of Impeachment Against President Richard M. Nixon

After Vice President Gerald Ford succeeded Nixon in August 1974, he established the policy of disclosing his tax returns, and all presidents since have done so even though not required to by law or regulation.
— Jim Byrne

Tyranny consists in the wanton and improper use of strength by the stronger, in the use of it to do things which one equal would not attempt against another. A majority is tyrannical when it forces men to contribute money to objects which they disapprove, and which the common interest does not demand.
— James Bryce

Now, as a public policy, is it or is it not advisable to have as many citizens as can economically do so contribute to the maintenance of the Government? Will they not have more interest in the expenditures and affairs of the Government if they are directly contributing something, no matter how small, toward its maintenance?
— Charles Crisp

Governments last as long as the under-taxed can defend themselves against the over-taxed.
— Bernard Berenson

The government's view of the economy can be summed up in a few short phrases. If it moves, tax it. If it keeps moving, regulate it. And if it stops moving, subsidize it.

— Ronald Reagan

There is a belief among some elected officials that if it moves, tax it. But oftentimes, when you tax it, it won't move.

— Paul Cellucci

Government is getting too big and too involved in our personal lives. We don't want government telling us what to eat or drink by taxing our food and beverages. We can decide what to buy without government help. If we let government tax beverages, who knows where it will end?

— Americans Against Food Taxes

There are two distinct classes of men in [England], those who pay taxes and those who receive and live upon taxes . . . . When taxation is carried to excess it cannot fail to disunite those two.

— Thomas Paine

[A]s many people as possible [should] be subject to tax, saving only the very poor, so that they can see that government is not a free good. Everyone who can do so should pay something toward the cost of government. It should not be possible for a majority of voters to shift a disproportionate share of the tax burden onto a minority of taxpayers.

— Lawrence A. Hunter and Stephen J. Entin

Who nothing has to lose, the war bewails;
And he who nothing pay, at taxes rails.

— William Congreve

When we proclaim that the necessity for revenue to support the government furnishes the only justification for taxing the people, we announce a truth so plain that its denial would seem to indicate the extent to which judgment may be influenced by familiarity with perversions of the taxing power.

— Grover Cleveland

The great Depression came about because of government intervention into the economy through monetary policies, short-sighted trade policies, and huge tax increases.

— William L. Anderson

Taxes are going up so fast that government is likely to price itself right out of the market.

— Dan Bennett

A spectre haunts the world's governments. They fear that the combination of economic liberalization with modern information technology poses a threat to their capacity to raise taxes.

— *Financial Times*

Americans now get less from their federal government than they used to. But most people pay about as much in taxes — or more — than they did in the past.

— Robert S. McIntyre

Resistance to taxation, although normal and healthy, is today also related to the belief that government is thoroughly sunk in self-dealing, indiscriminate meddling and the lunatic spending that lards police forces with devices designed for conquering Fallujah. People know what no normal person can know one-tenth of 1 percent of what the government is doing.

— George Will

Despite what lobbyists and think tanks would lead you to believe, the preponderance of evidence leans toward the conclusion that tax incentives have little effect on investment and economic growth.

— Martin A. Sullivan

The single most overlooked fact about tax incentives is that they do not create money out of thin air. In general, if they work at all, they work by moving private dollars from one use to another.

— Theodore P. Seto

The promises of yesterday are the taxes of today.
— William L. Mackenzie King
(attributed)

The trouble with being a breadwinner nowadays is that the Government is in for such a big slice.
— Mary McCoy

What makes the property tax palatable is that it is generally used to finance local government operations. It pays for local roads, police, and schools. There is a connection between what people pay and the public services they receive that is more obvious than at any other level of government. But when property taxes are increased and the excess revenue is diverted to other communities, that connection — or lack thereof — is equally obvious.
— David Brunori

Higher property taxes impose a double whammy on those at risk of losing their homes. First, they act as a tax surcharge on homeownership. And second, when the tax hikes aren't tied to better public services, they reduce housing values, thus reducing owner equity.
— *The Wall Street Journal*

God will surely punish anyone who reinstitutes an old tax, for that very day, the son of the man who reinstituted the land tax caught a fever and three days later died.
— Pope St. Gregory I

No government can exist without taxation .... This money must necessarily be levied on the people; and the grand art consists of levying so as not to oppress.
— Frederick the Great

Government is emphatically a machine: to the discontented a "taxing machine," to the contented a "machine for securing property."
— Thomas Carlyle

When a government is just, taxes are few.
— Thomas Paine

Taxes are the sinews of the State.

— Marcus Tullius Cicero

We must discard old notions that taxation is for revenue only. We must use taxation as an instrument of inflation control. We must recognize its function of distributing the economic burden of the war in a fair and equitable manner.

— Randolph Paul

The Treasury is constantly presented with proposals to accomplish all sorts of desirable social objectives through the tax system. In general, these objectives can be accomplished more effectively and economically by other means.

— Stanley S. Surrey

The function of taxation is to raise revenue. . . . I do not go along with the economists who think of taxation primarily as a means for . . . manipulating the economy.

— Wilbur Mills

[Tax laws are] the government's most effective device for modifying behavior.

— Ernest S. Christian and Gary A. Robbins

By re-creating the incentive to work, save, invest and take economic risks by reducing the percentage of reward for that economic activity taken by the federal government in the form of taxes, we will have more investment and more economic risk taking. That will expand the total economic activity, expanding the tax base from which federal tax revenues are drawn, providing additional revenues with which to offset federal budget deficits.

— Jack Kemp

Taxes tell you what not to do.

— Arthur B. Laffer

Tax rates matter. And what matters about them is what activities get taxed, not who gets taxed. When you increase the tax rate on an activity, you get less of it. The only question is how much less of it will you get.

— John Rutledge

Taxes create incentives. Incentives affect behavior. Flowers turn toward the sun — and they don't even have brains.

— Jeffery L. Yablon

[I]f you believe in free markets (and the endless tax debate illustrates how many people pretend to believe, but don't), you want takes to change people's incentives as little as possible.

In other words, you want them to behave as closely as possible to the way they would if there were no taxes. This means two things: Tax rates should be as low as possible, given the government's revenue needs, and tax rates on different ways to use your labor or your capital should be as similar as possible.

— Editors of Bloomberg.com

Perhaps the greatest reassurance for those who quake at the prospect of repealing contemporary drug prohibitions can be found in the era of prohibition outside of America. Other nations, including Britain, Australia and the Netherlands, were equally concerned with the problems of drink and eager for solutions. However, most opted against prohibition and for strict controls that kept alcohol legal but restricted its availability, taxed it heavily, and otherwise discouraged its use. The results included ample revenues for government coffers, criminals frustrated by the lack of easy profits, and declines in the consumption and misuse of alcohol that compared favorably with trends in the United States.

— Ethan A. Nadelman

One expects that the private equity industry thrives because of its expertise in making superior investments, not because it receives favorable tax treatment . . . . A fundamental principle that all business managers learn is that if a project makes sense only because of its tax treatment, then it is not a worthwhile project.

— Joann M. Weiner

I never made an investment decision based on the tax code. Good business people don't do something because of [tax] inducements.

— Paul O'Neill

[A]n investment's taxation can by itself make the difference between a winner and a loser.

— Jason Zweig

He that shall look into other countries and consider the taxes, tallages, and impositions, and assizes, and the like that are everywhere in use, will find that the Englishman is most master of his own valuation, and the better in the purse of any nation in Europe.

— Francis Bacon

The suppression of unnecessary offices, of useless establishments and expenses, enabled us to discontinue our internal taxes. These, covering our land with officers, and opening our doors to their intrusions, had already begun that process of domiciliary vexation which, once entered, is scarcely to be restrained from reaching, successively, every article of property and produce.

— Thomas Jefferson

The biggest borrower of them all, the U.S. Government, gets away with murder. It offers a crummy yield on its bonds, repays your principal with cheesy, inflated dollars and then has the gall to tax you on your nonexistent real return.

— William Baldwin

The income tax reflected a major transformation in prevailing economic thought and fundamentally altered the individual's relationship to the central state.

— Margaret Levi

The apportionment of taxes on the various descriptions of property is an act which seems to require the most exact impartiality; yet there is, perhaps, no legislative act in which greater opportunity and temptation are given to a predominant party to trample on the rules of justice.

— James Madison

The middle class are being told — and are of course always willing to believe — that they are being overtaxed .... [But] the American middle class is not overtaxed. The middle class collects most of the entitlements. Yet politicians of both parties cheerfully indulge the white middle-class illusion that every nickel of their taxes goes to support black welfare mothers.

— Lee A. Sheppard

But the general rule always holds good. In constitutional states liberty is a compensation for the heaviness of taxation. In despotic states the equivalent for liberty is the lightness of taxation.

— Charles Louis de Secondat,
baron de la Brede et de Montesquieu

If taxation is a badge of free men, let me assure my friend that poor people of this country are covered all over with the insignia of free men.

— William Jennings Bryan

Taxes are not to be laid on the people but by their consent in person or by deputation.

— James Otis

No man's life, liberty, or property are safe while the legislature is in session.

— Gideon J. Tucker

Between liberty and compulsory taxation there is no possible reconciliation.

— Auberon Herbert

It isn't as though it were my money — it's just the taxpayers' money.
— Senator Jack S. Phogbound (of Al Capp's *Li'l Abner* comic strip)

We do not commonly see in a tax a diminution of freedom, and yet it clearly is one. The money taken represents so much labor gone through, and the product of that labor being taken away, either leaves the individual to go without such benefit as was achieved by it or else to go through more labor.

— Herbert Spencer

[I]t is inseparably essential to the freedom of a people and the undoubted right of Englishmen that no taxes be imposed on them but with their own consent, given personally, or by their representatives.
— 1765 Resolution of Delegates
From Nine American Colonies

Governments are necessarily continuing concerns. They have to keep going in good times and in bad. They therefore need a wide margin of safety. If taxes and debt are made all the people can bear when times are good, there will be certain disaster when times are bad.
— Calvin Coolidge

Taxes are not debts in the sense that having once been established and paid all further liability of the individual to the government has ceased . . . . The obligation of the individual to the state is continuous and proportioned to the extent of the public wants. No human wisdom can always foresee what may be the exigencies of the future.
— David J. Brewer

There is only one way to kill capitalism — by taxes, taxes, and more taxes.
— Karl Marx

I don't like the income tax. Every time we talk about these taxes we get around to the idea of "from each according to his capacity and to each according to his needs." That's socialism. It's written into the *Communist Manifesto*. Maybe we ought to see that every person who gets a tax return receives a copy of the *Communist Manifesto* with it so he can see what's happening to him.
— T. Coleman Andrews

Despite its Marxist origins, many Americans and Western Europeans to this day consider a progressive tax fair and just.
— G. Thomas Sims

I am a fan of progressive taxation. I would say our country has prospered from using such a system — even at 70% rates to say nothing of 90%.
— Bill Gates Sr.

The way to crush the bourgeoisie is to grind them between the millstones of taxation and inflation.

— Vladimir I. Lenin

Inflation, which tends to induce a forcible shift of wealth from private to public hands, is the functional equivalent of a tax increase.

— Joseph Isenbergh

By a continuing process of inflation, governments can confiscate, secretly and unobserved, an important part of the wealth of their citizens.

— John Maynard Keynes

Whether the nominal taxpayers pay off the burdens of weak debtors or everyone pays the universal tax of inflation makes little difference.

— Thomas G. Donlan

Calculation has convinced me that circumstances may arise, and probably will arise, wherein all the resources of taxation will be necessary for the safety of the state.

— Thomas Jefferson

The foundation of the obligation to pay taxes is not the privileges enjoyed or the protection given to a citizen by government .... The necessity of money for the support of States in times of peace or war, fixes the obligation upon their citizens.

— James M. Wayne

No civilized government has ever existed that did not depend upon taxation in some form for the continuance of ... existence.

— Samuel F. Miller

Taxes are not good things, but if you want services, somebody's got to pay for them so they're a necessary evil.

— Michael Bloomberg

The American people on the one hand don't like taxes. None of us do. But, on the other hand, we expect the government to do certain things for us.

— Wesley Clark

I'm trying to campaign, since government ain't working [during a shut-down], we shouldn't have to pay taxes. Paying taxes is supposed to pay for the government, which in turn is not working, so if they're not working, I shouldn't have to pay taxes. And me being in the upper echelon of the tax bracket, [I] feel that the money I could be saving over the next couple of days could be very vital to my survival.

— Nelly

Ask the majority of Americans whether they support libraries, schools, housing, and health care and they will say, 'Yes.' However, ask if they are in favor of taxes, they will say, 'No.' This is because they no longer make a connection between the two.

— Fred Ciporen

Civil servants and priests, soldiers and ballet-dancers, schoolmasters and police constables, Greek museums and Gothic steeples, civil list and services list — the common seed within which all these fabulous beings slumber in embryo is taxation.

— Karl Marx

And priests are like soldiers. I've never met a member of the military who cared much about taxing and spending. Their general view is that taxes should be high enough to allow a great nation to support a first-rate military and keep you safe, end of story. Soldiers aren't really paid commensurate with their responsibility and importance; it's not as if they're in the 60% bracket. Priests tend to be like that, too. They're not paid much, they're housed and fed by their order or parish. Taxes are more or less abstract to them. How high should taxes be? High enough for a first-rate country to help its citizens get the good things they need, end of story.

— Peggy Noonan

For every benefit you receive a tax is levied.

— Ralph Waldo Emerson

Your Social Security "contributions" are made with after tax dollars, and it was promised that those benefits would be tax free, but Washington started chipping away at that vow back in the 1980s. Today millions of Social Security recipients find a portion of their benefits subject to the IRS.

— Steve Forbes

[W]e often do a very poor job of linking taxes with the public benefits that taxes buy. Taxes that are clearly tied to benefits are less subject to attack than those that are not. At the federal level, the Social Security tax is an example. But in the case of most other taxes, the burden is obvious but the link to public benefits is not. We need to do a much better job of explaining what we mean when we say that taxes are the price of civilization.

— Thomas F. Field

In American political culture, taxes are no longer the price of civilization — they are the lifeblood of a parasitic state.

— Joseph J. Thorndike

[P]olicymakers use the tax laws for diverse and often conflicting purposes. Among these are raising revenue, as a macroeconomic tool for directing the national economy, as a bipartisan tool for cultivating favor with constituents, and as a partisan tool for implementing party objectives. The use of the tax laws for these conflicting purposes leads to the undermining of the integrity and coherence of the income tax, and increases the gross complexity that already plagues the tax laws.

— Sheldon D. Pollack

'Tis true that governments cannot be supported without great charge, and it is fit everyone who enjoys a share of protection should pay out of his estate his proportion of the maintenance of it.

— John Locke

Taxes are the life-blood of government, and their prompt and certain availability an imperious need.

— Owen J. Roberts

It costs something to be governed.

— Joseph McKenna

Good government cannot be found on the bargain-counter. We have seen samples of bargain-counter government in the past when low tax rates were secured by increasing the bonded debt for current expenses or refusing to keep our institutions up to the standard in repairs, extensions, equipment, and accommodations.

— Calvin Coolidge

If it were not for the American taxpayer . . . we would be slaves instead of free men.

— Lyndon B. Johnson

Throughout the first half of our history, Americans hated tax with passion, something they inherited from the founding fathers.

— Charles Adams

I am in favor of cutting taxes under any circumstance and for any excuse, for any reason, whenever it's possible.

— Milton Friedman

[F]or most Americans, any tax is a bad tax.

— Joshua Rosenberg

Taxes owing to the Government . . . are the price that business has to pay for protection and security.

— Benjamin N. Cardozo

Rightful taxation is the price of social order. In other words, it is the portion of the citizen's property which he yields up to the government in order to provide for the protection of all the rest. It is not to be wantonly levied on the citizen, nor levied at all except in return for benefits conferred.

— Journal of the Senate of the State of Ohio (1847)

The government has been compelled to levy taxes which unavoidably hit large sections of the population. The Italian people are disciplined, silent, and calm. They work and know that there is a government which governs, and know, above all, that if this government hits cruelly certain sections of the Italian people, it does so not out of caprice, but from the supreme necessity of national order.

— Benito Mussolini

Citizens [of Peru] have to understand that if they don't pay their taxes, their children will not have a good education.

— Beatriz Merino

Take an Argentine man. His first loyalty is to his mother. His second loyalty is to his children. Then you have cousins, aunts, uncles. By the time you get to business associates, the concept of loyalty, or trust, is fairly dissipated. By the time you get to "the country" — forget it. No one here thinks that if he pays taxes, for example, he might get something back from it. He thinks, "if I pay taxes, I'm an idiot."

— Anonymous Diplomat

The complexity of the [Brazilian] tax system is no accident. It serves a political purpose: Every complication in the code produces multiple government jobs and at least as many opportunities to grant special favors for a price. This means that simplifying the code is likely to lower overall corruption — but it also means that efforts to simplify are likely to meet with significant resistance.

— *The Wall Street Journal*

The obsession of journalists with interest group politics has contributed to the widespread popular cynicism about policymaking, and in particular, about the tax system. Comfortable middle-class taxpayers who benefit from a host of tax preferences specifically designed for them are convinced that everyone else is avoiding taxes through "loopholes," while they are paying at exorbitant rates. They believe that the IRS is incompetent, and they know that policymakers in Washington have sold out to the special interests. On the whole, little of this is accurate. But you would never know it by reading any of our leading national newspapers.

— Sheldon D. Pollack

You can't have [a] government like this without an income tax, but we [Libertarians] don't want a government like this.

— Ronald E. Paul

Your guilty conscience may move you to vote Democratic, but deep down you long for a cold-hearted Republican to lower taxes, brutalize criminals, and rule you like a king.

— Character in *The Simpsons* television cartoon show

The best reason to reduce taxes is to reduce our ideas of the number of dollars the government can properly spend in a year, and thereby reduce inflated ideas of the proper scope of bureaucratic authority.

— Robert Taft

We must insist, for example, that there be a limit to the level of taxation, not only because excessive taxation undermines the strength of the economy but because taxation beyond a certain level becomes servitude. And in America, it is Government that works for the people and not the other way around.

— Ronald Reagan

The same prudence which in private life would forbid our paying our own money for unexplained projects, forbids it in the dispensation of the public monies.

— Thomas Jefferson

There were always those who told us that taxes couldn't be cut until spending was reduced. Well, you know, we can lecture our children about extravagance until we run out of voice and breath. Or we can cure their extravagance by simply reducing their allowance.

— Ronald Reagan

Jobs and wealth are created by those who are taxed, not by those who do the taxing. Government, by its very nature, doesn't create resources but redistributes resources.

— Arthur B. Laffer

People try to live within their income so they can afford to pay taxes to a government that can't live within its income.

— Robert Half

It takes no courage to cut taxes. Zero.

— Steny H. Hoyer

The Congressman who is afraid of taxing the people, is, and ought to be regarded as a public enemy.

— Anonymous Georgia Newspaper Editor

Taxation may run *pari passu* with expenditure. The constituted authorities may rightfully make one equal the other.

— David J. Brewer

Capitation [direct taxes on the individual] is more natural to slavery; a duty on merchandise is more natural to liberty, because it has not so direct a relation to the person.

— Charles Louis de Secondat,
baron de la Brede et de Montesquieu

To lay duties on a commodity exported, which our neighbors want, is a knavish attempt to get something for nothing. The statesman who first invented it had the genius of a pickpocket, and would have been a pickpocket if fortune had suitably placed him. The nations who have practiced it have suffered four-fold, as pickpockets ought to suffer. Savoy, by a duty on exported wines, lost the trade of Switzerland, which thenceforth raised its own wine; and (to waive other instances) Britain, by her duty on exported tea, has lost the trade of her colonies.

— Benjamin Franklin

As pressures for new revenues become more and more insistent, ways and means of meeting them present to a state not only the baffling task of tapping fresh sources of revenue but of doing so with due regard to a state's existing taxing system.

— Felix Frankfurter

Taxes are never welcome to a community. They seldom fail to excite uneasy sensations more or less extensive. Hence a too strong propensity, in the Governments of Nations, to anticipate and mortgage the resources of posterity, rather than encounter the inconveniences of a present increase in taxes. But this policy, when not dictated by very peculiar circumstances, is of the worst kind. Its obvious tendency is, by enhancing the permanent burdens of the people, to produce lasting distress, and its natural issue is in National Bankruptcy.

— Alexander Hamilton

[We should avoid] ungenerously throwing upon posterity the burden which we ourselves ought to bear.

— George Washington

The principle of spending money to be paid by posterity under the name of funding is but swindling futurity on a large scale.

— Thomas Jefferson

'Tis pleasant to observe, how free the present Age is in laying taxes on the next.

— Jonathan Swift

The methods and subjects of taxation are matters of governmental policy.

— Benjamin N. Cardozo

Tax subsidies, like their counterparts on the spending side, reduce economic efficiency by substituting political micromanagement for routine market decisions about how capital should be allocated across the economy.

— Progressive Policy Institute

Property is made the constitutional basis of taxation. This is not unreasonable. Governments are organized for the protection of persons and property and the expenses of the protection may very properly be apportioned among the persons protected according to the value of their property protected.

— Morrison Waite

What reason is there that he which laboreth much, and, sparing the fruits of his labor, consumeth little, should be more charged than he that, living idly, getteth little and spendeth all he gets, seeing the one hath no more protection from the commonwealth than the other?

— Thomas Hobbes

Those who do work are denied a fair return for their labor by a tax system which penalizes successful achievement and keeps us from maintaining full productivity.

— Ronald Reagan

Modern enterprise often brings different parts of an organic commercial transaction within the taxing power of more than one State, as well as of the nation. It does so because the transaction in its entirety may receive the benefits of more than one government.

— Felix Frankfurter

When everybody has got money they cut taxes, and when they're broke them [politicians] raise 'em. That's statesmanship of the highest order.

— Will Rogers

The tax law . . . is the primary link between the nation's citizens and their government. Many more people file tax returns than vote in presidential elections.

— Michael J. Graetz

Our colonial forbears knew more about the ways of taxing than some of their descendants seem to be willing to concede.

— Benjamin N. Cardozo

Printing money is merely taxation in another form. Rather than robbing citizens of their money, governments rob their money of its purchasing power.

— Peter Schiff

There are only three ways to meet the unpaid bills of a nation. The first is taxation. The second is repudiation. The third is inflation.

— Herbert Hoover

It is common to speak as though, when a Government pays its way by inflation, the people of the country avoid taxation. We have seen that this is not so. What is raised by printing notes is just as much taken from the public as is a beer-duty or an income-tax. What a Government spends the public pay for. There is no such thing as an uncovered deficit.

— John Maynard Keynes

In a democratic society, politicians are often unwilling to raise taxes because of the expected voter anger. For them, inflation and the devaluation of the currency serve much better because they constitute a hidden tax.

— Jack Weatherford

Higher taxes never reduce the deficit. Governments spend whatever they take in and then whatever they can get away with.

— Milton Friedman

Government can pay its bills with tax money, run up a budget deficit or print more cash, creating inflation. Inflation hurts the saver, deficits hurt the investor, taxes hurt the earner, and all three are usually the same person: you.

— P.J. O'Rourke

Solicitude for the revenues is a plausible but treacherous basis upon which to decide a particular tax case.

— Robert H. Jackson

In form, the tax is one upon the value of a privilege, and income is nothing but the measure.

— Benjamin N. Cardozo

Of all debts men are least willing to pay the taxes. What a satire is this on government! Everywhere they think they get their money's worth, except for these.

— Ralph Waldo Emerson

The construction which in our view the statute compels safeguards the interests of the Government, interprets a business transaction according to its tenor, and avoids gratuitous resentment in the relations between Treasury and taxpayer.

— Felix Frankfurter

The privilege of use is only one attribute, among many, of the bundle of privileges that make up property or ownership .... A state is at liberty, if it pleases, to tax them all collectively, or to separate the faggots and lay the charge distributively.

— Benjamin N. Cardozo

I want to cut tax rates; but if ... a particular cut in taxes increased revenue—then my conclusion would be that we hadn't cut tax rates enough, because what I want to cut is government revenue. That's what feeds government spending .... What they [the big spenders] want is to increase taxes so they will have more money to spend and won't have to cut spending.

— Milton Friedman

The state is the great fictitious entity by which everyone seeks to live at the expense of everyone else.

— Claude-Frederic Bastiat

It is time to start over from scratch and develop a new tax system in the United States. It must be a system that is designed on purpose, based on a clear and consistent set of principles, which everyone in the United States can understand.

— William Simon

Tax simplification is complicated stuff.

— Pam Olson

Simplicity is not a goal per se and it is definitely undesirable when it conflicts with the major objectives of a good tax system.

— Robert B. Eichholz

The notion that taxes should be simpler is one of the very few propositions in tax policy that generates almost universal agreement. The fundamental paradox of tax simplification is that despite this consensus, almost every year tax rules become more complex.

— William G. Gale

Nearly every politician on both sides of the aisle claims to want to make the tax code simpler and fairer, but each time Congress takes up so-called tax reform, the result is the exact opposite.

— Tom Coburn

Lots of people talk about simplifying the tax law. And lots of people agree that simplifying the tax law should be a policy priority. But the problem is that simplification is complicated, and it is politically dangerous work.

— George Guttman

The rise in complexity of the tax laws cannot be attributed solely to an increasingly complex economy and business world. Rather, the tax laws themselves contributed to the complexity in the business world.

— Sheldon D. Pollack

Complexity reduces taxpayers' perceptions of fairness of the Federal tax system by (1) creating disparate treatment of similarly situated taxpayers, (2) creating opportunities for manipulation of the tax laws by taxpayers who are willing and able to obtain professional advice, and (3) disillusioning taxpayers to Federal tax policy because of the uncertainty created by complex laws.

— Staff of the Joint Committee on Taxation

[T]axpayers appear to tolerate significant complexity in order to eliminate marginal horizontal inequity. More importantly, taxpayers generally are unwilling to sacrifice tax benefits to achieve simplicity.

— Deborah H. Schenk

Our tax law is a 1,598-page hydra-headed monster and I'm going to attack and attack and attack until I have ironed out every fault in it.

— Vivien Kellems

I hold in my hand 1,379 pages of tax simplification.

— Delbert L. Latta

Yet if there is one thing that Americans agree epitomizes failed government, it is the tax code.

— Kimberley A. Strassel

Progressivity and Equity

Any reasonable system of taxation would

be based on the slogan "Soak the Rich."

— Heywood Broun

Progressivity and Equity

[A] tax system can be defined as progressive if after-tax income is more equally distributed than before-tax income.

— Thomas Piketty and Emmanuel Saez

That which angers men most is to be taxed above their neighbours.
— Sir William Petty

Race has always been the curse and the blessing of South America. A curse because the Spanish colonial system was built entirely on race. Every time a child was born, they wrote down the shade of his or her skin. They taxed people by that same measure.

— Marie Arana

Tax preferences — which are legally known as tax expenditures — result in forgone revenue for the federal government because of preferential provisions in the tax code, such as exemptions and exclusions from taxation, deductions, credits, deferral of tax liability, and preferential tax rates.

— Stanley S. Surrey

The moment you abandon . . . the cardinal principle of exacting from all individuals the same proportion of their income or their property, you are at sea without rudder or compass, and there is no amount of injustice or folly you may not commit.

— J.R. McCulloch

But the argument based on the presumed justice of progressivism provides no limitation, as has often been admitted by its supporters, before all incomes above a certain figure are confiscated and those below left untaxed. Unlike proportionality, progressivism provides no principle which tells us what the relative burden of different persons ought to be. *It is no more than rejection of proportionality in favor of discrimination against the wealthy without any criterion for limiting the extent of this discrimination.*

— Friedrich A. Hayek

In a republican form of government, the true theory is to make no distinctions as to persons in the rates of taxation. Recognizing no class for special favors, we ought not to create a class for special burdens.

— Justin S. Morrill

Under wise and constitutional legislation, every citizen should contribute his proportion, however small the sum, to the support of government, and it is no kindness to urge any of our citizens to escape this obligation.

— Stephen J. Field

The tax expenditure concept posits that an income tax is composed of two distinct elements. The first element consists of structural provisions necessary to implement a normal income tax . . . . The second element consists of the special preferences found in every income tax. These provisions, often called tax incentives or tax subsidies, are departures from the normal tax structure and are designed to favor a particular industry, activity, or class of persons.

— Stanley S. Surrey and Paul R. McDaniel

Tax expenditures are similar to spending programs in their impact on the deficit; and like spending, are established to achieve specific national objectives. However, the effect of tax expenditures in achieving these goals is rarely studied.

— Senate Committee on Governmental Affairs

There is, to be sure, no clear division between tax cuts and tax expenditures. At one extreme, a cut in a tax rate from 20% to 15% is not an "expenditure" unless you believe that all income belongs to the government. At the other, the $8,000 refundable "tax credit" that goes to a first-time home buyer is hard to distinguish from a grant-in-aid.

— Brian Wingfield

The tax system has become the vehicle of choice for influencing economic policy, the distribution of the tax burden, the state of the economy, the social welfare of families, and almost anything else you want to mention.

— Gene Steuerle

Financial systems are bloated by implicit taxpayer guarantees, which allow banks, particularly large ones, to borrow money at interest rates that do not fully reflect the risks they take in search of outsized profits. Since that risk is then passed on to taxpayers, imposing taxes on financial firms in proportion to their borrowing is a simple way to ensure fairness.

— Kenneth Rogoff

Over the years, the progressive income tax has been used to comfort the afflicted and, on occasion, to afflict the comfortable. Ultimately, it has proven better suited to achieving the latter than the former (especially as its use to comfort the afflicted has itself been a source of affliction to many of the comfortable).

— J. Mark Iwry

We live in a society of one person, one vote, where progressive taxes have been enacted precisely to weaken the winners.

— Nassim Nicholas Taleb

Proportionate taxation we would gladly accept on the theory that those better able to pay should remove some of the burden from those less able to pay. The Bible explains this in its instruction on tithing. We are told that we should give the Lord one tenth and if the Lord prospers us ten times as much, we should give ten times as much. But, under our progressive tax, computing Caesar's share is a little different.

— Ronald Reagan

There appears to be a widespread consensus that an element of progression is desirable in the tax structure.

— William Simon

It is not very unreasonable that the rich should contribute to the public expense, not only in proportion to their revenue, but something more than in that proportion.

— Adam Smith

A progressive income tax is also the most complicated and difficult of taxes to maintain. It places a premium on sensitivity to economic changes and to public attitudes. It demands high technical skills on the part of those who shape the legislative structure, who administer and interpret its provisions, and who advise the public on how to order its business and family affairs under the tax. It requires a literate citizenry with a respect for law and a willingness to shoulder fiscal burdens.

— Joseph J. Thorndike

Is this not true — That in proportion to the value of their estates the extremely wealthy pay far less taxes than those of moderate means? Compare the amount paid by millionaires with the amount paid by ordinary citizens. I believe that in proportion to their estates they pay less than half as much as ordinary citizens, whereas they ought to pay more.

— Rutherford B. Hayes

The need for a progressive tax system is imprinted on the American DNA.

— James Q. Riordan

Progressive taxation of income and profits means that precisely those parts of the income which people would have saved and invested are taxed away.

— Ludwig von Mises

Another false remedy for poverty is the progressive income tax, as well as a very heavy burden of capital gains taxes, inheritance taxes, and corporate income taxes. All of these have the effect of discouraging production, investment, and capital accumulation. To that extent they must prolong rather than cure poverty.

— Henry Hazlitt

Desirable as it is to foster business recovery, we should not do so by creating injustices in the tax system, particularly injustices at the expense of the man who earns his income — injustices to the advantage of the man who does not.

— Franklin D. Roosevelt

Nothing is more calculated to make a demagogue popular than a constantly reiterated demand for heavy taxes on the rich. Capital levies and high income taxes on the larger incomes are extraordinarily popular with the masses, who do not have to pay them.

— Ludwig von Mises

There can be no moral justification of the progressive tax. Perhaps that is why the bureaucrats pretend it is proportional taxation.

— Ronald Reagan

I find it hard, as a liberal, to see any justification for graduated taxation solely to redistribute income. This seems a clear case of using coercion to take from some in order to give to others and thus to conflict head-on with individual freedom.

— Milton Friedman

He [Barack Obama] says that he is for a tax credit, which is when government takes your money in order to give it away to someone else.

— John McCain

The king employs a considerable part of the tribute in grants of largesse, bestowed by way of banquets or presents, to those whose support consolidates his authority, whereas their defection would endanger it. Do we not see modern governments as well using the public funds to endow social groups or classes, whose votes they are anxious to secure? Today the name is different, and it is called the redistribution of incomes by taxation.

— Bertrand de Jouvenel

The more we discourage productivity and saving, the poorer most Americans will be. We need to change the attitude that taxes on the rich do not matter, and that redistribution of wealth is a legitimate government function.

— Theodore R. Groom

As income tax initially enacted at low rates and later seized upon as a means to redistribute income in favor of the lower classes has become a facade covering loopholes and special provisions that render rates that are highly graduated on paper largely ineffective.

— Milton Friedman

The very first Social Security check, for $22.54, was paid in 1940 to a Vermont woman who had paid $22 in Social Security taxes. By the time she died, in 1974, aged 100, she had collected $20,944.42.

— Andrew Tobias

One of the basic principles of optimal taxation is that the government should tax less the goods which have a supply more elastic to tax rates. Women labor supply is more elastic than that of men to after tax wages. Therefore optimal taxation theory implies that tax rates on labor income should be lower for women than for men.

— Alberto Alesina and Andrea Ichino

Unlike proportionality, progression provides no principle which tells us what the relative burden of different persons ought to be . . . the argument based on the presumed justice of progression provides no limitation, as has often been admitted by its supporters, before all incomes above a certain figure are confiscated, and those below left untaxed.

— Friedrich A. Hayek

Whenever you have growth and [income tax rate] progressivity, people move into higher tax brackets and the government gets a larger take. The economy may expand fast, but government will expand even faster.

— *The Wall Street Journal*

To finance the Hundred Years' War, France imposed an income tax in 1355. Rates were set at four percent on the rich, five percent on the middle class, and ten percent on the poor. After all, at four percent, a rich man would pay more tax than a poor man at ten percent.

— Jay Starkman

In the matter of taxation, every privilege is an injustice.

— Voltaire

Taxation may not be universal, but it must be general and uniform.

— Thomas Cooley

To tax and to please is not given to me, but to tax and be fair is.

— N.A. Palkhivala

Moral hazard exists when a policy produces incentives for perverse behavior . . . . [For example] the policy of removing tens of millions of voters from the income tax rolls, thereby making government largess a free good for them.

— George Will

Highly graduated taxation realizes most completely the supreme danger of democracy, creating a state of things in which one class imposes on another burdens which it is not asked to share, and impels the State into vast schemes of extravagance, under the belief that the whole costs will be thrown upon others.

— W. E. H. Lecky

Our fixation on progressive taxation was simply the wrong target. What we really should care about is a progressive fiscal system.

— Edward D. Kleinbard

If you look at who precisely pays income taxes, the reason is clear . . . . the top 5% of taxpayers . . . paid over half the total tax revenue. Since it is exactly the rich who disproportionately pay most of the income tax, it would be impossible to lower taxes without benefiting them disproportionately. Hey, it's their money.

— *The Wall Street Journal*

I have no disposition to tax wealth unnecessarily or unjustly, but I do believe that the wealth of the country should bear its just share of the burden of taxation and that it should not be permitted to shirk that duty.

— Cordell Hull

Our tax system comes up short in a lot of areas. It doesn't foster economic growth. It isn't very simple. And it certainly isn't fair. The one place where it does excel is at redistributing income.

— Ari Fleischer

Increasingly, the income tax is codified envy.

— George Will

Like philanthropy, saving is an act of self-denial that enriches your neighbors (by leaving more goods available for them to consume). But unlike philanthropy, saving is punished by the tax system (via the taxes on interest, dividends, capital gains and inheritance). That's nuts.

— Steven E. Landsburg

[I]deas of fairness in taxation are usually nebulous.

— Roy Blough and Carl Shoup

Some laws have moral force of their own. That is less clear about tax laws than many other laws.

— Terence Floyd Cuff

Tax fairness is a social construction, and all that matters is how people feel about it.

— Joseph J. Thorndike

The only thing that hurts more than paying an income tax is not having to pay an income tax.

— Lord Thomas R. Dewar

You know, gentlemen, that I do not owe any personal income tax. But nevertheless, I send a small check, now and then, to the Internal Revenue Service out of the kindness of my heart.

— David Rockefeller

The Higher the Tax Bracket, the Better the View.

— Advertisement for Luxury Florida Real Estate Development

For most people, a lower capital gains rate is meaningless. For the upper middle class it is a nice little tax cut. For the rich it is a major tax cut. For the superrich it is the most important aspect of their federal income tax liability.

— Martin A. Sullivan

The rich don't mind high taxes because they already have their money.

— Barney Kilgore

Rich folks should pay their taxes, in part so their offspring will have less leeway to become idle and go off the rails.

— Lee A. Sheppard

[T]he illusion that by means of progressive taxation the burden can be shifted substantially onto the shoulders of the wealthy has been the chief reason why ... the masses have come to accept a much heavier load than they would have done otherwise.

— Friedrich A. Hayek

A person should be taxed according to his means.

— *Talmud*

Because most of us are risk averse, we would benefit from buying insurance against the risk of being poor. A progressive income tax is like an insurance plan against being poor.

— Martin A. Sullivan

When a rich man is taxed, he need only retrench his superfluities, but when a poor man is taxed that can only increase his miseries.

— George Mason

Social unrest and a deepening sense of unfairness are dangers to our national life which we must minimize by rigorous methods. People know that vast personal incomes come not only through the effort or ability or luck of those who receive them, but also because of the opportunities for advantage which Government itself contributes. Therefore, the duty rests upon the Government to restrict such incomes by very high taxes.

— Franklin D. Roosevelt

If we make taxes commensurate to the damage that an individual does to others when he earns more — [*i.e.*, the damage to others' self-image and happiness], then he will only work harder if there is a true net benefit to society as a whole. It is efficient to discourage work effort that makes society worse off.

— Richard Layard

Most states tax systems are regressive . . . but are balanced by a progressive federal tax system. It is important to maintain that balance.

— Robert Greenstein

It is simply wrong to say we don't have a progressive tax system. The best analysis shows that average federal tax rates rise steeply with income.

— Greg Mankiw

The fairness of taxing more lightly income from wages, salaries, or from investments is beyond question. In the first case, the income is uncertain and limited in duration; sickness or death destroys it and old age diminishes it; in the other, the source of income continues; the income may be disposed of during a man's life and it descends to his heirs.

Surely we can afford to make a distinction between the people whose only capital is their mental and physical energy and the people whose income is derived from investments.

— Andrew Mellon

People want *just* taxes more than they want *lower* taxes. They want to know that every man is paying his proportionate share according to his wealth.

— Will Rogers

If our government is going to be able to provide for the common good, everybody has to contribute his or her fair share in the form of taxes. And when I say "everybody," I mean, "not everybody." Because the truth is that a lot of people don't pay taxes. Poor people, for example. Also many rich people. Also a fair number of middle-income people.

— Dave Barry

From the Boston Tea Party to now, tax fairness is firmly parked in the American psyche.

— Richard Neal

Okay guys, one more thing, this summer when you're being inundated with all this American bicentennial Fourth of July brouhaha, don't forget what you're celebrating, and that's the fact that a bunch of slave-owning, aristocratic, white males didn't want to pay their taxes.
— Richard Linklater
(*Dazed and Confused* screenplay)

The Boston Tea Party . . . was a revolt against tax loopholes, not high taxes.

— Joseph J. Thorndike

The Boston patriots who threw the tea chests into the harbor were not calling for cheaper tea. They were demanding the right to decide for themselves, in their own colonial assembly, how to tax their own tea — and refusing to let somebody else's Parliament decide for them. They would have been stunned to see their protests interpreted two centuries later as attacks on taxation in general. They had no interest in renouncing their own power to tax themselves.

— Robin L. Einhorn

[T]he colonists did not protest taxation. To be clear: They protested against taxation without representation, an entirely different matter. During the summer of 1774, when Parliament punished the city of Boston for the destruction of the East India Company's tea, people throughout Massachusetts Bay continued to pay taxes to the colonial government. At this chaotic moment, rather than keep their money, colonists voted in town after town to no longer transfer tax revenue to Harrison Gray, a treasurer of loyalist sympathies, but instead to send "moneys which they then had, or in future might have in their hands, belonging to the Province" to one Henry Gardner. Anyone who misses this point risks missing the fact that ordinary American patriots accepted the legitimate burdens of supporting a government in which they enjoyed genuine representation.

— T.H. Breen

It was not because the three-penny tax on tea was so exorbitant that our Revolutionary fathers fought and died, but to establish the principle that such taxation was unjust. It is the same with this woman's revolution; though every law were as just to woman as to man, the principle that one class may usurp the power to legislate for another is unjust, and all who are now in the struggle from love of principle would still work on until the establishment of the grand and immutable truth, "All governments derive their just powers from the consent of the governed."

— Susan B. Anthony

Taxes were very much at the center of the American Revolution. The lack of representation added a convenient slogan, but the root of the problem is that the colonists did not like taxes; they did not seek representation.

— Terence Floyd Cuff

I had now formed a clear and settled opinion, that the people of America were well warranted to resist a claim that their fellow-subjects in the mother-country should have the entire command of their fortunes, by taxing them without their consent.

— James Boswell

It is difficult to distinguish between protests of men and women of the 1700's whom we now characterize as "patriots" and the claims of modern tax protestors whose claims we more readily dismiss.

— Terence Floyd Cuff

The United States Congress has labored for almost a hundred years to produce a fair tax code, with impressively awful results.

— Thomas G. Donlan

The man of great wealth owes a peculiar obligation to the State, because he derives special advantages from the mere existence of government.

— Theodore Roosevelt

I would be willing to pay a lot more taxes, because I make a lot more money, but I don't want to give them more to just fuck things up more.

— Cher

A tax system, to be workable in a democratic country, must in general appeal to the sense of fairness of the people.

— Roy Blough and Carl Shoup

Let's raise taxes on trust fund kids and lower taxes on workers.

— Jonathan Barry Forman

The more heavily a man is supposed to be taxed, the more power he has to escape being taxed.

— Paul Dickson

We need to get out of the rut. We need a new mindset for thinking about taxes and expenditures. Here are some ideas. First, tax systems are blunt instruments and are not particularly effective for redistributing income or wealth. Second, well-designed and administered programs for education, health, and income support are more likely to reduce disparities between the rich and the poor and to reduce poverty. Third, we need to move away from thinking about increasing the tax burden on the rich as the primary way to increase spending for the poor.

— Eric M. Zolt

The rich aren't like us; they pay less taxes.

— Peter De Vries

[I]t would be dangerous to entrust the power to determine tax policies to a class of citizens who have been granted blanket immunity from taxes. It breeds political irresponsibility.

— Talbot Brewer

Rich men are doing, and are willing to do, their part in this war. They are ready to pay, some of them have already paid, their children's lives to the defense of democracy; and they should be taxed, and are willing to be taxed, high. They ought not to be maligned in addition.

— *The New York Times*

One will hardly believe that in order to become noble it is sufficient to become rich; and to cease to pay taxes it is sufficient to become noble. So there is only one way of escaping taxation and that is to make a fortune.

— Pierre Samuel du Pont de Nemours

Those in power institute the regulations and rules, and then hire people to protect them from the burdens and demands of their legislation. There is no congressman passing tax law who doesn't have staffers in his office taking care of his own financial life and who will not, when he moves down the street into the lobbying firm, have an army of accountants to protect him there.

— Peggy Noonan

12 Years I am a Worker
I'm Not a Criminal
I Pay Income Taxes

— Sign on hat of Columbian immigrant
at political rally

The fundamental class division in any society is not between rich and poor, or between farmers and city dwellers, but between taxpayers and tax consumers.

— David Boaz

By impost and excise [taxes], the man of luxury will pay; and the middling and the poor parts of the community, who live by their industry, will go clear; and as this would be the easiest mode of raising a revenue, it was the most natural to suppose it would be resorted to.

— Nathaniel Gorham

Our modern federal government is spending [in 1991] $4,900 a year on every person in America. The average American household of 2.64 people receives almost $13,000 worth of federal benefits, services and protection per annum. These people would have to have a family income of $53,700 to pay as much in taxes as they get in goodies. Only 18.5 percent of the population has that kind of money. And only 4.8 percent of the population — 12,228,000 people — file income tax returns showing more than $50,000 in adjusted gross income. Ninety-five percent of Americans are on the mooch.

— P.J. O'Rourke

It is not too much to hope that some day we may get back on a tax basis of 10 percent, the old Hebrew tithe, which was always considered a fairly heavy tax.

— Andrew Mellon

What we need to do is come up with something simple. And when I pick up my Bible, you know what I see? I see the fairest individual in the universe, God, and he's given us a system. It's called a tithe.

We don't necessarily have to do 10% but it's the principle. He didn't say if your crops fail, don't give me any tithe or if you have a bumper crop, give me triple tithe. So there must be something inherently fair about proportionality. You make $10 billion, you put in a billion. You make $10 you put in one. Of course you've got to get rid of loopholes. Some people say, "well that's not fair because it doesn't hurt the guy who made $10 billion as much as the guy who made $10." Where does it say you've got to hurt the guy? He just put a billion dollars in the pot. We don't need to hurt him. It's that kind of thinking that has resulted in 602 banks in the Cayman Islands.

— Ben Carson

A 10 percent flat tax should be our goal. After all, back in Bible times, the people of Israel paid a "tithe" — that is, a 10 percent flat tax — to God. If God Himself only demands a tithe, who does Uncle Sam think he is, demanding more?

— Michael Reagan

Even King Solomon's thriving kingdom crashed once his son decided to impose onerous taxes.

— Aryeh Spero

If there is any truth to the biblical account of Solomon's wealth, it seems obvious that he overspent and overtaxed — breaking the most elementary rule in the book of political leadership. So why doesn't the Bible remember him as a fool rather than the wisest of kings? Whence this great, and apparently ancient, reputation for wisdom?

— James L. Kugel

[V]iewing narrowly what the Bible says about taxation tells us little about the tax policy that is most consistent with biblical principles. The specific references to taxation in the Bible are too dependent on particular historical circumstances to serve as a guide to taxation today. Rather, we must look at its broader philosophical, moral, and ethical principles, which are undeniably progressive because they represent that inequality and the welfare of the poorest members of society are paramount considerations.

— Bruce Bartlett

I believe in a graduated income tax on big fortunes, and . . . a graduated inheritance tax on big fortunes, properly safeguarded against evasion and increasing rapidly in amount with the size of the estate.

— Theodore Roosevelt

[The estate tax is] the cruelest of taxes, because why should the government help itself to half of a man's lifetime earnings?

— Art Linkletter

The estate tax has been historically part of our very fundamental belief that we should have a meritocracy.

— Hillary Clinton

When a government taxes a certain level of income or inheritance at a rate of 70 or 80 percent, the primary goal is obviously not to raise additional revenue . . . . it is rather to put an end to such incomes and large estates, which lawmakers have for one reason or another come to regard as socially unacceptable and economically unproductive.

— Thomas Piketty

Dynastic wealth, the enemy of a meritocracy, is on the rise. Equality of opportunity has been on the decline. A progressive and meaningful estate tax is needed to curb the movement of a democracy toward a plutocracy.

— Warren Buffett

The most effective weapon against Plutocratic policy is the graded income tax.

— Charles H. Jones

Advocates of estate tax repeal should be forced to spend a day in the company of [heiress] Paris Hilton and her compatriots. Once they see the corrosive effect of money on potential heirs, they would support confiscatory rates.

— Lee A. Sheppard

I'm changing my will. I've found a new way to beat the inheritance tax. I'm leaving everything to the government.
— Joseph Fields, Sam Hellman, James V. Kern and Wilkie Mahoney
(*The Doughgirls* screenplay)

The case for drastic progression in taxation must be rested on the case against inequality — on the ethical or aesthetic judgment that the prevailing distribution of wealth and income reveals a degree (and/or kind) of inequality which is distinctly evil or unlovely.

— Henry C. Simons

There seems to be an obvious solution to rising inequality: higher taxes. But there's an inconvenient fact here. The way most advanced, industrial countries have made real gains on inequality is through relatively regressive taxes that fund programs that reduce inequality.
— Cathie Jo Martin and Alexander Hertel-Fernandez

When people ask, "Why should the rich pay a larger percent of their income than middle-income people?" — my answer is not an answer most people get: It's because their power developed from laws that enriched them.

— Ralph Nader

Now that I'm 72 years old, I can look forward to paying a significant portion of my accumulated wealth in estate taxes to the federal government and, depending on the state I live in at the time, to that state government as well. Of my current income this year, I expect to pay 80%-90% in federal income taxes, state income taxes, Social Security and Medicare taxes, and federal and state estate taxes. Isn't that enough?

— Harvey Golub

If there is a principle that unites the left side of the political spectrum, it is a belief that an energetic government can effectively use progressive taxation to insure the poor, the unlucky and the elderly against undue hardship.

— E.J. Dionne Jr.

American history doesn't lend a lot of support to the idea that Americans think we should take money from rich people because they just have too much. What it does lend support to is that we should ask Americans to pay their fair share.

— Joseph J. Thorndike

As you have been enabled to accumulate this wealth by the blessings of free institutions, contribute something to perpetuate them.

— Benton McMillin

The estate tax is essentially a tax upon wealth. It operates on wealth and ability to pay regardless of geography or state lines. It is a question of exercising the right to levy a tax for the transfer of property.

— John Nance Garner

The purpose of the income tax law is to prevent the accumulation of enormous fortunes, and the control of industry and commerce that goes with such large fortunes.

— Fiorello H. La Guardia

The purpose of the estate tax is not primarily to raise revenue . . . . The purpose of the estate tax is to reduce wealth inequality.

— Martin J. McMahon Jr.

[For the supporters of the 1913 income tax] the revenue goals of the tax were far less important than the desire to use the tax to advance economic justice.

— Elliot Brownlee

[States progressing towards the ideals of the *Communist Manifesto* will enact] a heavy progressive income tax.

— Karl Marx and Friedrich Engels

The only effective design for diminishing the income inequality inherent in capitalism is the progressive income tax.

— John Kenneth Galbraith

What do you call it when someone steals someone else's money secretly? Theft. What do you call it when someone takes someone else's money openly by force? Robbery. What do you call it when a politician takes someone else's money in taxes and gives it to someone who is more likely to vote for him? Social Justice.

— Thomas Sowell

Not only is the revenue derived from the high rates levied on large incomes, particularly in the highest brackets, so small compared with the total revenue as to make hardly any difference to the burden borne by the rest; but for a long time . . . it was not the poorest who benefited from it but entirely the better-off working class and the lower strata of the middle class who provided the largest number of voters.

— Friedrich A. Hayek

Economic theory does not provide an answer as to how the tax burden should be distributed among people with unequal incomes. While few would argue that the tax system should be regressive, the degree to which it should be progressive involves subjective value judgments.

— David L. Brumbaugh, Gregg A. Esenwein, and Jane G. Gravelle

Here is my principle: Taxes shall be levied according to ability to pay. That is the only American principle.

— Franklin D. Roosevelt

When you don't have an argument against fair taxation, you come up with a slogan: Class Warfare.

— Lawrence O'Donnell

In a country of great industries like this, it ought to be easy to distribute the burdens of taxation without making them anywhere bear too heavily or too exclusively upon any one set of persons or undertakings. What is clear is that the industry of this generation should pay the bills of this generation.

— Woodrow Wilson

I have never viewed taxations as a means of rewarding one class of taxpayers or punishing another. If such a point of view ever controls our public policy, the traditions of freedom, justice and equality of opportunity, which are distinguishing characteristics of our American civilization, will have disappeared.

— Andrew Mellon

Using tax policy to punish people is a bad idea.

— Jamie Dimon

A basic and common-sense rule of tax policy is that we ought to have the same rate of tax apply across different occupations or investments. The relative profitability of different professions, or investments, ought to be dictated by the market, not the tax law.

— Joseph Bankman

The subjects of every state ought to contribute toward the support of government, as nearly as possible, in proportion to their respective abilities; that is, in proportion to the revenue which they respectively enjoy under the protection of the state.

— Adam Smith

[T]he old saw "freedom isn't free" applies at least as much to paying taxes as it does to the other ways in which we protect and defend our liberties.

— E.J. Dionne Jr.

Those who say that the poorer the people, the larger the families — the heavier the taxation placed upon them, the greater their effort to pay it blaspheme — against the human race. They ought to experience the bitter destitution to which they condemn their fellow citizen in order to determine how false and atrocious is their attitude.

— Désiré Joseph Mercier

[I favor] a progressive tax . . . to put it out of the power of the owner of one of these enormous fortunes to hand on more than a certain amount to any one individual.

— Theodore Roosevelt

Taxes should be proportioned to what may be annually spared by the individual.

— Thomas Jefferson

Many of those with income just above the welfare levels resent paying taxes to benefit people only slightly worse off than they are.

— Paul Starr

Most of the people in the upper income brackets are not rich and do not have wealth sheltered offshore. They are typically working people who have finally reached their peak earning years after many years of far more modest incomes — and now see much of what they have worked for siphoned off by politicians, to the accompaniment of lofty rhetoric.

— Thomas Sowell

I do not believe that the government should ask social legislation in the guise of taxation. If we are to adopt socialism, it should be presented to the people of this country as socialism and not under the guise of a law to collect revenue.

— Calvin Coolidge

Taxes are necessary. But the system of discriminatory taxation universally accepted under the misleading name of progressive taxation of income and inheritance is not a mode of taxation. It is rather a mode of disguised expropriation of the successful capitalists and entrepreneurs.

— Ludwig von Mises

The taxing power of government must be used to provide revenues for legitimate government purposes. It must not be used to regulate the economy or bring about social change. We've tried that, and surely we must be able to see it doesn't work.

— Ronald Reagan

Because the largest share of federal income taxes is paid by the highest earners, lower-earning households bear a much smaller share of the overall income tax burden, thereby creating progressivity in the federal income tax system. However, it also means that federal revenues devoted to general government operations are particularly sensitive to changes in the income of the top earners.

— Joint Economic Committee

It will be a sad day for the revenues if the goodwill of the people toward their taxing system is frittered away in efforts to accomplish by taxation moral reforms that cannot be accomplished by direct legislation.

— Robert H. Jackson

[T]aking and spending the fruits of someone else's labor or property is not the equivalent of disinterested virtue, even though many progressives believe that to be the case.

— Kip Dellinger

As long as most Americans accept the moral premise that the needs of some are a moral claim on the lives and property of others, taxation won't drop in any significant way. Taxes will be slashed only when Americans openly reject this premise and stand for the opposite proposition: that an individual's income is 100% his private property, not to be taxed and redistributed to other people.

— David Holcberg

I'm getting so *tired* of writing books for the benefit of the Treasury and I can't tell you how utterly I resent the squandering of *my* money on such fatuous things as Education and Making Life Easy and Luxurious for So-Called Workers.

— Georgette Heyer

Faced with a requirement to select a tax structure, an individual might choose a proportionate rate structure simply because no other rate structure comes immediately to mind. It is as if, in choosing a tax structure, the polity were a lost traveller faced with a selection of equally well-trodden paths. Lacking any convincing rationale to turn right or left, the traveler continues on the path that leads straight ahead. Perhaps we can do no better than the lost traveler and are condemned to raise and redistribute a substantial portion of the world's wealth on a formula selected through intuition. But before resigning ourselves to that fate, it would be worthwhile to examine theories of distributive justice that might shape the tax structure.

— Joseph Bankman and Thomas Griffith

A flat tax is a bad idea whose time has not come.

— Lawrence Summers

A ton of economists, both liberal and conservative, have argued for a flat tax, but nobody's ever had the nerve to do it. . . . It would be simplifying things, but simplification doesn't seem to be in the human psyche.

— Clint Eastwood

If everybody pays at a common rate, it will be harder to expand government and raise the rate, because a larger fraction of potential voters will have a stake in limiting the spending. The more progressive the tax system becomes and the more concentrated among the few taxes become, the easier it is to expand government at the expense of a minority paying the bulk of costs.

— Michael J. Boskin

I was working on a flat tax proposal and I accidentally proved there's no God.

— Homer Simpson
(of *The Simpsons* television cartoon show)

The Bible tells us to care for the poor. It doesn't say a thing about marginal tax rates.

— Jonathan Greenberg

We can't afford a fair tax system, so we go with an unfair one.
— Gerry Padwe

There is no simple tax, at least no simple tax that is also fair.
— Joel Slemrod

The expense of government to the individuals of a great nation is like the expense of management to the joint tenants of a great estate, who are all obliged to contribute in proportion to their respective interests in the estate. In the observation or neglect of this maxim consists what is called the equality or inequality of taxation.
— Adam Smith

Imagine a banquet attended by 100 random Americans. If the bill for the meal is distributed like the income tax, the richest person in the room is required to pay one-third of the tab — or more than all 50 attendees with a below-average income. The three richest people are charged as much as the other 97. And the 30 or so lowest-income people in the room . . . pay nothing and eat for free.
— *The Wall Street Journal*

As a matter of policy, it is advisable to have every citizen with a stake in his country. Nothing brings home to a man the feeling that he personally has an interest in seeing that government revenues are not squandered, but intelligently expended, as the fact that he contributes individually a direct tax, no matter how small, to his government.
— Andrew Mellon

The tax wisdom of the ancients that has survived, and thus in the classical sense is profoundly conservative, is that we tax the biggest winners the most and that if we redistribute, it is to those with a reduced or no ability to care for themselves.
— David Cay Johnston

I do not propose either to purchase or to confiscate private property in land. The first would be unjust; the second, needless. Let the individuals who now hold it still retain, if they want to, possession of what they are pleased to call their land. Let them continue to call it their land. Let them buy and sell, and bequeath and devise it. We may safely leave them the shell, if we take the kernel. It is not necessary to confiscate land; only to confiscate rent.

We already take some rent in taxation. We have only to make some changes in our modes of taxation to take it all.

— Henry George

[T]heoretically there is nothing that can stop the government from taxing 100 percent of income so long as the people get benefits from the government commensurate with their income which is taxed.

— Barack Obama Sr.

[The property tax] puts a premium on dishonesty and debauches the public conscience. It reduces deception to a system and makes a science of knavery. It presses hardest on those least able to pay. It imposes double taxation on one man and grants entire immunity to the next. In short, the general property tax is so flagrantly inequitable that its retention can be explained only through ignorance or inertia. It is the cause of such crying injustice that its abolition must become the battle cry of every statesman and reformer.

— Edwin R.A. Seligman

Those who pay [the federal income tax] are the exception, those who do not pay are millions; and the whole moral force of the law is a dead letter. The honest man makes a true return; the dishonest hides and covers all he can to avoid this obnoxious tax. It has no moral force. This tax is unequal, perjury-provoking, and crime encouraging, because it is at war with the right of a person to keep private and regulate his business affairs and financial matters. Deception, fraud, and falsehood mark its progress everywhere in the process of collection. It creates curiosity, jealousy, and prejudice among the people. It makes the tax gatherer a spy.

— Dennis McCarthy

There are two methods . . . whereby man's needs and desires can be satisfied. The production and exchange of wealth: economic means . . . and the uncompensated appropriation of wealth produced by others: political means.

— Albert Jay Nock

To tax the community for the advantage of a class is not protection: it is plunder.

— Benjamin Disraeli

In a system of taxation based on justice and equity it is fundamental that the burdens be proportioned to the capacity of the people contributing . . . . But the common good also requires the public authorities, in assessing the amount of tax payable, take cognizance of the peculiar difficulties of farmers.

— Pope John XXIII

A good prince will tax as lightly as possible those commodities which are used by the poorest members of our society; e.g., grain, bread, beer, wine, clothing, and all other staples without which human life could not exist.

— Desiderius Erasmus

Sugar, rum and tobacco are commodities which are nowhere necessaries of life, which are [sic] become objects of almost universal consumption, and which are therefore extremely proper subjects of taxation.

— Adam Smith

We cannot lose sight of the fact that complexity is the result of our struggle for fairness.

— Margaret Milner Richardson

The wisdom of man never yet contrived a system of taxation that operates with perfect equality.

— Andrew Jackson

Even tax administration does not as a matter of principle preclude considerations of fairness.

— Felix Frankfurter

How could we, in a free society of a bunch of Christians, have the worst, most unjust tax structure that you could ever have dreamed up?
— Susan Pace Hamill

To some liberal Catholics, social justice is measured almost solely in terms of federal spending. Their formula is simple — those who advocate higher taxes and more spending are for more social justice than those who advocate lower taxes and less spending.
— Ed Gillespie

The task of devising means for distributing the burdens of taxation equitably has always challenged the wisdom of the wisest financial statesmen.
— Stanley F. Reed

Give women the vote, and in five years there will be a crushing tax on bachelors.
— George Bernard Shaw

Bachelors should be heavily taxed. It is not fair that some men should be happier than others.
— Oscar Wilde

The Emperor Caesar Augustus taxed bachelors as part of his population policy .... Bachelor taxes also existed in some of the U.S. Northwest Territories in the 19th century, and in many of the former satellite countries, all in view of declining populations. The Third Reich attempted to achieve a similar result in a kinder, gentler fashion.
— Joel S. Newman

He who only has the base necessities of life should pay nothing; taxation on him who has a surplus may, if need be, extend to everything beyond necessities. He may urge that on account of his rank what is superfluous for a man in a lower position is necessary for him, but that is untrue, for a nobleman has only two legs like a cowman, and each has only one belly.
— Jean Jacques Rousseau

[I]f I'm a moderate income person and I pay $2,000 in tax and get $10,000 in benefits versus I pay nothing in tax and get $8,000 in benefits, I'm getting the same amount of redistribution from that society.

— Gene Steuerle

If we enjoyed the freedom of the framers it is possible that we might, in the light of experience, devise a more equitable system of taxation than that which they gave us.

— Harlan F. Stone

Revenue laws are notoriously not expressions of an ordered system of reason and fairness. There has probably never been a revenue statute which, by design or oversight, has not favored some groups and laid the basis for a claim of unfairness to others similarly situated.

— Felix Frankfurter

I am well aware that these tax privileges are sometimes defended on the grounds that they encourage the production of strategic minerals. It is true that we wish to encourage such production. But the tax bounties distributed under present law bear only a haphazard relationship to our real need for proper incentives to encourage the exploration, development and conservation of our mineral resources. A forward-looking resources program does not require that we give hundreds of millions of dollars annually in tax exemptions to a favored few at the expense of the many.

— Harry Truman

Do we imagine that our assessments operate equally? Nothing can be more contrary to the fact. Wherever a discretionary power is lodged in any set of men over the property of their neighbors, they will abuse it.

— Alexander Hamilton

When the same man, or set of men, holds the sword and the purse, there is an end of liberty.

— George Mason

Nothing is more familiar in taxation than the imposition of a tax upon a class or upon individuals who enjoy no direct benefit from its expenditure, and who are not responsible for the condition to be remedied.

— Harlan F. Stone

Uniform taxation upon those equally able to bear their fair shares of the burdens of government is the objective of every just government.

— Hugo L. Black

By squeezing the destitute of their bare subsistence the state deprives them of all strength. Of the poor man it makes a beggar, of the workman an idler, of an unfortunate a rogue, and thus leads through starvation to the gallows.

— Guillaume Thomas Francois Raynal

Those who are wealthier should consider their higher tax bracket as part of their Biblical obligation to tend to the "widow and the orphan."

— Iowa Catholic Conference

Perfect equality and perfect uniformity of taxation as regards individuals or corporations, or the different classes of property subject to taxation, is a dream unrealized. It may be admitted that the system which most nearly attains this is the best.

— Samuel F. Miller

There is . . . no constitutional guaranty of equality of taxation.

— Harlan F. Stone

Equity is the privilege of paying as little as somebody else.

— Louis Eisenstein

It is fair that each man shall pay taxes in exact proportion to the value of his property; but if we should wait before collecting a tax to adjust the taxes upon each man in exact proportion with every other man, we should never collect any tax at all.

— Abraham Lincoln

Any reasonable system of taxation would be based on the slogan "Soak the Rich."

— Heywood Broun

The income tax is nothing more than another tool of redistributing wealth during life; the estate tax is nothing more than a tool for redistributing wealth after death. They are both taxes of envy.

— Christopher W. Hesse

History shows that tax hikes bring in far less revenues than expected. It's easy to see why: Raising taxes on those with lots of wealth shrinks the amount of capital available for investment, which means fewer new jobs, slower growth in incomes and lower overall productivity. Hardly a policy for prosperity. This is envy, pure and simple, and a tax policy based on envy is the worst kind. It sets neighbor against neighbor and downplays the contributions of skill and entrepreneurial gusto that those we derisively call the rich bring to our economy. In economics, as in most religions, envy is among the deadliest of sins.

— *Investor's Business Daily*

The issue of nonpayers is dangerous because the income tax is more than just a way to raise money. It's really about connection to the government, to the polity. To not be a part of that shared experience is a problem. If you want to protect the income tax, you need to make it feel like a shared burden.

— Joseph J. Thorndike

Suppose a star has reached the peak and can get $150,000 for his services in a picture. If he makes two pictures a year the Federal Government charges him $164,000 for being so snooty, to which the State of California adds a moderate tax of $36,000, for the use of its valuable climate. The net result is that each year, the star is allowed to work four months for himself on condition that he work eight months, free of charge, for the people. Under these circumstances, one might think that the Government would have nothing but encouraging smiles for these public benefactors. On the contrary, it matters deeply that such incomes are indecent and that people who have the ability to pay such heavy taxes should be reduced to the more democratic condition of inability to pay.

— William C. De Mille

Mathematical equality . . . cannot be reached in any system of taxation, and it is useless and idle to attempt it.

— Rufus W. Peckham

Let us not make the income tax so high that the man whose money we want to use in business prefers not to take the risk.

— Wendell L. Willkie

Any attempt to tax away new fortunes in the name of preventing inequality is certain to have adverse effects on further technology creation and niche exploitation by entrepreneurs — and harm job creation as a result. The reason is one of the laws of economics: Potential reward must equal the risk or the risk won't be taken.

— John Steele Gordon

A highly progressive income tax structure tends to discourage investment in human capital because it reduces take-home pay and the reward to highly skilled, highly paid occupations.

— Gary S. Becker, Edward P. Lazear, and Kevin M. Murphy

All taxes upon the transference of property of every kind, so far as they diminish the capital value of that property, tend to diminish the funds destined for the maintenance of productive labor.

— Adam Smith

The American Tax system is supposed to be progressive. Yet, for the very rich, nothing could be further from the truth.

— Dorothy A. Brown

Don't soak the rich, soak the poor. There's more of them.

— Eric Wright

Through the tax code, there has been class warfare waged, and my class has won.

— Warren Buffett

A sound tax policy must lessen, so far as possible, the burden of taxation, on those least able to bear it; and it must also remove those influences which might retard the continued steady development of business and industry on which, in the last analysis, so much of our prosperity depends.

— Andrew Mellon

Corporate taxes are found to be most harmful for growth, followed by personal income taxes and then consumption taxes.

— The Organization for Economic Cooperation and Development

People understand that corporations are powerful and that the corporate tax is one way in which the state, as representative of the people, can limit their power.

— Reuven S. Avi-Yonah

Most Americans see the corporate income tax as a way that corporations bear the cost of government services. However, corporations treat the tax as a cost of business, which is passed on to consumers in the form of higher prices, to workers in the form of lower wages, and to shareholders in the form of lower dividends.

In other words: Corporations don't pay taxes, people pay taxes.

— Bryan Taylor

I was reminded earlier this week of a House floor exchange between two Congressmen. The first said, "Corporations don't pay tax; people do." And the second retorted, "That's the problem!" If we are going to succeed in reforming the tax laws, we must have more thought leadership grounded in sound economics from our politicians and the media.

— Pamela F. Olson

[A]s an economic matter, it is far better to tax people instead of corporations. But the public seems to like the corporate income tax — a levy that economists hate because it is the most detrimental tax for economic growth.

— Michael J. Graetz

A tax on corporate income is merely a tax at the source on the income of the corporation's stockholders, and a small corporation may be owned by one rich stockholder, while a great corporation may be owned by hundreds of thousands of stockholders with a moderate average income.

— *The New York Times*

Corporate taxes are simply costs. The method of their assessment does not change this fact. Costs must be paid by the public in prices, and corporate taxes are thus in effect concealed sales taxes.

— Enders M. Vorhees

In reality, the corporate income tax is a tax on customers, assessed randomly. It weighs more heavily on the customers who buy from profitable companies, more lightly on the customers of businesses that are struggling — which seems exactly backward.

— Thomas G. Donlan

I don't think we should be embarrassed that a large corporation pays nothing in tax. I've never seen a corporation enjoy a good meal. I've never seen a corporation go on vacation.

— Andrew Lyon

Given the ability of economic actors to adjust, the burden of the corporate income tax spreads beyond corporate shareholders' sector to all owners of capital, including owners of corporate debt, non-corporate business, and owner-occupied housing.

This picture of the long-run burden of the corporate tax has implications for the vertical equity of the tax system — that is, its distribution across income classes. Because capital ownership is greater at upper-income levels, the corporate income tax is itself progressive and makes the overall tax system more progressive than it would otherwise be.

— Donald J. Maples

Democrats object to cutting the U.S. 35% corporate tax rate — which is higher than in all of Europe, undermines economic growth and discourages job creation — for all companies on grounds that it favors the rich and powerful. But Democrats will carve out tax loopholes for businesses they like and that write them campaign checks.

— *The Wall Street Journal*

Alert citizens should realize that the main purpose of the corporate tax is to provide a matrix from which crony capitalism and corruption can create loopholes. It's easier to compete for customers and capital if your competitors pay more taxes.

— Thomas G. Donlan

Corporations don't pay taxes, they collect them.

— Paul H. O'Neill

As regards income-tax, I am, thank goodness, an individual. I pray that I may never become a corporation. It seems to me that some society for the prevention of cruelty to things ought to step in between the authorities and the corporations. I have never gone deeply into the matter, having enough troubles of my own, but a casual survey of the laws relating to the taxing of corporations convinces me that any corporation that gets away with its trousers and one collar-stud should offer up Hosannas.

— P.G. Wodehouse

American business is complaining enormously about the level of corporate income tax. I would have you take that with a grain of salt.

— Warren Buffett

The real friends of property are not those who would exempt the wealth of the country from bearing its fair share of the burdens of taxation, but rather those who seek to have every one, without reference to his locality, contribute from his substance, upon terms of equality with all others, to the support of the government.

— John Marshall Harlan

There is no fairness in taxing the salaried man and the merchant upon their incomes, and taxing at far lower rates the profits on the capital of the speculator.

— Franklin D. Roosevelt

Eccentricities of incidence are common, and perhaps inevitable, in every system of taxation.

— Benjamin N. Cardozo

Those who are subject to be taxed cannot complain that they are denied the equal protection of the law because those who cannot legally be taxed are not taxed.

— Joseph McKenna

Protection and taxation are not necessarily correlative obligations, nor precise equality of burden attainable, however desirable.

— Horace H. Lurton

Systems of taxation are not framed, nor is it possible to frame them, with perfect distribution of benefit and burden. Their authors must be satisfied with a rough and ready form of justice.

— Benjamin N. Cardozo

It is fairer to tax people on what they extract from the economy, as roughly measured by their consumption, than to tax them on what they produce for the economy, as roughly measured by their income.

— Thomas Hobbes

Consumption taxes are better for economic growth because they create stronger incentives to save and invest than do income taxes. Under an income tax, a person who consumes what he earns immediately is taxed once, specifically on the earnings that he receives in that year. If instead he invests what he earns, the interest on that investment, which is compensation for deferring consumption, is also taxed. This pushes him toward consuming more now and saving less.

— Edward P. Lazear

It is a signal advantage of taxes on articles of consumption that they contain in their own nature a security against excess.

— Alexander Hamilton

All taxes upon the articles of consumption, because of the power that must necessarily be vested in the officers who collect them, will in the end destroy the liberty of any people that permits them to be introduced.

— Albert Gallatin

It may be true that plaintiff does not receive the same amount of benefit from some of these taxes, or from any of them, as do citizens living in the heart of the City . . . . But who can undertake to adjust with precise accuracy the amount which each individual in an organized civil community shall contribute to sustain the organization?

— Samuel F. Miller

One might as well compare the federal income tax of a banker whose net earnings are in the millions with that of a thousand clerks who by reason of exemptions are to pay no tax whatever. The comparison proves nothing unless it be the obvious fact that taxpayers are few when the count is at the highest level.

— Benjamin N. Cardozo

Taxes generally are imposed upon persons for the general advantages of living within the jurisdiction, not upon property, although generally measured more or less by reference to the riches of the person taxed.

— Oliver Wendell Holmes Jr.

The state is not called upon to explain the reasons for taxing the members of the one class more heavily than it does the members of the other.

— Benjamin N. Cardozo

Wealth has long been accepted as a fair measure of a tax assessment.

— Stanley F. Reed

Of all burdens imposed upon mankind that of grinding taxation is the most cruel.

— Ward Hunt

Justice requires that the burdens of government shall as far as is practicable be laid equally on all; and if property is taxed once in one way, it would ordinarily be wrong to tax it again in another way, when the burden of both taxes falls on the same person.

— Morrison Waite

I am in favor of an income tax. When I find a man who is not willing to bear his share of the burdens of the government which protects him, I find a man who is unworthy to enjoy the blessings of a government like ours.

— William Jennings Bryan

Income tax, intrinsically the most just of all taxes.

— Justin S. Morrill

[T]he wit of man never devised a fairer or juster tax than a graduated income tax.

— Champ Clark

The income tax is a just law. It simply intends to put the burdens of government justly upon the backs of the people.

— William Jennings Bryan

There is no tax which, in its essence, is more just and equitable than an income tax.

— John Marshall Harlan

Where there is an income tax, the just man will pay more and the unjust less on the same income.

— Plato

The Income Tax is the most odious, vexatious, inquisitorial, and unequal of all our taxes.

— *New York Tribune*

[Americans should] pull the income tax out by its roots and throw it away so it can never grow back.

— Bill Archer

We're going to close the unproductive tax loopholes that have allowed some of the truly wealthy to avoid paying their fair share. In theory, some of those loopholes were understandable, but in practice they sometimes made it possible for millionaires to pay nothing, while a bus driver was paying 10 percent of his salary, and that's crazy. It's time we stopped it.

— Ronald Reagan

I believe [the income tax] is the most easily concealed of any tax that can be laid, the most difficult of enforcement, and the hardest to collect .... [I]t is, in a word, a tax upon the income of honest men and an exemption, to a greater or lesser extent, of the income of rascals.

— Sereno Payne

Simply stated, the income tax was a necessary condition for the creation of the welfare state and the resulting social pathologies. The income tax also is the most economically destructive way politicians have ever developed for financing government.

— Daniel J. Mitchell

We do not believe there is a tax levied by the Government so onerous upon so large a class of people as the Income Tax.

— *New York Daily Tribune*

In every civilized country there is an exemption of small incomes which it would be manifest cruelty to tax.

— Henry B. Brown

I'm convinced that, if you use income as the base of taxation, you have inherent in the system a magnet that draws all kinds of complexities. That's what I think we've learned from history — that you cannot keep a simple income tax.

— Bill Archer

A fair tax system should consistently tax spending, not work or savings, and should use progressive rates to meet whatever liberal or redistributive objectives it has.

— Edward J. McCaffery

It has long troubled me, however, that even when a consumption tax is mentioned by an economist or a politician, there is never expressed the fundamental reason why such a tax is the fairest kind of tax: that it taxes the use — and hence the inability of anyone else to use — the resources of the earth, which once belonged to no one, or to all mankind, or (arguably) to all creatures.

— Edgar C. Keller

If middle-class Americans had any realistic sense of how rich the rich really are, policy moves that cater specifically to the wealthy — like the repeal of the inheritance tax — would face a much rougher ride.

— Paul Krugman

The wise and correct course to follow in taxation and all other economic legislation is not to destroy those who have already secured success but to create conditions under which every one will have a better chance to be more successful.

— Calvin Coolidge

Where there's a will, there's an inheritance tax.

— Anonymous

The taking of possession of inherited property is one of the most ancient subjects of taxation known to the law.

— Harlan F. Stone

Death is the most convenient time to tax rich people.

— David Lloyd George

It is not fair to tax the same earnings twice — once when you earn them and again when you die — so we must repeal the death tax.

— George W. Bush

Taxing people after they die just doesn't seem fair.

— Bob Schaffer

Those who support the death tax generally do so not for economic reasons but for political ones. They want to make the tax code "fair" by taxing away the lifetime wealth of others.

— William Beach

No more certain sign exists that a nation has chosen to step off its historic upward path than the creation of wealth taxes. A nation imposes a wealth tax when it wakes up one day to conclude that it has become embarrassed, rather than proud of, its wealth, which is to say, its national success.

— Daniel Henninger

Naturally our tax system is not neutral to social values. Look at the values that are penalized when a government imposes a death tax: Thrift. Conservation. Entrepreneurship. Ingenuity. Family businesses. Family farms. Families.

— Jennifer Dunn

The best reason to repeal the death tax is moral: It punishes a lifetime of thrift for the inevitability of death and no purpose but punishment.

— *The Wall Street Journal*

[The estate tax] has its roots in socialism.

— Richard C. Shelby

Some conservatives have claimed that taxing dead rich people is immoral. It is even more immoral to tax live poor people, who need the money for food, housing, and other necessities.

— Robert Michaelsen

I'd like somebody to get rid of the death tax. That's what I want. I don't want to get taxed just because I died. I just don't think it's right. If I give something to my kid, I already paid the tax. Why should I have to pay it again because I died?

— Whoopi Goldberg

Indeed, it is difficult to set bounds to the share of a rich man's estate which should go at his death to the public through the agency of the state, and by all means such taxes should be graduated, beginning at nothing upon moderate sums to dependents, and increasing rapidly as the amounts swell . . . . Nor need it be feared that this policy would sap the root of enterprise and render men less anxious to accumulate, for to the class whose ambition it is to leave great fortunes and be talked about after their death, it will attract more attention, and, indeed, be a somewhat nobler ambition to have enormous sums paid over to the state from their fortunes.

— Andrew Carnegie

The estate tax raises very little, if any, net revenue for the federal government. The distortionary effects of the estate tax result in losses under the income tax that are roughly the same size as estate tax revenue.

— Joint Economic Committee

[T]he prime objective [of estate taxation] should be to put a constantly increasing burden on the inheritance of those swollen fortunes which it is certainly of no benefit to this country to perpetuate.

— Theodore Roosevelt

In short, the estate and gift taxes in the United States have failed to achieve their intended purposes. They raise little revenue. They impose large excess burdens. They are unfair.

— Henry Aaron and Alicia Munnell

[Anti-estate tax slogan:] No taxation without respiration.

— Bob Schaffer

[Estate taxes are not really taxes but] penalties imposed on those who neglect to plan ahead or who retain unskilled estate planners.

— Henry Aaron and Alicia Munnell

. . . Americans like "sin" taxes, such as those on cigarettes and alcohol. But the estate tax is the opposite case: it is an anti-sin, or a virtue, tax. It is a tax on intergenerational altruism, on thrift.

— Edward J. McCaffery

Spend your money on riotous living — no tax. Leave your money to your children — the tax collector gets paid first . . . . The basic argument against the estate tax is moral. It taxes virtue — living frugally and accumulating wealth. It discourages saving and asset accumulation and encourages wasteful spending.

— Milton Friedman

A well-timed death is the acme of good tax planning, better even than a well-timed marriage.

— Donald C. Alexander

Succession duties first of all possess the grave economic fault of tending to fall on capital or accumulated wealth rather than on income; they therefore may retard progress.

— C.F. Bastable

[T]he history of modern taxation is the history of . . . class antagonisms.

— Edwin R.A. Seligman

Opinions about death taxes vary greatly in a society relying on private incentives for economic growth. Some believe that these taxes hurt economic incentives, reduce saving, and undermine the economic system. But even they would concede that death taxes have less adverse effects on incentives than do income taxes of equal yield. Income taxes reduce the return from effort and risk taking as income is earned, whereas death taxes are paid only after a lifetime of work and accumulation and are likely to be given less weight by individuals in their work, saving, and investment decisions.

— Joseph Pechman

The relevant question is whether the inheritance tax is more or less harmful than the other taxes that have to be levied to pay for what our government spends. Are inheritance taxes worse than higher income taxes that discourage work and innovation? Are they worse than higher property taxes that discourage the accumulation of wealth? Are they worse than higher corporate profits taxes that discourage issuing equity and shift business offshore? Clearly not.

— Hendrick Van den Berg

The policy behind estate tax legislation . . . is the diversion to the purposes of the community of a portion of the total current of wealth released by death.

— Felix Frankfurter

The idea that some people would pay half of their estate, after some substantial exemptions, to the federal government seems to me entirely appropriate.

— William Gates Sr.

Our nation has always held itself out as a meritocracy and a land of opportunity, and an estate tax helps avoid accumulation on inherited economic and political power that is antithetical to this historical vision of our society.

— Robert Rubin

The growing disposition to tax more and more heavily large estates left at death is a cheering indication of the growth of a salutary change in public opinion . . . . Of all forms of taxation, this seems the wisest.

— Andrew Carnegie

If rich people care about their kids, they should spend money on them while they're alive, not wait till they're in their graves before family values kick in. Better still, tell the kids to work for a living and give money to people who really need it, in donations to charity. Thus truly compassionate conservatives should have little truck with efforts to abolish the death tax. Conservatism should be about rewarding work, not inheritance, and encouraging success, not genetic dumb luck.

— Andrew Sullivan

Leo: They [the Republicans] have the votes for repeal [of the estate tax]? . . . Where are they getting them? . . . Where are the other 7 votes against us?

Josh: That's the thing.

Toby: It's from inside the Black Caucus. That's where the 7 votes are . . . .

Josh: These are members of the Congressional Black Caucus . . . . Can you think of any reason why they'd oppose the estate tax?

Leo: Sure.

Josh: What?

Leo: The first generation of black millionaires is about to die.

— Scene from *The West Wing* television series

The estate tax helps keep America more of a democracy than a veiled plutocracy. Meritocracy and the estate tax go hand in hand.

— Daniel J. Kornstein

Although we can't know all the diverse motivations people have for giving, the estate tax is certainly an inducement for high-net-worth families to extend their generosity.

— William Gates Sr. and Chuck Collins

I am sure I give away more because it is deductible than if it was not, because I am sharing it with Uncle Sam. Instead of a congressman telling me where my dollars are going to go, I am telling them where their dollars can go.

— Anonymous Millionaire

I would be dishonest if I claimed that this consideration [the estate-tax deduction] had nothing to do with my decision [to donate to charity] . . . . . Abolishing the estate tax would remove one of the main incentives for charitable giving.

— George Soros

The estate tax exerts a powerful and positive effect on charitable giving. Repeal would have a devastating impact on public charities.

— William Gates Sr.

I never can pass by the Metropolitan Museum of Art in New York without thinking of it not as a gallery of living portraits but as a cemetery of tax-deductible wealth.

— Lewis H. Lapham

Usually people contribute to charities and educational objects out of their surplus. After they have done everything else they want to do, after they have educated their children and traveled and spent their money on everything they really want or think they want, then, if they have something left over, they will contribute it to a college or to the Red Cross or for some scientific purposes. Now when war comes [and taxes therefore rise] . . . that will be the first place where wealthy men will be tempted to economize, namely in donations to charity.

— Henry French Hollis

If the government takes all or nearly all of one's disposable income or surplus income, it must undertake the responsibility for spending it, and it must then support all those works of charity and mercy and all the educational and religious works which in this country have heretofore been supported by private benevolence.

— *The Washington Post*

The losses in federal and state revenues from charitable deductions far exceed donor transfers to the needy. Redistribution has been demonstrated to be far better achieved through government appropriations than through tax remission or deduction measures.

— Julian Wolpert

I don't see why a man shouldn't pay an inheritance tax. If a country is good enough to pay taxes to while you are living, it's good enough to pay in after you die. By the time you die you should be so used to paying taxes, that it would be almost second nature to you.

— Will Rogers

[I]f we must tax, it is better to tax him who merely receives than him who earns.

— Edwin R.A. Seligman

But why should the frugal and thrifty among the rich be taxed heavily on their deathbeds, while the spendthrifts who live luxuriously are not?

— Edward J. McCaffery

Since the accumulation of a substantial estate is one of the motivations that drive people to work hard, a death tax on saving is indirectly a tax on work.

— Richard A. Posner

[The estate tax is] an act of economic waste which is damaging to all.

— Joseph Schumpeter

[Slogan on button:] "Death taxes steal from America's family-owned businesses."

— Food Distributors International

The notion that a man's personal property upon his death may be regarded as a universitas and taxed as such, even if qualified, still is recognized both here and in England.

— Oliver Wendell Holmes Jr.

[O]f 60 major nations around the world, only two have higher death tax rates than the U.S. and 24 have no inheritance tax at all . . . . America is about the most expensive place to die on the planet.

— *The Wall Street Journal*

While we object to the power of making laws being transferred from father to son by inheritance, we do permit the acquisition by inheritance of a financial power which confers the right to legislate for industry, commerce, finance, and to shape the life of the country. As a matter of public policy, and not only as a source of revenue for the support of the government, the tax on inheritance should be increased.

— Meyer London

Huge estates are precisely those that should be taxed most heavily, because the larger the estate, the more likely it is to be made up of investment gains that were never taxed during the owner's lifetime.

— *The New York Times*

I've always been impressed by the attention paid to the dead. The Democrats make sure they get to vote. The Republicans give them a tax cut.

— Bob Somerby

By taxing estates heavily at death the state marks its condemnation of the selfish millionaire's unworthy life.

— Andrew Carnegie

If breaking up large concentrations of wealth is the intention of the death tax, then it is a miserable failure.

— Edward J. McCaffery

Many of the people who favor repealing the estate tax undoubtedly do so because they mistakenly believe that they are subject to it.

— Marjorie E. Kornhauser

Sometimes we hear an argument that the children of the wealthy are more worthy than the other possible beneficiary of wealth — the government. Rarely is there any explanation of that rationale.

— Charles Davenport

General taxation to maintain public schools is an appropriation of property to a use in which the taxpayer may have no private interest, and, it may be, against his will. It has been condemned by theorists on that ground. Yet no one denies its constitutionality. People are accustomed to it and yet accept it without doubt.

— Oliver Wendell Holmes Jr.

Countries, therefore, when lawmaking falls exclusively to the lot of the poor cannot hope for much economy in public expenditure; expenses will always be considerable, either because taxes cannot touch those who vote for them or because they are assessed in a way to prevent that.

— Alexis de Tocqueville

Capital gains income is often discussed as if it were somehow different from other forms of income. Yet, for purposes of income taxation, it is essentially no different from any other form of income from capital.

— Gregg A. Esenwein

In time of this grave national danger, when all excess income should go to win the war, no American citizen ought to have a net income, after he has paid his taxes, of more than $25,000 a year.

— Franklin D. Roosevelt

A woman's income chargeable to income tax shall . . . (for any year) during which she is a married woman living with her husband be deemed for income tax purposes to be his income and not to be her income.

— UK Income and Corporation Taxes Act, 1970, section 37

Once a woman is married, the tax laws really don't want her to work.

— Virginia Postrel

A tax against the depositors which is recoverable only from the bank looks like a tax against the bank.

— John Marshall Harlan

"Equity" and "equitable" are appealing words. They conjure up visions of "doing right", of "mercy", and of Solomon-like wisdom. Certainly, none of us wants this Court to be perceived as "inequitable". However, this connotation of "equity" and "equitable", and awareness of the antonym, should not be allowed to affect the nature and work of the [Tax] Court or our decision-making process.

— Herbert Chabot

Exemption

Donors who are only interested in the tax benefits of their gifts may give philanthropy a bad name, but their money still helps.

— Mark Litzler

Exemption

Joseph made it a law over the land of Egypt unto this day, that Pharaoh should have the fifth part; except the land of priests only, which became not Pharaoh's . . . .

— *Old Testament*

The Rosetta Stone, . . . whose text in hieroglyphics, demotics [sic], and Greek was the key to revealing the stories of ancient Egypt, was in fact a grant of tax immunity. Which is why, of course, it was engraved in stone and not written on papyrus.

— Alvin Rabushka

[A] main branch in [the Daoist] tradition is *Quanzhen (Chuanchen)*, which is usually translated as "Complete Perfection" or "Perfect Realization" Daoism. Founded in the twelfth century by a solder-turned-ascetic named Wang Chongyang (1113-70), this tradition is now the official, state-sponsored monastic order on the mainland and China's largest Daoist school. . . .

Wang attracted seven disciples (six men and one woman), also known as the "Seven Immortals," each of whom founded his or her own lineage. One of the followers . . . Qiu Chuji, met with the Mongol warlord Chinggis (Genghis) Khan and convinced him to give Complete Perfection monasteries the imprimatur of tax exemption.

— Stephen Prothero

I would suggest the taxation of all property equally whether church or corporation, exempting only the last resting place of the dead and possibly, with proper restrictions, church edifices.

— Ulysses S. Grant

Piety is no defense to the assessments of the tax collector.
— John Marvin Jones

Every tax exemption constitutes a subsidy . . . .
— William J. Brennan Jr.

Tax exemption is a privilege derived from legislative grace, not a constitutional right.
— Lapsley W. Hamblen Jr.

You have no authority to impose taxes, tribute, or duty on any of the priests . . . at this house of God.
— *Old Testament*

Churches have nothing to fear from tax reform and, like most people and institutions, would have much to gain from better economic conditions brought about by reform. Despite their dominant position in gifts, churches are not the leaders in fighting a tax reform that denies deductions. Instead, institutions serving the absolute economic and social elite — universities, symphonies, opera companies, ballets, and museums — are protesting the loudest. No compelling case has ever been made that these worthy undertakings should be financed by anyone but their customers. A glance at the crowd in any of them will tell you that it is perverse to tax the typical American to subsidize the elite institutions.
— Robert Hall and Alvin Rabushka

The pressures upon [Christians and Jews living in the Mideast during the spread of Islam] to convert came not from the "sword" as Christian polemicists used to maintain, but rather from the purse: Christians and Jews paid a special tax from which Muslims were exempt.
— Malise Ruthven

[I]n the United States, rules on charitable giving have made it harder for Muslims to fulfill their religious obligation [because contributions to foreign charities generally create no U.S. income tax benefit]. That is why I am committed to working with American Muslims to ensure that they can fulfill zakat.
— Barack Obama

I invite you to embrace Islam. There are no taxes in Islam, but rather there is a limited zakat [alms] totaling 2.5 percent.

— Osama bin Laden

Dhimmis are permitted to practice their religion and preserve their culture, but only if they pay a special *jizya*, or poll tax, not required of Muslims. The Dhimmis pay the tax in exchange for protection by the state. As such, they are outside the political community. So it is not that the Dhimmis are second-class citizens — essentially, Dhimmis are not citizens at all. Even if certain Muslim regimes treat them tolerably, they still live largely at the government's whim, as designated outsiders.

— Alan Dershowitz

[Arab Spring Revolutionary]: We are willing to *die* for a new way of life — one like yours in America!

[American]: You're willing to die for tax breaks?

[Arab Spring Revolutionary]: For sure! And loopholes! We *dream* of such things!

— Garry Trudeau
("Doonesbury")

Fight those who do not believe in Allah . . . nor follow the religion of truth . . . until they pay the tax in acknowledgment of superiority and they are in a state of subjection.

— *Koran*

Take the case of my [son] Huzziya. I made him lord of Tappassanda. But he listened to the people there, saying, "If you give us tax exemptions, we will support you in a rebellion against your father." So I deposed Huzziya.

— Hittite King Hattusili I
(c. 1640-1610 B.C.)

All Israel was "dismayed and terrified" [at Goliath's challenge] and, not surprisingly, there were no volunteers until the young harpist and poet, David, stepped forward. Now why would he be that foolish? Because Saul promised that the man who slays Goliath will receive riches, the king's daughter, *and exemption from all taxes!* "Riches" is a relative term that could mean anything, and we all know that most women were virtually chattel, a dime a dozen, in the Bible, *so it had to be the tax exemption that drove David to risk his life!*

— Conrad Rosenberg

If you go, for example, to the Old Testament of the Bible, to the Joseph story about the Pharaoh setting aside grain for the lean times that would come, he exempted the land of the priests from that requirement of collecting grain to be ready for the lean times. So even back at that time, there are indications of this interaction between tax exemption and government.

— Marcus S. Owens

Why should one who enjoys all the advantages of a society purchased at a heavy expense, and lives in affluence upon an income derived exclusively from interest on government stock, be exempted from taxation?

— John Marshall

It is very different for 90 per cent of the population to vote taxes on themselves and an exemption for 10 per cent, than for 90 per cent to vote punitive taxes on the other 10 per cent — which is in effect what has been done in the United States.

— Milton Friedman

[P]eople who don't pay taxes aren't worried about the tax burden.

— Karl Rove

The exemption of property from taxation is a question of policy and not of power.

— John McLean

Exemptions from the operation of a tax always create inequalities. Those not exempted must, in the end, bear an additional burden or pay more than their share.

— Stephen J. Field

When the Government grants exemptions or allows deductions all taxpayers are affected; the very fact of the exemption or deduction for the donor means that other taxpayers can be said to be indirect and vicarious "donors."

— Warren E. Burger

I don't know of a single foreign product that enters this country untaxed, except the answer to prayer.

— Mark Twain

What it 't to us, if taxes rise or fall,
Thanks to our fortune, we pay none at all.
Let muckworms who in dirty acres deal,
Lament those hardships which we cannot feel,
His grace who smarts, may bellow if he please,
But must I bellow too, who sit at ease?
By custom safe, the poets' numbers flow,
Free as the light and air some years ago.
No statesman e'er will find it worth his pains
To tax our labours, and excise our brains.
Burthens like these with earthly buildings bear,
No tributes laid on castles in the air.

— Charles Churchill

Taxation is the rule, and exemption the exception.

— William Eich

Strong considerations of fiscal and social policy view tax exemptions with a hostile eye.

— Frank Murphy

[E]ven people such as Henry Ford — who objected to the very concept of a foundation and strongly believed that such an institution would ultimately pervert good, effective charity — found that for purposes of estate planning and control of their companies, tax policy left them no choice.

— Heather R. Higgins

The [19th century] period of unrestrained, rugged individualism was a period when the modern type of non-profit community hospital was first established and developed. It was the period of the Carnegie Libraries and their spread through the philanthropy of Andrew Carnegie. It was the period when so many colleges were founded throughout the country. It was the period of the founding of the Society for Prevention of Cruelty to Animals, and the spread of foreign missions. There was no income tax, no deductibility of contributions, so what people spent on charity came out of their pocket and not, as now, largely out of taxes they would otherwise pay. And yet, in every aspect of private charitable activity, it was a boom period.

— Milton Friedman

People hear "nonprofit" and they think "white hat public interest," but all it really means is a tax designation. Most Washington nonprofits are either industry fronts or rely on industry money and good will.

— John Stauber

Nonprofit is a tax status, not a business model.

— Old Saying within the Nonprofit Community

We take judicial notice of the fact that General Motors Corporation is not a non-profit corporation and that it does not consciously sell and buy trucks except for the purposes of making a profit.

— Irving Loeb Goldberg

The taxpayers of this country deserve a break, and the tax-exempt foundations and charitable trusts can give it to them by contributing their gross revenues to the Federal Government for the duration of the Vietnam War.

— Wright Patman

Who is it that takes up these ideas against the working man, the auto worker, and the businessman and the farmer? It's usually some fellow from one of those multi-billion dollar tax-exempt foundations, that when the taxes are raised, they don't pay any taxes because they were tax exempt.

— George Wallace

The real motive behind most private foundations is keeping control of wealth (even while the wealth itself is given away).

— *Business Week* Magazine

[T]he Internal Revenue Service has drafted fantastically intricate and detailed regulations in an attempt to thwart the fantastically intricate and detailed efforts of taxpayers to obtain private benefits from foundations while avoiding the imposition of taxes.

— D. Dortch Warriner

[T]ax laws intended to encourage charity have had the unintended effect of spawning a foundation priesthood funded into perpetuity and insulated from public accountability.

— *The Wall Street Journal*

[S]hould foundations be scrutinized? I think they should. After all, it's tax-free money.

— Elizabeth J. McCormack

Nonprofits, by definition, have no profit motive; profits cannot legally be distributed to a nonprofit's owners. Nonprofits have no private shareholders who bear the brunt of bad management and improper oversight. Indeed, the real shareholders are at least partly the public-at-large, who subsidize nonprofits through grants, tax exemptions, and revenues forgone on tax-deductible donations — in return for the public benefits provided by the organizations.

— Arthur C. Brooks

Whether the property of the United States shall be taxed under the laws of a State depends upon the will of its owner, the United States, and no State can tax the property of the United States without their consent.

— Horace Gray

Just what instrumentalities of either a state or the Federal government are exempt from taxation by the other cannot be stated in terms of universal application.

— Harlan F. Stone

The exemption from taxation of money or property devoted to charitable and other purposes is based upon the theory that the government is compensated for the loss of revenue by its relief from financial burden which would otherwise have to be met by appropriations from public funds, and by the benefits resulting from the promotion of the general welfare.

— House Ways and Means Committee

The government gives me a relief from my taxes in order to encourage me to spend it on philanthropy. I am spending money that the government allows me to keep, which means that I have a responsibility to use the money more effectively than the government would. The alternative is for me to pay my taxes and let the government allocate the money in whatever manner it chooses. So philanthropists must do a better job than the government, given a realistic assessment of the government's performance, either in the choice or in the execution of their programs.

— Andrew Grove

[T]ax exemption for public charities should be restricted to those areas where the quality or quantity of goods and services that would be produced strictly through market forces is inadequate.

— O. Donaldson Chapoton

It is easier to admire the motives for [a religious tax] exemption than to justify it by any sound argument.

— William Z. Stuart

Every year, with renewed vigor, many citizens seek sanctuary in the free exercise clause of the first amendment. They desire salvation not from sin or temptation, however, but from the most earthly of mortal duties — income taxes.

— Irving R. Kaufman

The grant of a tax exemption is not sponsorship since the government does not transfer part of its revenue to churches but simply abstains from demanding that the church support the state. No one has ever suggested that tax-exemption has converted libraries, art galleries, or hospitals into arms of the state or put employees "on the public payroll."

— Warren E. Burger

I think it is high time [worship of comedy troupe Monty] Python was recognized as a religion. People say it changed their lives. It seems to give people hope. They gather together in groups to chant mass quotes. We have all spent three days on a cross. And it would give us a very decent tax break .... [I]f Scientology can be rated a religion then Pythology ought to qualify under any decent tax system.

— Eric Idle

Many nonprofit groups strive for a just and humane life for the people they serve, yet at the same time have people on staff who are eligible for food stamps.

— John Pratt and Sondra Reis

Nonprofits are an artifice of the law, and what's special about them is not that they do different things or that they are organized in a special way, it's that they don't pay taxes.

— Anonymous Libertarian

As I am working with small and medium businesses to lessen their tax burden, it is astonishing to me how often I see them having to compete with a tax-exempt entity doing basically the same work.

— Dean Zerbe

[G]overnment relieves from the tax burden religious, educational, and charitable activities because it wishes to encourage them as representing the highest and noblest achievements of mankind.

— Chauncey Belknap

Institutions which teach morality, respect for law, good health practices, and so forth, do much good for society, but they do not necessarily have any greater claim to a state property-tax exemption than do parents who teach their children such things.

— Joan E. O'Bannon

A grant of exemption is never to be considered as a mere gratuity — a simple gift from the legislature . . . A consideration is presumed to exist. The recipient of the exemption may be supposed to be doing part of the work which the state would otherwise be under obligations to do. A college, or an academy, furnishes education to the young, which it is a part of the state's duty to furnish.

— David J. Brewer

Donors who are only interested in the tax benefits of their gifts may give philanthropy a bad name, but their money still helps.

— Mark Litzler

As you journey through life . . . always try to give something back . . . . But be *sure* whatever you give back qualifies as a tax deduction.

— Chris Browne
("Hagar the Horrible")

A charity ball is like a dance except it's tax deductible.

— P.J. O'Rourke

Taxpayers who want to game the system and the charities that assist them will be called to account.

— Mark Everson

Most charities comply with the tax laws. Of course, it's the ones that don't that make the headlines.

— Fred Stokeld

Nearly three-quarters of Americans make charitable contributions, with those toward the lower end of the income scale donating a higher percentage of their income than any other group. We have tailored our tax system to reinforce this national trait. Americans donate more money per capita than any other people . . . . No other nation has such a private non-profit sector.

— David Brooks

Most philanthropy is tax-motivated. The notion that charity wouldn't be hurt if you eliminated the death tax is absurd.

— William Zabel

Yes, Christians and Jews are supposed to be charitable, but we're supposed to be charitable as individuals . . . . [I]f government forces me to be charitable I'm not being charitable, I'm being coerced. There is no merit in heaven in paying your tax because you don't want to go to jail.

— Stephen J. Entin

A widespread foreign misconception is that Americans contribute because gifts are tax-deductible; in fact, the reverse is true; gifts are deductible *because* Americans contribute and because our government, which regards the charitable world as its partner, wants to encourage private charitable giving . . . . Every one of our nation's major universities, art museums, and hospitals was created before taxes were a factor in giving.

— Daniel Rose

The legislative reasons for granting immunity from taxes to . . . charitable institutions . . . prominent among which would doubtless be the fact, that the support and maintenance extended to the objects of the charity relieves the State from a burden which would involve a much larger amount of taxation than that which it waives by granting the exemption.

— Joseph P. Bradley

[B]usiness people on charity boards frequently approve decisions that ignore the very sense and insights they use in their own businesses.

— Randy Richardson

[Z]oning regulations very properly forbid nonprofit organizations, such as universities, to have shops in their buildings, on pain of losing their tax-exempt status. The result is that whole quarters come to consist of nothing but university buildings that, being deserted after hours, form a splendid rearing ground for crime.

— Charles Issawi

Big business never pays a nickel in taxes, according to Ralph Nader, who represents a big consumer organization that never pays a nickel in taxes.

— Dave Barry

[T]he majority of tax-exempt bonds are held by schools that have large investment assets. These schools are using their tax exemption to amass investments, receive tax-deductible donations, and float tax-exempt bonds. These benefits are unique to tax-exempt entities. The federal government forgoes the revenue from tax-exempt entities in exchange for the social benefit from these institutions. . . . Does the expense of debt service take money away from student aid or academic service? Do bond issuances occur even as universities raise tuition and build investment assets?

— Charles Grassley

I didn't see why the schoolmaster should be taxed to support the priest, and not the priest the schoolmaster.

— Henry David Thoreau

What knight errant ever paid a tax, a queen's levy, a tribute, a tariff, or a toll?

— Miguel De Cervantes
(*Don Quixote*)

Because Judaism sees *tzedaka* [charitable giving] as a form of self-taxation rather than as a voluntary donation, the Jewish community regards publicizing donors' gifts in the same spirit as the American practice of asking political candidates to release their tax returns. In both cases, public scrutiny causes people to act more justly.

— Joseph Telushkin

[The House Ways and Means] Committee intends that an individual need not necessarily accept reduced compensation merely because he or she renders services to a tax-exempt, as opposed to a taxable, organization.

— House Ways and Means Committee

The public appears uneasy about, if not hostile to, the increasing nonprofit commercialism. So far, charities have enjoyed a "halo effect" in our political economy. The rationalized myth of charities as selfless, donative, and volunteer-run deliverers of services to the poor has never entirely been true, but it underlies society's grant of tax exemption and tax deductibility for contributions. To the extent, however, that this quid depends on the idealized quo, should charity's core myth change — in a way that becomes visible to the public — society's willingness to alter the subsidies could also change.

— Evelyn Brody

Looking backward it is easy to see that the line between the taxable and the immune has been drawn by an unsteady hand.

— Robert H. Jackson

Like a photo-negative, the tax treatment of charities presents a reverse image of normal incentives. Nominally peripheral to the tax system, charities actually benefit from a tax structure that imposes high rates on their for-profit competitors and their donors. The greater the regular corporate tax burden, the greater the relative value of the charity's tax exemption. The higher the individual income-tax rates, the lower the price of giving to charity.

— Evelyn Brody

The tax-exempt privilege is a feature always reflected in the market price of bonds. The investor pays for it.

— Louis D. Brandeis

Those tax-exempt bonds were put in so that a town or a state or a government could sell more bonds than it ought to.

— Will Rogers

Another means of silently lessening the inequality of property is to exempt all from taxation below a certain point, and to tax the higher portions of property in geometrical progression as they rise.

— Thomas Jefferson

Unless . . . savings are exempted from income tax, the contributors are twice taxed on what they save, and only once on what they spend.

— John Stuart Mill

An asset will rise in value today if there is an increase in what people expect the asset to earn in the future. If the asset does in fact earn the higher expected income in the future, that higher income will be taxed when it is earned. To also tax the rise in the present value of that increased future after-tax income stream (the present-day capital gain) is to tax the future earnings twice.

— Stephen J. Entin

Trying to understand the various exempt organization provisions of the Internal Revenue Code is as difficult as capturing a drop of mercury under your thumb.

— Stephen J. Swift

Why you don't marry that girl? She lives in Monte Carlo and you can live tax free.

— Richard M. Nixon

Old MacDonald had an agricultural real estate tax abatement.

— Anonymous

Collection and Administration

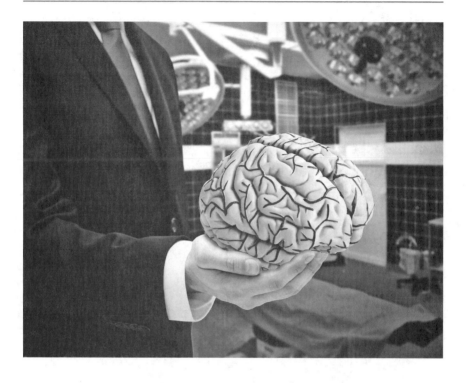

[Speaking of the IRS:] Thank God they're not doing brain surgery.

— Fred Allen

Collection and Administration

It is now actually proposed to place a tax on incomes! . . . It is a vile, Jacobin, jumped up Jack-in-office piece of impertinence — is a true Britton to have no privacy? Are the fruits of his labour and toil to be picked over, farthing by farthing, by the pimply minions of Bureaucracy?

— John Knyveton

It may be the pleasure and pride of an American to ask, what farmer, what mechanic, what laborer, ever sees a tax-gatherer of the United States?

— Thomas Jefferson

It's income tax time again, Americans: time to gather up those receipts, get out those tax forms, sharpen up that pencil, and stab yourself in the aorta.

— Dave Barry

The only time most straight men get anal stimulation is during a physical exam. Then and at tax time.

— Paul Joannides

Two years ago it was impossible to get through on the phone to the IRS. Now it's just hard to get through. That's progress.

— Charles O. Rossotti

It's tax time. I know this because I'm staring at documents that make no sense to me, no matter how many beers I drink.

— Dave Barry

This [*i.e.*, preparing my tax return] is too difficult for a mathematician. It takes a philosopher.

— Albert Einstein

Nuclear physics is much easier than tax law. It's rational and always works the same way.

— Jerold Rochwald

It will be of little avail to the people, that the laws are made by men of their choice, if the laws be so voluminous that they cannot be read, or so incoherent that they cannot be understood; if they be repealed or revised before they are promulgated, or undergo such incessant changes that no man, who knows what the law is today, can guess what it will be tomorrow. Law is defined to be a rule of action; but how can that be a rule, which is little known, and less fixed?

— James Madison

It's often said that the Middle East peace process is very complicated. That's not exactly true. The tax treaty between Canada and the United States: That's complicated. The federal-state tax treatment of undistributed timber royalties alone is enough to crack the jaw. But nobody is detonating bombs over Canada-U.S. timber taxes.

— David Frum

[The Internal Revenue Code] has become *lex incognita*. Bad things happen when law is occult. In the private sector, taxpayers seek out the most optimistic advice. Conservative advisors are driven out by the bold. On the government side, delays and gaps grow in providing guidance, which, when it comes, may be defensively arbitrary with little more foundation in the statute than the aggressive advice of some private practitioners on the opposite side. In frustration, Congress has yielded to IRS calls for new, no-fault penalties to increase the effective tax rates for taxpayers who guess wrong on how the law will be applied. But penalties do not clarify.

— M. Carr Ferguson

The income tax has spawned an intrusive bureaucracy, creating so much complexity and red tape that millions of ordinary citizens have to go get some accountant to fill out the forms for them — and then sign under penalty of perjury that it was done right. If you knew how to do it right, you wouldn't have to go to somebody else to have it done, would you?

— Thomas Sowell

Trying to translate the tax law into plain English is a very difficult task.

— Benson Goldstein

I don't care anymore whether I pay more taxes or less taxes, as long as I don't have to understand it.

— Bob Thaves
("Frank & Ernest")

Citizens should be able to comply with the tax code without having to spend absurd amounts of money to do so. The fact that there is such a large compliance markup in our tax system indicates that the tax system has gone awry.

— Arthur B. Laffer

I am amazed at the serenity at which we accept another (near) mandate: That we must pay somebody to help us do our taxes. The government does not specifically require us to hire paid tax preparers or buy commercial software, of course. But it has, in effect, left millions of taxpayers with no real choice. Congress has created a tax code that makes it nearly impossible for many Americans to file returns without paid help.

— Howard Gleckman

The one area of the economy where the tax system is a robust job-creating machine is the area of tax return preparation and software, tax planning, tax controversies and tax compliance. The distortions in our tax law are so numerous, so rewarding to the well-advised, and frequently so complex to comprehend and comply with that they serve to produce millions of well-paying indoor jobs that not only require no heavy lifting, but also are immune from the ups and downs of the business cycle.

— Michael J. Graetz

Every time the government changes things, [my tax return preparation] business does increase. Every year a few more people throw up their hands and say "I can't prepare my return any more."

— Henry Bloch

Why can't Americans do their own taxes? Because the federal Tax Code is out of control, that's why. It's gigantic and insanely complex, and it gets worse all the time. Nobody has ever read the whole thing. IRS workers are afraid to go into the same ROOM with it.

— Dave Barry

If tax compliance were an industry, it would be one of the largest in the United States. To consume 6.1 billion hours, the "tax-industry" requires the equivalent of more than three million full-time workers.

— Nina E. Olson

I have long been concerned that a basic high school or college education does not teach someone how to fill out a tax return. This seems to me to be a basic life skill that should be taught somewhere. We provide sex education, drug education, and harassment education . . . but no tax education.

— Terence Floyd Cuff

If taxes are so important, and taxes are math, how come nobody in the history of this country has taught taxes in a math class? No! Instead they teach you stuff like Geometry which is no help at all. I still can't play pool!

— Lewis Black

[Preparing a tax return is] not a mechanical process. . . . You're interpreting, you're giving advice . . . you're even a psychiatrist, to some degree.

— William Stevenson

Linking federal and state taxation systems makes inherent sense. . . . Reducing differences between the two systems saves resources for taxpayers and states alike, while also improving compliance.

— David A. Super

Convenience of payment is important in helping to ensure compliance with the tax system. The more difficult a tax is to pay the more likely that it will not be paid.

— Tax Division of the American
Institute of Certified Public Accountants

I'm 33 years old; I haven't outgrown the problems of puberty, I'm already facing the problems of old age. I completely skipped healthy adulthood. I went from having orgasms immediately, to taking forever. You could do your taxes in the time it takes me to have an orgasm.

— Scene from *Seinfeld* television series

If the Lord had meant us to pay income taxes, he'd have made us smart enough to prepare the return.

— Kirk Kirkpatrick

But the tax collector stood at a distance and dared not even lift his eyes to heaven as he prayed. Instead, he beat his chest in sorrow, saying, "O God, be merciful to me, for I am a sinner."

— *New Testament*

The tax which each individual is bound to pay ought to be certain, and not arbitrary. The time of payment, the manner of payment, the quantity to be paid, ought all to be clear and plain to the contributor, and to every other person, so that the tax payer is not put in the power of the tax gatherer.

— Adam Smith

The Pharisee stood and prayed thus to himself, "God, I thank thee that I am not like other men, extortioners, unjust, adulterers, or even like this tax collector."

— *New Testament*

You can have a Lord, you can have a King, but the man to fear is the tax collector.

— Anonymous Citizen of Lagash,
a city-state that existed approximately
6,000 years ago in what is now Iraq

[T]he phrase "beating it out of you" comes from ancient Egypt where if you could not pay your taxes, you could go to the priests, who were the civil servants of the pharaohs, and they would give you a beating proportionate to the taxes that you owed and could not pay.

— David Cay Johnston

The Spanish used to burn people they didn't like. In England they once cut off your ears for stealing a penny. Russia had the whip. But for sheer ingenuity in instruments of torture, America wins again. We refer to income tax Form 1040.

— Announcer on *Fibber McGee and Molly* radio series

Beware of strong drink. It can make you shoot at tax collectors . . . and miss.

— Robert A. Heinlein
(*The Notebooks of Lazarus Long*)

Experimentation with the income tax yielded mixed results at first. Virginia enacted a tax in 1909, but many citizens refused to pay it. After some tax agents sent to rural areas were never heard from again, Virginia repealed the tax, having collected less than $100,000.

— Steven R. Weisman

If you make any money, the government shoves you in the creek once a year with it in your pockets, and all that don't get wet you can keep.

— Will Rogers

Love will find you when you least expect it. Which makes it more like the IRS than we think.

— Jeff MacNelly
("Shoe")

Even if you are sure you are right and have all the records to prove it, fighting the IRS, one of the most powerful government bureaucracies on the planet, can be the ultimate nightmare. Seemingly routine struggles can drag on for years, leading to endless frustration and sleepless nights. Even those who eventually triumph may wonder if the fight was worth all the time, effort and expense.

— Tom Herman

Fact: The birth agonies of the new IRS led to one of the great and terrible PR discoveries in modern democracy, which is that if sensitive issues of government can be made sufficiently dull and arcane, there will be no need for officials to hide or dissemble, because no one not directly involved will pay enough attention to cause trouble.

— David Foster Wallace

[I]f the IRS took 100 taxpayers at random and sent each an incorrect notice that they owed an extra $92.35 in taxes and interest, more than two-thirds would probably just send in a check without investigating further.

— George Guttman

The income tax allows the government to confiscate the wealth of its citizens. The curse of the withholding tax is that it allows the government to commit this crime systematically, effortlessly, painlessly, and benevolently.

— Laurence M. Vance

In connection with the payment of taxes due, no person shall fear that he will suffer, at the hand of perverse and enraged judges, imprisonment, lashes of leaded whips, weights, or any other tortures devised by the arrogance of judges. Prisons are for criminals .... In accordance with this law, taxpayers shall proceed with security.

— Constantine

[I]n an area as complex as the tax system, the agency Congress vests with administrative responsibility must be able to exercise its authority to meet changing conditions and new problems.

— Warren E. Burger

The IRS fully recognizes its potential for instilling fear, and quite deliberately uses intimidation tactics to make us more docile and unquestioning taxpayers.

— Vernon K. Jacobs

[T]he IRS attracts as employees, for the obvious reasons, a disproportionate share of bullies, sadists, incompetents and those who have no understanding of the importance of the rule of law and liberty.

— Richard W. Rahn

The tax agencies have no right to terrorize business . . . .

— Vladimir Putin

Amos: After all, with millions of people paying taxes, the government has got to work like a machine.
Andy: Oh, they work like a machine, all right — a vacuum cleaner.

— Scene from *Amos and Andy* radio series

Bad things happen to people who ignore IRS correspondence.

— Nina E. Olson

Why do you think we [IRS enforcement agents] go after the little guys? They can't fight back.

— Anonymous IRS Lawyer

To meet revenue needs, the tax collection process has focused on easily measured sources of income, leaving many transactions either partially taxed or untaxed.

— Ralph B. Tower

If the IRS used only the maximization of yield approach, it would meet its goals of using its resources most effectively to yield the most revenue. The purpose, however, of the audit program, is not to produce the greatest revenue but to produce the greatest level of voluntary compliance . . .

— IRS Commissioner's Advisory Group Study (1978)

The fear of an Internal Revenue Service audit ranks right with the fear of death, visiting the dentist or speaking in public. Most taxpayers don't know what an audit involves, but they know they don't want to find out.

— Mike McDevitt

Now, we would like to think that there is no such thing as left-wing or right-wing tax enforcement, but there is.

— Lee A. Sheppard

In almost every administration since the IRS's inception the information and power of the tax agency have been mobilized for explicitly political purposes.

— David Burnham

Most voters would rather have their purse or wallet stolen than be audited by the IRS.

— Frank Luntz

[Ralph receives a letter from the I.R.S.]

Ralph: Don't you realize how serious this is? They're investigating me!

Alice: Ralph, being investigated is not the end of the world. You are not the first person who was ever investigated.

Norton: You're darn right! The jails are full of them!

— Scene from *The Honeymooners* television series

[The Head of the Internal Revenue Service] points out that when we sign our tax returns, we are in effect taking a legal oath. "This means," he sternly reminds us, "that the information you provide must meet the same standard of truth and accuracy that President Clinton met when he testified under oath about alleged acts of internship with Monica Lewinsky." For example, if you have three dependents, when you fill in the box that says "Number of Dependents," the following answers would meet the Clinton Accuracy Standard:
"Three."
"Four."
"Around twenty-seven."
"I don't recall."
"It depends what you mean by 'dependent.'"

— Dave Barry

The taxpayer-rights provisions of the Internal Revenue Code are like the civil-rights provisions of the former Soviet Union's constitution. On paper, they tell a wonderful story. In practice, for many taxpayers there is no effective protection against government abuse.

— Bob Kamman

The time has come when an honest man can't take an honest drink without having a gang of revenue officers after him.

— Zebulon Vance

We [Internal Revenue Service employees] are not the bosses of taxpayers; they are ours.

— T. Coleman Andrews

I personally believe that the relationship between taxpayer and tax administrator will always be adversarial. This isn't a good thing or a bad thing; it's just the way it is.

— Mary Lou Fahey

One of the underlying problems is that too many of us think that tax policy is made at the National Office in Washington. The real tax policy is made by that auditing agent who is sitting in your client's office. He can miss issues that are screaming, or he can dig in on absurd issues, but it can be very expensive to get him back on the right track.

— Terence Floyd Cuff

The reality, as you must know, is that about half the IRS work force is of little use to management, either because of a lack of motivation or ability.

— Paul Streckfus

If [your brother] refuses to listen to [two or three people who try to correct him], tell it to the church; and if he refuses to listen even to the church, let him be to you as a gentile or a tax collector.

— *New Testament*

To think that the IRS can become a modern financial services institution while administering the current income tax is to believe that you can turn a Winnebago around without taking it out of the garage.

— Michael J. Graetz

The scary thing is that the IRS is, relatively speaking, one of the more efficient federal agencies.

— Paul Streckfus

We must get rid of the IRS. It's a bureaucracy fraught with totalitarianism.

— Sonny Bono

[The Internal Revenue Service] is not the root of all evil in Washington, or even all evil in the tax system. In fact, that distinction belongs to Congress.

— Joseph J. Thorndike

Another way of verbally masking elite preemption of other people's decisions is to use the word "ask" — as in "We are just asking everyone to pay their fair share." Of course governments do not ask, they *tell*. The Internal Revenue Service does not "ask" for contributions. It takes. It can confiscate bank accounts and other assets and it can put people behind bars for not paying.

— Thomas Sowell

Some proudly refer to our tax system as "voluntary." Others cannot help but observe that voluntary systems seem to work best when backed up by mandatory withholding, mandatory reporting, and criminal sanctions.

— J. Mark Iwry

The fact is that the government, like a highwayman, says to a man: "Your money, or your life." And many, if not most, taxes are paid under the compulsion of that threat.

— Lysander Spooner

You don't pay taxes — they *take* taxes.

— Chris Rock

People try to argue that government isn't really force. You believe that? Try not paying your taxes. . . . When they come to get you for not paying your taxes, try not going to court. Guns will be drawn. Government is force — literally, not figuratively.

— Penn Jillette

It is difficult to imagine greater government control of a person's life than forcing the person to give half or more of his honorably earned money to the state under threat of being imprisoned.

— Dennis Prager

Liberals love to say things like, "We're just asking everyone to pay their fair share." But government is not about asking. It is about telling. The difference is fundamental. It is the difference between making love and being raped, between working for a living and being a slave.

— Thomas Sowell

I want the people of America to be able to work less for the government and more for themselves. I want them to have the rewards of their own industry: That this is the chief meaning of freedom.

— Calvin Coolidge

Unofficial Motto of the Internal Revenue Service: "We have what it takes to take what you have."

— Anonymous

[D]espite having an arsenal of weapons, no IRS agent has ever fired a shot at anyone.

— David Cay Johnston

Helpful Hints When Choosing a Return Preparer
- Avoid tax preparers who claim they can obtain larger refunds than other preparers.
- Avoid preparers who base their fee on a percentage of the amount of the refund.
- Use a reputable tax professional who signs your tax return and provides you with a copy for your records.

— Internal Revenue Service

A remarkable and potentially far-reaching byproduct of America's voluntary system of taxation is a tax collector that actually aspires to be popular.

— J. Mark Iwry

A tax audit should be an educational experience, in terms of learning something useful for future tax planning and when preparing future tax returns.

— Vernon K. Jacobs and Charles W. Schoeneman

Tax law complexity confounds those who want to comply, provides numerous opportunities for those who don't, and creates a dense fog that permeates the entire tax administration system making detection of non-compliance, whether accidental or intentional, exceedingly difficult.

— IRS Oversight Board

I want to begin by saying we have had good experience with the Internal Revenue Service; it's the Internal Revenue Code that doesn't work.

— Brian Gloe

Complexity [in the tax laws] obscures understanding and creates a sense of "distance" between taxpayers and the government, undermining taxpayer morale and leading to lower levels of voluntary compliance.

— Nina E. Olson

Because of the immense size and complexity of the tax system and the difficulty of measuring how effectively it is operating, its deterioration will not become totally evident until things get so bad that the cost of recovery will be immense.

— Charles O. Rossotti

Simplicity in modern taxation is a problem of basic architectural design. Present legislation is insufferably complicated and nearly unintelligible. If it is not simplified, half of the population may have to become tax lawyers and tax accountants.

— Henry C. Simons

There is a big constituency in the country for tax reduction but not for tax reform, except as reform is used as a code word for reduction.

— Michael Blumenthal

People don't give a damn about tax reform.

— Dick Cheney

Most Americans would not tolerate a tax system that collected all the taxes it was supposed to!

— Lawrence M. Stone

[Tax] law is not what is written in the statute books. Law is what you are willing to enforce. We all get to know the tolerance allowed and the area of enforcement and will live up or down to that.

— Sheldon S. Cohen

[N]othing can be more ruinous to a state or oppressive to individuals than a partial and dilatory collection of taxes.

— Anonymous Citizen of Colonial Philadelphia

A perfect revenue law, if improperly administered or resisted by a hostile public, will soon become a practical monstrosity; but an imperfect law, if wisely administered with a reasonable public, will produce very satisfactory results.

— Aubrey R. Marrs

I don't suppose we will ever get to the point where people are pleased to pay taxes, but we owe it to them to see that the collection is done as efficiently as possible, as courteously as possible, and always honestly.

— Lyndon B. Johnson

No other branch of the law [*i.e.*, tax law] touches human activities at so many points. It can never be made simple, but we can try to avoid making it needlessly complex.

— Robert H. Jackson

Gross inequalities may not be ignored for the sake of ease of collection.

— Owen J. Roberts

When part of the economy is informal, and untaxed, the burden falls heavily on legitimate business.

— William Lewis

[Speaking of the IRS:] Thank God they're not doing brain surgery.
— Fred Allen

All that happens is, you take your financial records to the IRS office and they put you into a tank filled with giant, stinging leeches. Many taxpayers are pleasantly surprised to find that they die within hours.

— Dave Barry

[I]t's easy to overstate the lineal relationship between taxes and extortion. Unchecked, the metaphor runs to facile versions of the "taxation as theft" argument best left to undergraduate political theory classes. In the real world — the present world of real governments with real power, authority, and legitimacy — taxes are best viewed as taxes, not protection money.

— Joseph J. Thorndike

The income tax has made more liars out of the American people than golf has. Even when you make a tax form out on the level, you don't know when it's through if you are a crook or a martyr.

— Will Rogers

For voluntary self-assessment to be both meaningful and productive of revenues, the citizens must not only have confidence in the fairness of the tax laws, but also in their uniform and vigorous enforcement of these laws. If non-compliance by the few continues unchecked, the confidence of the many in our self-assessment system will be shaken and one of the cornerstones of our government weakened.

— John F. Kennedy

The IRS spends God knows how much of your tax money on these toll-free information hot lines staffed by IRS employees, whose idea of a dynamite tax tip is that you should print neatly. If you ask them a real tax question, such as how you can cheat, they're useless.

— Dave Barry

[It] is important that there be broad public support for the system. In the U.S. . . . taxpayers make the first determination of their liabilities through the returns they prepare and file . . . . [W]ith the low IRS audit coverage that currently prevails, that first determination is usually the last. . . . [Thus] it is important that taxpayers have sufficient commitment to the system that their returns bear [a] reasonable relation to reality.

— Steven R. Johnson

No one is above the tax laws. If you don't want to see your name posted on our site along with other tax delinquents, be sure to keep up with your tax obligations.

— "Shaming Website" of Comptroller of Maryland

Noncompliance breeds disrespect for the tax system. And nonpursuit of noncompliance breeds resentment toward government.

— Max Baucus

No fact speaks so well for the loyalty of the American people, and in support of their determination to pay their debts as the readiness with which they submit [in late 1865] to the payment of war taxes in times of peace.

— *The Nation* Magazine

There is untold wealth in America — especially at income tax time.

— Anonymous

Three factors affect the dollar amount that can be collected by increased enforcement. First, much of the gross tax gap for individual income tax filers is due to types of unreported income that are difficult to detect. Second, some of the detected tax liability cannot be easily collected, particularly from those taxpayers who are currently unable to pay. Third, many detected tax liabilities are so small relative to enforcement costs that it is not deemed cost-effective to pursue collection.

— James M. Bickley

An accountant once told me that the definition of fair market value for tax purposes is the value arrived at in negotiations between a willing tax lawyer and a willing revenue agent, neither of whom has ever bought or sold anything of consequence in his life.

— Paul H. Asofsky

Nothing makes a man and wife feel closer, these days, than a joint tax return.

— Gil Stern

On my income tax [Form] 1040 it says "Check this box if you are blind." I wanted to put a check mark about three inches away.

— Tom Lehrer

This year, it is important for you to know that the Internal Revenue Service now has a positive, taxpayer-friendly image. What does this mean to you, the individual taxpayer? According to [the Head of the IRS] it means you are now expected to tip: "If you're a married taxpayer filing jointly, tucking a $50 bill inside your tax return will definitely cause the IRS employee serving you to feel appreciated and be less likely to select you for the auditing procedure we call 'The Closet Full of Snakes.'"

— Dave Barry

There was wisdom as well as wit in the cynical wag's remark that the lawyers had transformed the ancient principle of "no taxation without representation" into a doctrine of "no taxation without litigation."

— Robert H. Jackson

At first, few lawyers considered income tax a profitable vocation. That changed after World War I. Excess-profits tax and high income tax rates generated controversies that made tax practice highly lucrative, and accountants handled most of it. Lawyers took notice.

— Jay Starkman

Any client with enough money to hire lawyers to go to court to argue about taxes is too fat a cat for juries. In good times, the regular folks don't mind that big shots pay no tax. In bad times, they mind very much.

— Lee A. Sheppard

[N]o suit for the purpose of restraining the assessment or collection of any tax shall be maintained in any court by any person, whether or not such person is the person against whom such tax was assessed.

— *Internal Revenue Code*
(Anti-Injunction Act)

[T]here is no constitutional right to bring frivolous suits . . . . People who wish to express displeasure with taxes must choose other forums, and there are many available.

— Frank H. Easterbrook

The prompt payment of taxes is always important to the public welfare. It may be vital to the existence of a government. The idea that every taxpayer is entitled to the delays of litigation is unreason.

— Noah Haynes Swayne

Few of us ever test our powers of deduction, except when filling out an income tax form.

— Laurence J. Peter

You first have to decide whether to use the short or the long form. The short form is what the Internal Revenue Service calls "simplified," which means it is designed for people who need the help of a Sears tax preparation expert to distinguish between their first and last names . . . . The IRS wants you to use the short form because it gets to keep most of your money. So unless you have pond silt for brains, you want the long form.

— Dave Barry

Next to being shot at and missed, nothing is quite as satisfying as an income tax refund.

— F.J. Raymond

The tax farmer would advance money to the monarch — the equivalent of planting his seeds — and then go about collecting it from the citizenry — the equivalent of gathering in a harvest whose ultimate value, as with all farmers, he hoped would exceed the cost of the seeds.

— Peter L. Bernstein

It would be nice if we could all pay our taxes with a smile, but normally cash is required.

— Anonymous

As I sit in my poverty-stricken home, looking at the place where the piano used to be before I had to sell it to pay my income tax, I find myself in a thoughtful mood.

— P.G. Wodehouse

Uncle claims that if he files his income tax wrong he'll go to jail, and if he files it right he'll go to the poor house.

— Nonnee Coan
("Small Fry Diary")

All money nowadays seems to be produced with a natural homing instinct for the Treasury.

— Prince Philip,
Duke of Edinburgh

Every child born in America can hope to grow up to enjoy tax loopholes.

— TRB
(Richard Stout)

Income taxes are the most imaginative fiction written today.

— Herman Wouk

Certain states are out-and-out aggressive. But in most, you can drive a Mack truck through the revenue department and no one will notice. They're often clueless about how to question our tax planning strategies and techniques.

— Anonymous Oil Company
Tax Director

Students of federal taxation agree that the tax system suffers from delay in getting the final word in judicial review, from retroactivity of the decision when it is obtained, and from the lack of a roundly tax-informed viewpoint of judges.

— Robert H. Jackson

If [a United States Supreme Court Justice is] in the doghouse with the Chief [Justice], he gets the crud. He gets the tax cases.

— Harry Blackmun

A tax . . . may obstruct the industry of the people, and discourage them from applying to certain branches of business which might give maintenance and employment to great multitudes. While it obliges the people to pay, it may thus diminish, or perhaps destroy, some of the funds which might enable them more easily to do so.

— Adam Smith

I will tell you a secret, which I learned many years ago from the commissioners of the customs in London: They said, when any commodity appeared to be taxed above a moderate rate, the consequence was to lessen that branch of the revenue by one half; and one of those gentlemen pleasantly told me, that the mistake of Parliaments, on such occasions, was owing to an error in computing two and two to make four; whereas in the business of laying heavy impositions, two and two never make more than one; which happens by lessening the import, and the strong temptation of running such goods as paid high duties.

— Jonathan Swift

You don't have to be chairman of a Wall Street investment bank to grasp that higher taxes on capital lead to a lower level of investment and slower growth.

— Henry M. Paulson Jr.

Governments likely to confiscate wealth are unlikely to find much wealth to confiscate in the long run.

— Thomas Sowell

High taxes . . . frequently afford a smaller revenue to the government than what might be drawn from more moderate taxes.

— Adam Smith

The proliferation of bureaucrats and its invariable accompaniment, much heavier tax levies on the productive part of the population, are the recognizable signs, not of a great, but of a decaying society.

— William Chamberlin

In the sixth year of his reign Constantine visited the city of Autun, and generously remitted the arrears of tribute, reducing at the same time the proportion of their assessment from twenty-five to eighteen thousand heads, subject to the real and personal capitation. Yet even this indulgence affords the most unquestionable proof of the public misery. This tax was so extremely oppressive, either in itself or in the mode of collecting it, that, whilst the revenue was increased by extortion, it was diminished by despair: a considerable part of the territory of Autun was left uncultivated; and great numbers of the provincials rather chose to live as exiles and outlaws than to support the weight of civil society.

— Edward Gibbon

[As the Roman Empire declined] the resources of the farmers were exhausted by outrageous burdens of all taxes, the fields were abandoned, and the cultivated land reverted to waste.

— Lactantius

States with high and rising tax burdens are more likely to suffer economic decline; those with low and falling tax burdens are more likely to enjoy strong economic growth.

— Lawrence Kudlow

By the time of Diocletian, many Roman subjects were not earning enough money to pay their annual taxes. In order to meet their annual tax assessments, they were forced to sell their animals, tools, or even the land itself. Increasingly, those smaller merchants who lacked land had no alternative but to sell their own children, and sometimes even themselves, into slavery to pay their taxes. Thus more and more families were reduced to poverty.

— Jack Weatherford

If, as the rate of a particular duty is increased, the revenue yielded increases, the duty is predominantly a tax. But when the rate is increased above the point at which the yield in revenue is a maximum, it is clear that some element of penalty is present, and we finally reach a duty of prohibitive amount, whose yield is very small or non-existent. This is closely akin to a simple prohibition of production or importation, with a penalty for infraction.

— Hugh Dalton

At the beginning of the dynasty, taxation yields a large revenue from small assessments. At the end of the dynasty taxation yields a small revenue from large assessments.

— Ibn Khaldun

If you tax too high, the revenue will yield nothing.

— Ralph Waldo Emerson

High tax rates on paper, that many people avoid, often does not bring in as much tax revenue as lower tax rates that more people actually pay, after it is safe to come out of the tax shelters and earn higher rates of taxable income.

— Thomas Sowell

There is a distinct pattern throughout American history: When tax rates are reduced, the economy's growth rate improves and living standards increase. Good tax policy has a number of interesting side effects. For instance, history tells us that tax revenues grow and "rich" taxpayers pay more tax when marginal tax rates are slashed. This means lower income citizens bear a lower share of the tax burden — a consequence that should lead class-warfare politicians to support lower tax rates.

— Daniel J. Mitchell

It is a paradoxical truth, that tax rates are too high today, and tax revenues are too low, and the soundest way to raise the revenues in the long run is to cut the tax rates.

— John F. Kennedy

If Congress decides to increase tax rates to 70% next week on this year's income, tax revenues will increase for this year because most people will not be able to respond. People will go to great lengths to avoid paying high tax rates, including reducing work effort and taxable savings and investments; or even finding illegal means to avoid the tax collector. But it takes time for them to do so. A big tax increase on the job-creating and investing class this year will almost certainly kill economic growth and job creation next year, resulting in less tax revenue.

— Richard W. Rahn

Although the economy grows in response to tax reductions (because of higher consumption in the short run and improved incentives in the long run), it is unlikely to grow so much that lost tax revenue is completely recovered by the higher level of economic activity.

— Council of Economic Advisors (2003)

But it isn't true that cutting taxes always raises revenue, and that raising taxes always reduces revenue.

— David Wessel

To put it most simply, tax cuts do not pay for themselves; all they do is lose revenues.

— Richard Kogan

The notion that tax cuts are free or painless is flawed and misleading. Tax cuts have to be paid for with either reduced, current, or future spending or increased future taxes, relative to what would have occurred in the absence of the tax cuts.
— William G. Gale, Peter R. Orszag, and Isaac Shapiro

The high duties which have been imposed upon the importation of many different sorts of foreign goods, in order to discourage their consumption in Great Britain, have in many cases served only to encourage smuggling; and in all cases have reduced the revenue of the customs below what more moderate duties would have afforded. The saying of Dr. Swift, that in the arithmetic of the customs two and two, instead of making four, make sometimes only one, holds perfectly true with regard to such heavy duties.
— Adam Smith

There is a limit to the taxing power of the state beyond which increased rates produce decreased revenues.
— Calvin Coolidge

[U]sing tax cuts to stimulate the economy is probably a waste of time and money.
— Allan Sloan

[T]he fairy tale of supply-side economics insists that taxes are always too high, especially on the rich.
— E.J. Dionne Jr.

Any man of energy and initiative in this country can get what he wants out of life. But when initiative is crippled by legislation or by a tax system which denies him the right to receive a reasonable share of his earnings, then he will no longer exert himself and the country will be deprived of the energy on which its continued greatness depends.
— Andrew Mellon

The relative stability of profits after taxes is evidence that the corporation profits tax is in effect almost entirely shifted; the government simply uses the corporation as a tax collector.
— K.E. Boulding

[Suggested simplified tax form:] How much money did you make last year? Mail it in.

— Stanton Delaplane

I have *no idea* what was in my federal tax return. Like 93 percent of all U.S. taxpayers, I just sign it and send it in. For all I know, it states that I am a professional squid wrangler.

— Dave Barry

The arm of the tax-gatherer reaches far.

— Wiley B. Rutledge

But the act demands that you pay a tax on your total net income, no matter where it is derived. Ridiculous! I will not pay it.

— Harry Gordon Selfridge

It is the part of the good shepherd to shear his flock, not flay it.

— Tiberius Caesar

Kings ought to shear, not skin their sheep.

— Robert Herrick

Taxation: how the sheep are shorn.

— Edward Abbey

In levying taxes and in shearing sheep it is well to stop when you get down to the skin.

— Austin O'Malley

What is the difference between a taxidermist and a tax collector? The taxidermist takes only your skin.

— Mark Twain

There is one difference between a tax collector and a taxidermist — the taxidermist leaves the hide.

— Mortimer Caplin

It is of course idle to expect that the complexities of our economic life permit revenue measures to be drawn with such simplicity and particularity as to avoid much litigation.

— Felix Frankfurter

[The IRS] may take some solace in the fact that Matthew was a tax collector before he became a saint.

— Donald C. Alexander

As I went about with my father when he collected taxes, I knew that when taxes were laid some one had to work to earn the money to pay them.

— Calvin Coolidge

Never has it come to my attention or been part of my experience that a revenue agent, a tax collector, has put humanity above regulation. They are, again in my experience, the most abjectly humorless, dehumanized, order taking, weak-charactered, easily vicious, almost casually amoral people I have met.

— Karl Hess

Those who make their living by collecting taxes cause the people to starve; when the people starve, the tax collectors, having no one to tax, starve also.

— Lao Tzu

Herr Louis Dobermann was a German tax collector who needed an alert, companion dog to protect him when he was doing his rounds.

Because he was also the keeper of the local animal shelter, he had a continuous supply of breeding stock to help him develop just such an animal. This "put together" breed was subsequently named after him, as a tribute to his creation.

— *The Dog Pages*

In the time of Emperor Vespasian, the government provided urinals in the streets of Rome and charged a fee for their use. The emperor, seeking to reduce his budget deficit, decided to raise the fee. His son, a finicky fellow, asked the emperor whether the additional receipts should be considered a tax increase or a reduction of government expenditure for the provision of the facilities. To this the emperor made his famous reply (in Latin, the only language he spoke): *"Non Olet!"* The literal translation is, "It doesn't smell." But the meaning is, "It's all money, and it doesn't matter which side of the ledger you put it on."
— Herbert Stein

It is impossible to escape nice distinctions in the application of complicated tax legislation.
— Felix Frankfurter

Sophisticated tax practitioners do not, in fact, benefit when tax practitioner incompetence and tax avoidance succeed. Quite the reverse, as the profession discovered in the tax shelter era.
— Burgess J.W. Raby and William L. Raby

My company [AT&T] fills out 39,000 tax forms a year; that's one every three and a half minutes.
— Michael Armstrong

As a taxpayer, you are required to be fully in compliance with the Untied States Tax Code, which is currently the size and weight of the Budweiser Clydesdales.
— Dave Barry

Elaborate machinery, designed to bring about a perfect equilibrium between benefit and burden, may at times defeat its aim through its own elaboration.
— Benjamin N. Cardozo

I recently heard a CPA remark that the only accounting principle which the Internal Revenue Service regards as "generally accepted" is "A bird in the hand is worth two in the bush." Although my friend overstates his case a bit — quite a bit — I cannot dismiss the thrust of his comment without some soul searching.
— Sheldon S. Cohen

The Opera reminds me of my tax audit. It was in a language I didn't understand. And it ended in tragedy.

— Chris Cassatt and Gary Brookins
("Jeff MacNelly's Shoe")

Taxes must be laid by general rules.

— Harlan F. Stone

I wouldn't mind paying taxes — if I knew they were going to a friendly country.

— Dick Gregory

Judicial efforts to mold tax policy by isolated decisions make a national tax system difficult to develop, administer or observe.

— Robert H. Jackson

Tax statutes and tax regulations never have been static. Experience, changing needs, changing philosophies inevitably produce constant change in each.

— William O. Douglas

The *first* matter to consider in *any* tax case is: What are the exact words of the statute? There is no use in thinking great thoughts about a tax problem unless the thoughts are firmly based on the controlling statute.

— Erwin N. Griswold

[W]hat the ratifiers understood themselves to be enacting must be taken to be what the public of that time would have understood the words to mean. It is important to be clear about this. The search is not for a subjective intention. If someone found a letter from George Washington to Martha telling her that what he meant by the power to lay taxes was not what other people meant, that would not change our reading of the Constitution in the slightest.

— Robert H. Bork

We [Judges of the U.S. Tax Court] have from time-to-time complained about the complexity of our revenue laws and the almost impossible challenge they present to taxpayers or their representatives who have not been initiated into the mysteries of the convoluted, complex provisions affecting the particular corner of the law involved . . . . Our complaints have obviously fallen upon deaf ears.

— Arnold Raum

Like Theseus of old we are compelled to enter this labyrinth [*i.e.*, the Tax Code] — but without his ball of thread.

— Joseph McLaughlin

I have something my tax doctor calls "narcotaxis." Within 20 seconds of hearing someone launch into an explanation of tax laws, my eyes become glassy, my body loses all feeling, and I go into a shallow coma.

— Russell Baker

A distinction between bonds and stocks for the essentially practical purposes of taxation is more fanciful than real.

— George Sutherland

Many inequities are inherent in the income tax. We multiply them needlessly by nice distinctions which have no place in the practical administration of the law.

— William O. Douglas

It is reasonable that a man who denies the legality of a tax should have a clear and certain remedy . . . . Courts sometimes, perhaps, have been a little too slow to recognize the implied duress under which payment is made.

— Oliver Wendell Holmes Jr.

If any person shall complain in court that payment has been unduly exacted of him or that he has sustained any arrogance and if he should be able to prove this fact, a severe sentence shall be pronounced against such tax collector.

— Constantine

The Constitution does not require uniformity in the manner of collection. Uniformity in the assessment is all it demands.
— Morrison Waite

No government could exist, that permitted the collection of its revenue to be delayed by every litigious man or every embarrassed man, to whom delay was more important than the payment of costs.
— Ward Hunt

A member in public practice shall not . . . Prepare an original or amended tax return or claim for a tax refund for a contingent fee for any client.
— American Institute of Certified Public Accountants

Conflicts are multiplied by treating as questions of law what really are disputes over proper accounting. The mere number of such questions and the mass of decisions they call forth becomes a menace to the certainty and good administration of the law.
— Robert H. Jackson

It would be an extreme if not an extravagant application of the Fifth Amendment to say that it authorized a man to refuse to state the amount of his income because it had been made in crime.
— Oliver Wendell Holmes Jr.

I'm sick and tired of politicians beating up on the IRS. We have the best and fairest tax-collection system in the world.
— Charles B. Rangel

The IRS has a new way to get ordinary decent folks to comply with the tax code: Throw other ordinary, decent folks in jail.
— *Forbes* Magazine

To you taxpayers out there, let me say this: Make sure you file your taxes on time! And remember that, even though income taxes can be a "pain in the neck," the folks at the IRS are regular people just like you, except that they can destroy your life.
— Dave Barry

The tax laws produce more revenue when they are enforced than when they are not enforced.

— Donald C. Alexander

We need tax systems where all pay what they owe, because when taxes aren't collected, it is the poor who suffer.

— David Cameron

Increasing enforcement not only catches tax cheats, but discourages others from avoiding paying their taxes.

— John Snow

The higher a taxpayer believes the rate of tax cheating to be, the more likely that taxpayer is to cheat, too. In fact, a taxpayer's perception of compliance by others is a more powerful predictor of whether the taxpayer will act honestly than is the taxpayer's assessment of the risk of an audit or the likely penalty for evasion.

— Jason Mazzone

Since the government lacks the means to investigate and prosecute every suspected violation of the tax laws, it makes good sense to prosecute those who will receive or are likely to receive, the attention of the media.

— Terrell Hodges

Large continued avoidance of tax on the part of some has a steadily demoralizing effect on the compliance of others.

— John F. Kennedy

Under penalties of perjury, I declare that I have examined this return and accompanying schedules and statements, and to the best of my knowledge and belief, they are true, correct, and complete.

— Required Declaration,
IRS Form 1040

They can't collect legal taxes from illegal money.

— Al Capone

The IRS has had substantial success in Chicago. Al Capone was convicted on tax evasion charges here, and that was probably the last time a majority of Americans applauded the IRS on anything.

— Sheldon I. Banoff

It took an IRS accountant to catch Al Capone.

— IRS Recruiting Poster

They [*i.e.*, the enemies of Bill Clinton] got him on sex for the same reason the Feds got Al Capone on tax evasion: Because they could.

— Richard Cohen

Just as the tax code has become an instrument of social engineering for politicians, over and above its primary purpose of raising revenue for the government, so too has the tax-enforcement process become an instrument of general law enforcement for law-enforcement stretching far beyond the enforcement required to collect the taxes levied by the code.

— Dan R. Mastromarco and Lawrence A. Hunter

Last year I had difficulty with my income tax. I tried to take my analyst off as a business deduction. The Government said it was entertainment. We compromised finally and made it a religious contribution.

— Woody Allen

Over the years my taxes have become more complex, and my annoyance with the complexity and ambiguity makes it harder for me to focus on taxes as part of my role and duty as a citizen of this amazing country.

So what can we do to make tax day better? The word *mitzvah* in Hebrew means both a duty and a privilege, and one thing I try to do (not always successfully) is to think about taxes as a mitzvah.

— Dan Ariely

If Congress may tax one citizen to the point of discouragement for making an honest living, it is hard to say that it may not do the same to another just because he makes a sinister living. If the law-abiding must tell all to the tax collector, it is difficult to excuse one because his business is lawbreaking.

— Robert H. Jackson

The question where an income is earned is always a matter of doubt when the business is begun in one country and ended in another.

— William Howard Taft

The [Tax Court] is independent, and its neutrality is not clouded by prosecuting duties. Its procedures assure fair hearings. Its deliberations are evidenced by careful opinions. All guides to judgment available to judges are habitually consulted and respected. It has established a tradition of freedom from bias and pressures. It deals with a subject that is highly specialized and so complex as to be the despair of judges. It is relatively better staffed for its task than is the judiciary.

— Robert H. Jackson

[Taxpayer]: As God is my Judge, I do not owe this tax!
[Tax Court Judge]: He's not. I am. You do.

— Apocryphal Story Involving
U.S. Tax Court Judge J. Edgar Murdock

The tight net which the Treasury Regulations fashion is for the protection of the revenue.

— Felix Frankfurter

Men must turn square corners when they deal with the Government.

— Oliver Wendell Holmes Jr.

The payment of taxes is an obvious and insistent duty, and its sanction is usually punitive.

— Joseph McKenna

Suggesting that the IRS outsource its enforcement activities is like suggesting that the FBI outsource its manhunts and the Pentagon outsource its wars.

— Tax Executives Institute

When a revenue agent confronts the taxpayer with an apparent deficiency, the latter may be more concerned with a quick settlement than an honest search for the truth.

— Tom C. Clark

Many tax collectors, in their zeal to catch those among us who don't pay their taxes, seem to have lost sight of the most important truth about our tax system — that citizens have rights that must be protected.

— Max Baucus

"I pay my taxes," says somebody, as if that were an act of virtue instead of one of compulsion.

— Robert G. Menzies

Dear Mr. President, Internal Revenue regulations will turn us into a nation of bookkeepers. The life of every citizen is becoming a business. This, it seems to me, is one of the worst interpretations of the meaning of human life history has ever seen. Man's life is not a business.

— Saul Bellow
(*Herzog*)

This tax problem has made a bookkeeper of me too. I'm really not supposed to paint, I guess. Instead, I'm supposed to sit here and scribble figures in a book. If the figures don't balance I'll be put in prison. I don't care about money. All I want to do with the limited time I have left is to use it to paint a few pictures in peace and quiet. By now, I've learned a good deal about painting and ought to be able to contribute my best. The country might benefit from giving me time to paint. But does anyone care?

— Edvard Munch

As a cop, the IRS has to balance customer service and law enforcement. Stated another way, the agency's motto could be: "We're your friend. But if you push that friendship too far, we'll ruin your life and then throw you in jail."

— Christopher Bergin

[E]very stick crafted to beat on the head of a taxpayer will metamorphose sooner or later into a large green snake and bite the [IRS] commissioner on the hind part.

— Martin D. Ginsburg

No other nation in the world has ever equaled this record [of voluntary tax compliance]. It is a tribute to our people, their tradition of honesty, and their high sense of responsibility in supporting our government.

— Mortimer Caplin

One of the major characteristics of our tax system, and one in which we can take a great deal of pride, is that it operates primarily through individual self-assessment.

— John F. Kennedy

Our tax system depends on each person who is voluntarily meeting his or her tax obligations having confidence that his or her neighbor or competitor is also complying.

— Charles O. Rossotti

[I]t is far preferable from a public policy standpoint when taxpayers pay voluntarily rather than pursuant to enforcement action. We should strive to make sure taxpayers understand how tax dollars they pay are used to protect and benefit them, and we should make compliance as easy as possible.

— Nina E. Olson

[I]t is my business to find out whether you are making me pay an abnormal part of the taxes by reason of the fact that you are conducting a swindling game to save yourself from paying your rightful share.

— Huey Long

Each citizen has a personal interest, a pecuniary interest, in the tax return of his neighbor. We are members of a great partnership, and it is the right of each to know what every other member is contributing to the partnership and what he is taking from it.

— Benjamin Harrison

America's tax system depends upon our voluntary declaration of taxes owed and a patriotic willingness to pay our fair share.

— J. Robert Kerrey

Our self-enforcement system depends in large part on the tax practitioners being wise and ethical enough not to push things too far. Unfortunately, that idealistic solution has failed since tax practitioners, not unlike all humans, are not angels.

— Lawrence M. Stone

[W]e do not have, and never had, and could not have a "voluntary" tax system.

— Donald C. Alexander

[T]here are some nice experimental results showing that if you ask people to take an active role and vote on where a small part of their taxes goes (education, infrastructure, military, health, etc.), this improves their attitude toward taxes.

— Dan Ariely

I don't believe in the Government reaching down into your pocket and taking money by force, by police state methods, but that's what it is doing every day under our tax system.

— T. Coleman Andrews

The American compliance record stems from a combination of civic obligation, fear of audit, and confidence that everyone else on the block is chipping in. Remove any one of those, and you could quickly undermine the whole system.

— Fred Hiatt

The United States has a system of taxation by confession. That a people so numerous, scattered and individualistic annually assesses itself with a tax liability, often in highly burdensome amounts, is a reassuring sign of the stability and vitality of our system of self-government. What surprised me in once trying to help administer these laws was not to discover examples of recalcitrance, fraud or self-serving mistakes in reporting, but to discover that such derelictions were so few.

— Robert H. Jackson

The smuggling of tobacco undoubtedly began when it first become profitable, when James I, out of his hatred of the weed, placed an imposition of six shillings and eightpence upon each pound of it imported.

— Alfred Rive

We can trace the personal history of a man, and his successes and failures, just by looking at his tax returns from his first job to his retirement.

— Charles A. Church

Every good citizen . . . should be willing to devote a brief time during some one day in the year, when necessary, to the making up of a listing of his income for taxes . . . to contribute to his Government, not the scriptural tithe, but a small percentage of his net profits.

— Cordell Hull

It is the small owner who offers the only really profitable and reliable material for taxation . . . . He is made for taxation . . . . He swarms; he is far more tied to his place and his calling than the big owner; he has less skill, and ingenuity as regards escape; and he still has a large supply of "ignorant patience of taxation."

— Auberon Herbert

People hate the salt tax, because they are obliged to have the salt, and cannot evade the tax: governments love the tax for the same reason — because people are obliged to pay it.

— Thomas Hart Benton

Excise: A hateful tax levied upon commodities, and adjudged not by the common judges of property, but wretches hired by those to whom excise is paid.

— Samuel Johnson

Income tax, if I may be pardoned for saying so, is a tax on income.

— Lord Macnaghten

. . . I'm continually amazed at the attitude people have toward their tax refund. There seems to be in most people's minds — and I'm talking about intelligent, educated people who understand the tax system — a disconnect between the refund they get and the amount of taxes they pay. It's like a lottery. People want that check!

— Verenda Smith

Intaxication: euphoria at getting a refund from the IRS, which lasts until you realize it was your money to start with.

— Greg Oetjen

Internal Revenue Service: The world's most successful mail order business.

— Bob Goddard

U.S. Internal Revenue Service: an agency modeled after the revenue raising concepts of the 19th century economist, Jesse James.

— Robert Brault

The United States may become the first great power to falter because it lost its ability to collect taxes.

— American Bar Association

[Old Mission Statement:] The purpose of the Internal Revenue Service is to collect the proper amount of tax revenue at the least cost; serve the public by continually improving the quality of our products and services; and perform in a manner warranting the highest degree of public confidence in our integrity, efficiency and fairness.

— Internal Revenue Service

The Internal Revenue Service shall review and restate its mission to place a greater emphasis on serving the public and meeting taxpayers' needs.

— The Internal Revenue Service
Restructuring and Reform Act of 1998

[New Mission Statement:] The IRS mission is to provide America's taxpayers top quality service by helping them understand and meet their tax responsibilities and by applying the tax law with integrity and fairness to all.

— Internal Revenue Service

No one likes paying taxes, but at least the taxpaying public trusts that when they send a payment to the IRS, it is properly credited and accounted for. They do not worry that an IRS employee stole it.

— Steven Jones

The Power to Tax

The power to tax is the power to destroy
only in the sense that those who have power
can misuse it.

— Felix Frankfurter

The Power to Tax

It is proper here to remark, that the authority to lay and collect taxes is the most important of any power that can be granted; it connects with it almost all other powers, or at least will in process of time draw all others after it; it is the great mean of protection, security, and defense, in a good government, and the great engine of oppression and tyranny in a bad one.

— "Brutus," Anonymous Author of
Anti-Federalist Paper Number 17

Many of the opposition [to the new Federal Constitution] wish to take from Congress the power of internal taxation. Calculation has convinced me that this would be very mischievous.

— Thomas Jefferson

Representatives and direct Taxes shall be apportioned among the several States which may be included within this Union, according to their respective Numbers, which shall be determined by adding to the whole Number of free Persons, including those bound to Service for a Term of Years, and excluding Indians not taxed, three fifths of all other Persons.

— Section 2 of Article I of the U.S. Constitution

The Congress shall have Power To lay and collect Taxes, Duties, Imposts and Excises, to pay the Debts and provide for the common Defence and general Welfare of the United States; but all Duties, Imposts and Excises shall be uniform throughout the United States . . . .

— Section 8 of Article I of the U.S. Constitution

No Capitation, or other direct, Tax shall be laid, unless in Proportion to the Census or Enumeration herein before directed to be taken.
— Section 9 of Article I of the U.S. Constitution

Congress shall have the power to lay and collect taxes on income, from whatever source derived . . . .
— 16th Amendment to the U.S. Constitution

Article 1 of the Constitution forbids Congress to impose a direct tax on property without "apportioning it among the states in accordance with population." Needless to say, this requirement would make any direct tax on property almost impossible to impose. That is why in 1913, the states ratified the 16th Amendment, which allows Congress to impose an "income tax" on U.S. residents without apportioning it among the states. And it is for that reason that Congress cannot impose a tax on accumulated wealth, financial or otherwise. There must be at least a reasonable basis for asserting that what is being taxed is "income," rather than wealth per se.
— David P. Hariton

Contrary to popular belief, Congress was not prohibited from taxing incomes prior to the Sixteenth Amendment.
— Bruce Bartlett

The payment of poll taxes as a prerequisite to voting is a familiar and reasonable regulation long enforced by many States and for more than a century in Georgia.
— Pierce Butler

An unlimited power to tax involves, necessarily, the power to destroy.
— Daniel Webster

That the power to tax involves the power to destroy; that the power to destroy may defeat and render useless the power to create; that there is plain repugnance, in conferring on one government a power to control the constitutional measures of another, which other, with respect to those very measures is declared to be supreme over that which exerts the control, are propositions not to be denied.
— John Marshall

No one imagines . . . that a law professing to tax, will be permitted to destroy.

— John Marshall

The power to tax is the power to destroy only in the sense that those who have power can misuse it.

— Felix Frankfurter

The power to tax is not the power to destroy while this court sits.

— Oliver Wendell Holmes Jr.

The power to tax is the one great power upon which the whole national fabric is based. It is as necessary to the existence and prosperity of a nation as is the air he breathes to the natural man. It is not only the power to destroy, but it is also the power to keep alive.

— Rufus W. Peckham

The power to tax carries with it the power to embarrass and destroy.

— Willis Van Devanter

The power to tax the exercise of a privilege is the power to control or suppress its enjoyment.

— William O. Douglas

The power to tax is the power to govern.

— Maurice L. Duplessis

The power to tax is the power to rule.

— Brooks Atkinson

A state's power to tax property is plenary.

— Owen J. Roberts

[The] power to tax is virtually without limitation.

— Lewis F. Powell Jr.

The power to tax, to seize wealth with or without the owner's approval, is a key feature distinguishing a government from a business or an individual. Many of us feel a natural resentment toward that unique power.

— Hanno Beck, Brian Dunkiel, and Gawain Kripke

The power to tax is . . . the strongest, the most pervading of all the powers of government reaching directly or indirectly to all classes of the people.

— Samuel F. Miller

The power to tax is indeed one of the most effective forms of regulation. And no more powerful instrument for centralization of government could be devised.

— William O. Douglas

The power to tax, once conceded, has no limits; it contains until it destroys.

— Robert A. Heinlein

You can do anything under [the Constitution's] taxing power.

— Harlan F. Stone

The Constitution is first a tax document, a pro-tax document, written by nationalists to allow the federal government to tax people and things directly without going through the states.

— Calvin H. Johnson

[The states] have no power, by taxation or otherwise, to retard, impede, burden or in any manner control the operations of the constitutional laws enacted by Congress.

— John Marshall

O that there might in England be
A duty on hypocrisy
A tax on humbug, an excise
On solemn plausibilities.

— Henry Luttrell

[T]he power of taxing the people and their property is essential to the very existence of government . . . .

— John Marshall

The power to tax may be exercised oppressively upon persons, but the responsibility of the legislature is not to the courts, but to the people by whom its members are elected.

— Salmon P. Chase

That the power of taxation is one of vital importance; that it is retained by the States; that it is not abridged by the grant of a similar power to the government of the Union; that it is to be concurrently exercised by the two governments: are truths which have never been denied.

— John Marshall

What happens if the political entity in which you are located no longer corresponds to a job that takes place in cyberspace, or no longer really encompasses workers collaborating with other workers in different corners of the globe, or no longer really captures products produced in multiple places simultaneously? Who regulates the work? Who taxes it? Who should benefit from those taxes?

— David Rothkopf

The right to tax "in its nature acknowledges no limits."
— Oliver Wendell Holmes Jr.

The government's power to control one's life derives from its power to tax. We believe that power should be minimized.
— Americans for Tax Reform Mission Statement

There is no worse tyranny than to force a man to pay for what he does not want merely because you think it would be good for him.
— Robert A. Heinlein

We cannot be happy without being free; we cannot be free without being secure in our property; we cannot be secure in our property if, without our consent, others may, as by right, take it away; taxes imposed on us by Parliament do thus take it away.

— John Dickinson

The collection of any taxes which are not absolutely required, which do not beyond reasonable doubt contribute to the public welfare, is only a species of legalized larceny. Under this republic the rewards of industry belong to those who earn them. The only constitutional tax is the tax which ministers to public necessity. The property of the country belongs to the people of the country. Their title is absolute.

— Calvin Coolidge

Those who create the wealth naturally want to keep it and devote it to their own purposes. Those who wish to expropriate it look for ever more-clever ways to acquire it without inciting resistance. One of those ways is the spreading of an elaborate ideology of statism, which teaches that the people are the state and that therefore they are only paying themselves when they pay taxes.

— Sheldon Richman

The powers of taxation are broad, but the distinction between taxation and confiscation must still be observed.

— George Sutherland

A tax may be so "arbitrary and capricious," its "inequality" so "gross and patent," that it will not stand . . . .

— Learned Hand

To lay with one hand the power of government on the property of the citizen, and with the other to bestow it on favored individuals . . . . is none the less a robbery because it is done under the forms of law and is called taxation.

— Samuel F. Miller

[I]t is no more immoral to directly rob citizens than to slip indirect taxes into the price of goods that they cannot do without.

— Albert Camus

Many thinkers are apt to make common cause with the Socialists in demanding the complete abolition of the so-called indirect taxes. This is a mistake. There is nothing inherently bad about an indirect tax, nor is there anything inherently good about a direct tax. It depends entirely upon what kind of direct or indirect tax it is. A direct tax on the laborer is not necessarily good because it is direct; an indirect tax on the luxury of the rich is not necessarily bad because it is indirect. It happens, indeed, that most of the indirect taxes of the past have been devised by the powerful in order that their burden might fall on the weak; but it is by no means impossible to frame a system of taxes on consumption which will supplement other taxes and do substantial justice to all.

— Edwin R.A. Seligman

When there's a single thief, it's robbery. When there are a thousand thieves, it's taxation.

— Vanya Cohen

The prime objection to these "canons" [of tax justice] is that the writers have first to establish the justice of taxation itself. If this cannot be proven, and so far it has not been, then it is clearly idle to look for the "just tax." If taxation itself is unjust, then it is clear that no allocation of its burdens, however ingenious, can be declared just.

— Murray Rothbard

Taxation has surrounded itself with doctrines of justification; it had to; no miscreant can carry on without a supporting philosophy. Until recent times this pilfering of private property sought to gain the approval of its victims by protesting the need for maintaining social services. The growing encroachments of the state upon property rights necessarily brought about a lowering of the general economy, resulting in disaffection, and now taxation is advocated as a means of alleviating this condition; we are now being taxed into betterment.

— Frank Chodorov

People who relieve others of their money with guns are called robbers. It does not alter the immorality of the act when the income transfer is carried out by government.

— Cal Thomas

If you refuse to pay unjust taxes, your property will be confiscated. If you attempt to defend your property you will be arrested. If you resist arrest, you will be clubbed. If you defend yourself against clubbing, you will be shot dead. These procedures are known as the Rule of Law.

— Edward Abbey

Try not to think of it as "your" money.

— Apocryphal IRS Agent

The supreme power of every community has the right of requiring from all its subjects such contributions as are necessary to the public safety or public prosperity.

— Samuel Johnson

A State cannot tax a stranger for something that it has not given him.

— Felix Frankfurter

Orthodox concepts of ownership fail to reflect the outer boundaries of taxation.

— Frank Murphy

The new technologies should not be used as a justification to create new taxes.

— Glen A. Kohl

A state may not impose a charge for the enjoyment of a right granted by the federal constitution.

— William O. Douglas

The notion that a city has unlimited taxing power, is, of course, an illusion.

— Felix Frankfurter

Due process requires some definite link, some minimum connection, between a state and the person, property or transaction it seeks to tax.

— Robert H. Jackson

A State must not play favorites in the operation of its taxing system between business confined within its borders and the common interests of the nation expressed through business conducted across State lines.

— Felix Frankfurter

The right of the citizens of the United States to vote in any primary or other election for President . . . or for Senator or Representative in Congress, shall not be denied or abridged . . . by reason of failure to pay any poll tax or other tax.

— 24th Amendment to the U.S. Constitution

What the individual does in the operation of a business is amenable to taxation just as much as what he owns, at all events if the classification is not tyrannical or arbitrary.

— Benjamin N. Cardozo

It is one thing to impose a tax on the income or property of a preacher. It is quite another thing to exact a tax from him for the privilege of delivering a sermon.

— William O. Douglas

The encouragement or discouragement of competition is an end for which the power of taxation may be exerted.

— Louis D. Brandeis

Those of us who understand human history know the role taxation has played in shaping the destiny of mankind. The matter of taxes — more specifically, the right to tax — is clearly no stranger to controversy and has frequently served as the catalyst for revolutionary change.

— Owen Arthur

The validity of a tax depends upon its nature, and not upon its name.

— Benjamin N. Cardozo

One of the first signs of the breaking down of free government is a disregard by the taxing power of the right of the people to their own property. It makes little difference whether such a condition is brought about through the will of a dictator, through the power of a military force, or through the pressure of an organized minority. The result is the same. Unless the people can enjoy that reasonable security in the possession of their property, which is guaranteed by the Constitution, against unreasonable taxation, freedom is at an end.

— Calvin Coolidge

Of all the powers conferred upon government that of taxation is most liable to abuse . . . . This power can as readily be employed against one class of individuals and in favor of another, so as to ruin the one class and give unlimited wealth and prosperity to the other, if there is no implied limitation of the uses for which the power may be exercised.

— Samuel F. Miller

I want to be sure he [the Commissioner of the Internal Revenue Service] is a ruthless son of a bitch, that he will do what he is told, that every income tax return I want to see I see, that he will go after our enemies and not go after our friends.

— Richard M. Nixon

Nowhere is the federal government's mighty hand felt more directly than when the Internal Revenue Service comes calling with a demand for unpaid taxes. Taxation, admittedly a necessary element of any form of civilized government, places unparalleled power in the hand of the sovereign. When that power is unleashed in an inconsistent, threatening, and arrogant manner, the powerless taxpayer, who for all practical purposes is at the mercy of the government, has little recourse to remedy such abuses.

— Clay D. Land

It is wise to remember that the taxing and licensing power is a dangerous and potent weapon which, in the hands of unscrupulous or bigoted men, could be used to suppress freedoms and destroy religion unless it is kept within appropriate bounds.

— Frank Murphy

In determining whether the tax is in truth a tax on property, we are to consider, not its form or label, but its practical operation.

— Benjamin N. Cardozo

One of our basic rights is to be free of taxation to support a transgression of the constitutional command that the authorities "shall make no law respecting an establishment of religion, or prohibiting the free exercise thereof."

— Robert H. Jackson

Taxes on the circulation of ideas have a long history of misuse against freedom of thought.

— Frank Murphy

[T]o compel a man to furnish contributions of money for the propagation of opinions which he disbelieves, is sinful and tyrannical.

— Thomas Jefferson

The taxes that have an invidious incidence are those which historically were known in America as "taxes on knowledge."

— William O. Douglas

Several millennia ago, tribal lords discovered the advantages of collecting some of their people's property in return for a few identifiable benefits, such as not killing them. Over the centuries, tax collection gained in sophistication, including the relatively novel personal income tax. The new millennium shows no sign of abandoning this system.

— Sanford C. Bernstein & Company

The objection to double taxation by a single sovereign is no more potent under the Fourteenth Amendment than the objection that a tax otherwise valid has been doubled.

— Harlan F. Stone

Not even the power of [the Supreme] Court can make income of outgo. To speak of "a tax on corporate income that is paid out" is as self-contradictory as to speak of round squares.

— Robert H. Jackson

As far as I know, the Supreme Court has never declared war, nor has it raised taxes.

— Arthur J. Goldberg

[I]t is abundantly clear the Constitution does not guarantee that individuals may avoid taxation through inactivity. A capitation, after all, is a tax that everyone must pay simply for existing, and capitations are expressly contemplated by the Constitution. The Court today upholds that our Constitution protects us from federal regulation under the Commerce Clause so long as we abstain from regulated activity. But from its creation, the Constitution has made no such promise with respect to taxes.

— John Roberts

The burden of Federal taxation necessarily sets an economic limit to the practical operation of the taxing power of the States, and vice versa.

— Harlan F. Stone

State law creates legal interests and rights. The federal revenue acts designate what interests or rights, so created, shall be taxed. Our duty is to ascertain the meaning of the words used to specify the thing taxed. If it is found in a given case that an interest or right created by local law was the object intended to be taxed, the federal law must prevail no matter what name is given to the interest or right by state law.

— Owen J. Roberts

The right to possess private property is derived from nature, not from man; and the state has the right to control its use in the interests of the public good alone, but by no means to absorb it altogether. The state would therefore be unjust and cruel if under the name of taxation it were to deprive the private owner of more than is fair.

— Pope Leo XIII

The power of collecting and disbursing money at pleasure is the most dangerous power that can be trusted to man.

— Davy Crockett

I have paid no poll-tax for six years. I was put into a jail once on this account, for one night; and, as I stood considering the walls of solid stone, two or three feet thick, the door of wood and iron, a foot thick, and the iron grating which strained the light, I could not help being struck with the foolishness of that institution which treated me as if I were mere flesh and blood and bones, to be locked up. I wondered that it should have concluded at length that this was the best use it could put me to, and had never thought to avail itself of my services in some way. I saw that, if there was a wall of stone between me and my townsmen, there was a still more difficult one to climb or break through before they could get to be as free as I was. I did not for a moment feel confined, and the walls seemed a great waste of stone and mortar. I felt as if I alone of all my townsmen had paid my tax.

— Henry David Thoreau

If we can tax it, we will.

— City Income Tax Form of
Middleton, Ohio

Avoidance, Evasion, and Planning

The rich, indeed, are different from the rest of us; they have shiftier tax lawyers.

— Jim McTague

Avoidance, Evasion, and Planning

Any one may so arrange his affairs that his taxes shall be as low as possible; he is not bound to choose that pattern which will best pay the Treasury; there is not even a patriotic duty to increase one's taxes.

— Learned Hand

A taxpayer may engineer his transactions to minimize taxes, but he cannot make a transaction appear to be what it is not.

— Irving Loeb Goldberg

I will not pay a dime more of individual taxes than I owe, and I won't pay a dime more of corporate taxes than we owe. And that's very simple.

— Warren Buffett

I'm spending a year dead for tax reasons.

— Douglas Noel Adams

The legal right of a taxpayer to decrease the amount of what otherwise would be his taxes, or altogether avoid them, by means which the law permits, cannot be doubted.

— George Sutherland

[I]t is not the [Canadian] courts' role to prevent taxpayers from relying on the sophisticated structure of their transactions, arranged in such a way that the particular provisions of the Act are met, on the basis that it would be inequitable to those taxpayers who have not chosen to structure their transactions that way .... Unless the Act provides otherwise, a taxpayer is entitled to be taxed based on what it actually did, not based on what it could have done, and certainly not based on what a less sophisticated taxpayer might have done.

— Beverley McLachlin

Over and over again courts have said that there is nothing sinister in so arranging one's affairs as to keep taxes as low as possible. Everybody does so, rich or poor; and all do right, for nobody owes any public duty to pay more than the law demands: taxes are enforced exactions, not voluntary contributions. To demand more in the name of morals is mere cant.

— Learned Hand

Every man is entitled if he can to order his affairs so as that the tax attaching under the appropriate Acts is less than it otherwise would be. If he succeeds in ordering them so as to secure this result, then, however unappreciative the Commissioners of Inland Revenue or his fellow taxpayers may be of his ingenuity, he cannot be compelled to pay an increased tax.

— Lord Tomlin

[T]here is nothing wrong with a strategy to avoid the payment of taxes. The Internal Revenue Code doesn't prevent that.

— William H. Rehnquist

Day in and day out, your tax accountant can make or lose you more money than any single person in your life, with the possible exception of your kids.

— Harvey Mackay

Anybody who does not minimise his tax wants his head read. [*i.e.,* should go to a psychiatrist.]

— Kerry Packer

Nowhere on any tax form does it say you can't be crafty.
— Nuveen Investments
(advertisement)

[T]he more complicated the rules, the more taxpayers will find ways to avoid paying taxes.
— Martin Lobel

There's no line on the tax return that asks, "What are you not telling us?"
— Robert Goulder

A taxpayer need not arrange its affairs so as to maximize taxes as long as the transaction has a legitimate business purpose.
— Cornelia G. Kennedy

[I]t is axiomatic that taxpayers lawfully may arrange their affairs to keep taxes as low as possible. Nevertheless, at the same time the law imposes certain threshold duties which a taxpayer may not shirk simply by manipulating figures or maneuvering assets to conceal their real character.
— Morton I. Greenberg

Avoidance of taxes is not a criminal offense. Any attempt to reduce, avoid, minimize, or alleviate taxes by legitimate means is permissible. The distinction between evasion and avoidance is fine yet definite. One who avoids tax does not conceal or misrepresent. He shapes events to reduce or eliminate tax liability and upon the happening of the events, makes a complete disclosure. Evasion, on the other hand, involves deceit, subterfuge, camouflage, concealment, some attempt to color or obscure events, or making things seem other than what they are.
— Internal Revenue Service

You've got too many companies ending up making decisions based on what their tax director says instead of what their engineer designs or what their factories produce. And that puts our entire economy at a disadvantage.
— Barack Obama

Tax-motivated behavior ought to be discouraged . . . . This is because tax planning produces nothing of value to society. It may benefit the taxpayer whose taxes are reduced, but the social product is not increased.

— Martin J. McMahon Jr.

The tax code is a road map for law-abiding citizens and businesses to pay what they fairly owe, not an obstacle course to be gamed and gotten around.

— Max Baucus

[T]he very wealthy, because they can afford tax lawyers and all kinds of loopholes, really don't pay nearly as much as you think they do.

— John McCain

The really rich people figure out how to dodge taxes anyway.

— George W. Bush

Members of the *Monty Python* [British comedy] group have incorporated for tax reasons in the United States. The name of their company: EvadoTax, Incorporated.

— *Mother Jones* Magazine

Shall we devote the few precious days of our existence only to buying and selling, only to comparing sales with the sales of the same day the year before . . . only to seek pleasures and fight taxes, and when the end comes to leave as little a taxable estate as possible as the final triumph and achievement of our lives? Surely there is something finer and better in life.

— Julius Rosenwald

In tax shelter transactions, an elaborate series of formal steps is contrived to lead to an unreasonably beneficial tax result, usually flowing from some defect or ambiguity in the tax law.

— Peter C. Canellos

[T]ax shelters [involve] uncommon combinations of steps, the claimed tax consequence of which might be correct as a technical matter, but in totality producing a tax outcome which is absurd and unintended . . . .
— George K. Yin

A byzantine, loophole-riddled high-statutory-rate tax code encourages companies to construct byzantine, Rube-Goldberg-like strategies to minimize their tax burdens. Our legislators have created a system in which it's easier to boost profits through tax strategy innovation than actual product innovation, and firms respond accordingly.
— Catherine Rampbell

[Definition of a corporate tax shelter:] A deal done by very smart people that, absent tax considerations, would be very stupid.
— Michael J. Graetz

[A tax shelter] is a deal done by very smart people who are pretending to be rather stupid . . . .
— David P. Hariton

The best definition of a "tax shelter" is a transaction that has *higher* rate of return after tax than before tax.
— Calvin H. Johnson

As a teacher of this funny subject [tax law], I deeply regret the passing of the great American Tax Shelter Phenomenon. In a commendable zeal to pay no more tax than the law required, and preferably a good deal less, otherwise sane men and women invested their money, or at least money they had borrowed, in computers obsolescent on the day acquired, films that could not in one's lifetime turn a profit, master recordings to which none would listen, and a scheme delightfully entitled "the Mexican vegetable rollover." As Forbes magazine with rare accuracy suggested a dozen years ago, tax shelter economics were so bad that nineteen out of twenty investments could only be sold to groups of doctors. The twentieth scheme was awful beyond belief and could be sold only to dentists.
— Martin D. Ginsburg

When I was a young tax associate, a tax partner told me that there were about 20 pages in the Internal Revenue Code and about 50 pages of Treasury Regulations that boiled down to one sentence: "If you are in the real estate business, and if you have a good tax lawyer and a good accountant, you don't pay taxes."

— Jeffery L. Yablon

Tax planning is driven by the fact that under a non-neutral tax law, transactions or arrangements whose economic differences are minor can have significantly different tax consequences.

— James W. Wetzler

The law should not be such a [sic] idiot that it cannot prevent a taxpayer from changing the historical facts from year to year in order to escape a fair share of the burdens of maintaining our government. Our tax system depends upon self assessment and honesty, rather than upon hiding of the pea or forgetful tergiversation.

— Ferdinand F. Fernandez

In America, in 1913, an income tax law was passed and the rich have been devising tax dodging rackets ever since.

— Elliot Paul

Overall, the complexity of the tax code leads to perverse results. On the one hand, taxpayers who honestly seek to comply with the law often make inadvertent errors, causing them to either overpay their tax or become subject to IRS enforcement action for mistaken underpayments. On the other hand, sophisticated taxpayers often find arcane provisions that enable them to reduce or eliminate their tax liabilities.

— Nina E. Olson

There is an organized tax cheaters lobby.

— Robert S. McIntyre

There is no moral argument for cheating on taxes, especially calculated cheating that requires the use of tax professionals and planning. If you do not like our tax system, then work to elect a different Congress.

— David Cay Johnston

[M]any tax officials and scholars believe that the biggest noncompliance issues exist at lower income levels, especially in sole proprietorships and in the cash economy generally.

— Marjorie E. Kornhauser

The rich, indeed, are different from the rest of us; they have shiftier tax lawyers.

— Jim McTague

Tax lawyers are at the top end of the service-provider class, and janitors are at the bottom end. Tax lawyers are at the top, up there with the astrologers and interior decorators, because the *rentier* class values their services in keeping their money away from government.

— Lee A. Sheppard

At the heart of every abusive tax shelter is a tax lawyer or accountant.

— Charles Grassley

Rendering tax advice often involves moral considerations.

— Dennis J. Ventry Jr.

Any man of ethics should examine himself and not seek ways to lighten his tax burden in any manner whatsoever . . . if he does not strictly comply . . . he will have stolen from the public, and his sin will be grave in the extreme.

Nor should he find loopholes, congratulating himself and rationalizing that others, too, present incorrect . . . reports, and that he too can do as they do, maintaining earnings "on the side."

— 1695 Assessment Ledger of
Jewish Community of Mantue, Italy

By the late 1970s, the vast majority of the public had come to believe that everybody else was engaging in tax avoidance or outright tax evasion.

— Michael J. Graetz

Everybody thinks that the other guy is beating the tax code, and they're being suckered. They are the schnooks, and the other people are getting away with it.

— Alan Blinder

The hazards and inconveniences of dishonest dough are too numerous to make it worth while. You not only run the risk of going to the can, but there is the matter of conscience that produces sleepless nights and waking hours of fear and brooding like an income tax return full of lies.

— Damon Runyon

Being told over cocktails that someone had used arguably legal means to avoid paying taxes, someone less sophisticated might reasonably feel foolish and justified in resorting to illegal means to evade taxes.

— Charles E. McLure Jr.

Hating the Yankees is as American as pizza pie, unwed mothers, and cheating on your income tax.

— Mike Royko

The American people as taxpayers have begun in wholesale numbers to cheat, out of resentment of a tax system they think is unfair, too complicated and wasteful of their money. The so-called underground economy is growing rapidly — people working for cash only, reporting nothing, paying nothing.

— David Brinkley

There is plenty of evidence to suggest that we are facing a rising tide of corporate and individual behavior that makes going to any lengths to not pay taxes an acceptable activity.

— Larry R. Levitan

According to a Gallup Organization poll, 64% of the public think that at least half of all big-company executives cheat on their taxes.

— *The Wall Street Journal*

Rich people get their tax planning ideas from their friends.
— Lee A. Sheppard

Where there is at least a general suspicion of much unnecessary expense, and great misapplication of the public revenue, the laws which guard it are little respected.
— Adam Smith

The underground economy is to a large extent a tax-driven phenomenon. Its size has important consequences for revenue collection, requiring the attention of tax officials at both the national and the state and local levels. It may also represent an area in which tax reform can raise more revenue without raising tax rates.
— Bruce Bartlett

We'll try to cooperate fully with the IRS, because, as citizens, we feel a strong patriotic duty not to go to jail.
— Dave Barry

Tax Returns Prepared — Honest Mistakes Are Our Specialty.
— Apocryphal Chicago Storefront Window Sign

Wherever the olive tree grows [*i.e.*, southern Europe], you won't find much tax being collected.
— Anonymous Mayor of a small town in southern Spain

As several cash-strapped European countries can confirm, rampant tax evasion has a tendency to drive statutory tax rates higher so that the government can extract more money from those poor saps still obeying the law.
— Catherine Rampell

In America, if you cheat on your taxes your neighbor won't talk to you. In Italy, they'll ask you how you did it.
— Beppe Severgnini

In Italy, there is no real public pressure for a new, fairer tax system. People simply figure out ways to evade the one they already have.
— Beppe Severgnini

If they [*i.e.*, the Italian tax authorities] want upward of 50% of my income in taxes, I feel that's an unfair demand. [Although I am Prime Minister,] I feel morally authorized to evade as much as I can.

— Silvio Berlusconi

In this nation where tax evasion can be considered part of a solid business plan, even dentists and hairdressers demand payment in cash — payments that then frequently vanish from accounting books like so many Cheshire cats.

But no problem is more glaring than Italy's thriving "shadow economy," where evaded taxes on legal commerce coupled with lost taxes from illicit or under-the-table deals are costing the national treasury about $340 billion a year. If collected annually, that amount could pay back every last cent of Italy's $2.6 trillion debt in just under eight years.

Yet in Italy, as a saying goes, "only fools pay."

— Anthony Faiola

The U.S. underground economy is relatively small compared with other major countries, where it is roughly two-thirds larger, except in Italy, where it is three times larger . . . .

— Bruce Bartlett

[O]bserving the evident perversity of public life, its general atmosphere of free-for-all in every department, the average Italian is tempted to feel that tax evasion is his inalienable right.

— Tim Parks

Many Greeks ask themselves: "If politicians are corrupt, if there is corruption, why should I pay my taxes? I don't know where my money is going."

— George Papandreou

In most of these countries [*e.g.*, Spain, Portugal, and Greece], what matters is your family. . . . There is less of a sense of duty towards the state. Evading taxes is something you can freely talk about — and be proud of — at a dinner party in these countries.

— Alberto Alesina

Athens, after all, is a city in which 364 people told tax authorities they owned swimming pools — and in which satellite photographs reveal the existence of 16,974 swimming pools.

— Anne Applebaum

It's become a cultural trait. The Greek people never learned to pay their taxes. And they never did because no one is punished. No one *has ever been* punished. It's a cavalier offense — like a gentleman not opening a door for a lady.

— Anonymous Greek Tax Official

Our top priority will be to implement a new tax system [here in Greece] which will put an end to the provocative injustice that makes those who do not evade tax the ones who pay.

— Evangelos Venizelos

In contrast to the compulsory taxes of other countries, the giving of donations has always been practised in Tibet. The main difference is that here everyone decides for himself how much he can and will give.

— Clemens Kuby

Unless the government is standing right next to me doing one-third to one-half of my labor, they don't have a right to one-third or one-half of my compensation. There is no law that compels me to file a tax return. I have a choice, as every American has a choice.

— Lynne Meredith

[T]here is no law that requires Americans to pay taxes, but the government and the media have tricked people into thinking they have to pay.

— Nick Jesson

There have always been individuals who, for a variety of reasons, argue that various taxes are illegal. They use false, misleading, or unorthodox tax advice to gain followers . . . . The promoters of this tax advice often charge hefty fees or commissions to subscribe to their philosophies. Unfortunately, in the end, you may pay more in penalties, interest, and legal fees for following their bad advice. Their philosophies have lead to the financial ruin of innocent taxpayers deceived by false information. Believe it or not — a number of individuals who market these ideas actually pay taxes.

— Internal Revenue Service

No man in this country is under the smallest obligation, moral or other, so to arrange his legal relations to his business or to his property as to enable the Inland Revenue to put the largest possible shovel into his stores.

— Lord Clyde

Methods of escape or intended escape from tax liability are many. Some are instances of avoidance which appear to have the color of legality; others are on the borderline of legality; others are plainly contrary even to the letter of the law.

All are alike in that they are definitely contrary to the spirit of the law. All are alike in that they represent a determined effort on the part of those who use them to dodge the payment of taxes which Congress based on ability to pay. All are alike in that failure to pay results in shifting the tax load to the shoulders of others less able to pay, and in mulcting the Treasury of the Government's just due.

— Franklin D. Roosevelt

During his first term in office, [President Franklin D. Roosevelt] repeatedly claimed that he was exempt from the high tax rates on personal income that Congress had enacted — and Roosevelt had approved — in the revenue acts of 1934 and 1935.

In a series of letters to internal revenue officials, Roosevelt insisted that he could not be taxed at the heavy rates imposed on rich taxpayers during the mid-1930s. Article II, section 1 of the Constitution forbids any reduction in the president's compensation during his term in office, Roosevelt pointed out. Since the new rates enacted in 1934 and 1935 effectively reduced that compensation, they could not be applied to the president's salary.

— Joseph J. Thorndike

Anybody has a right to evade taxes if he can get away with it. No citizen has a moral obligation to assist in maintaining the government. If Congress insists on making stupid mistakes and passing foolish tax laws, millionaires should not be condemned if they take advantage of them.

— J. Pierpont Morgan

Hitler owed tax but didn't pay . . . . He was constantly challenging tax office rulings on his income tax between 1925 and 1932 . . . . After taking power he didn't pay tax anymore.

— Klaus-Dieter Dubon

The rabbis asked: Is it ever permitted to evade a tax? Two answers are given: Tax evasion is permitted where the tax collector is authorized to collect any sum he wishes or, according to a different opinion, where the tax collector is self-appointed and does not represent the king.

— Amy Wallk Katz

Why would any U.S. citizen wish to go through the time and expense required to establish an offshore account unless it was for the evasion of taxes or the hiding of funds?

— John Mathewson

A key to our tax system is that it contains enough loopholes that nearly everyone can cheat a little and be happy.

— Terence Floyd Cuff

At least in the United States, conservative politicians cheating on their spouses is similar to liberal politicians cheating on their taxes. The hypocrisy is so rank. And you can depend upon seeing it fairly often.

— Jeffery L. Yablon

Tax havens are not the little parasites they once were. Would that they were merely whorehouses on the edge of town that could be easily shut down! So much money is sloshing through them, and their use is so pervasive, that they functionally constitute the banking system.

— Lee A. Sheppard

It does not surprise anyone when I tell them that the most important tax haven in the world is an island. They are surprised, however, when I tell them that the name of the Island is *Manhattan*. Moreover, the second most important tax haven in the world is located on an island. It is a city called *London in the United Kingdom.*

— Marshall J. Langer

For years, we've talked about shutting down overseas tax havens that let companies set up operations to avoid paying taxes in America. That's what our budget will finally do. On the campaign, I used to talk about the outrage of a building in the Cayman Islands that had over 12,000 . . . businesses claim this building as their headquarters. And I've said before, either this is the largest building in the world or the largest tax scam in the world. And I think the American people know which it is. It's the kind of tax scam that we need to end. That's why we are closing one of our biggest tax loopholes.

— Barack Obama

The interdependence of the world economy makes trying to impose high income tax rates on multinational corporations and business partnerships counterproductive. Deductions flock to high-tax-rate countries, and income flocks to those with low rates. There is only so much the United States can do unilaterally to address this problem.

— Michael J. Graetz

Switzerland is a respectable developed European country that acts like a tropical island that feeds off tax evasion by U.S. citizens. Switzerland is a rich country because its currency is propped up by the conversion of tax evaders' euros and dollars into Swiss francs. Tax evasion banking is the mainstay of the Swiss economy.

— Lee A. Sheppard

[Indicia of a Tax Haven:]
(1) no or nominal income tax;
(2) rules that prevent the effective exchange of information with foreign tax authorities;
(3) a lack of transparency in the operation of legislative, legal, or administrative provisions; and
(4) the absence of a requirement for a substantive local presence.

— The Organization for Economic Cooperation and Development

There is a sizable and statistically robust association between being a tax haven and the presence of high-quality government institutions.

— James Hines

"International financial centers." That's Orwellian Newspeak for tax havens.

— Lee A. Sheppard

Tax day is the day that ordinary Americans send their money to Washington, D.C., and wealthy Americans send their money to the Cayman Islands.

— Jimmy Kimmel

Campione is an island measuring only one square mile in Lake Lugano (Italy). The Italian tax authorities do not enforce taxes on the worldwide income of foreigners establishing residence there. Residency is established by renting, buying, or acquiring a time-share in a property.

— Ronen Palan

We [the Organisation for Economic Co-operation and Development] were so worried about avoiding double taxation, we created double nontaxation. Nobody pays anywhere.

— Ángel Gurría

We cannot allow an environment to develop where wealthy individuals can go offshore and avoid tax without consequence. We cannot allow an environment where large corporations can pay hefty fees and salaries for top talent to engage in overly aggressive shifting of taxable activities to low tax jurisdictions.

— Douglas Shulman

Everyone is entitled to conduct their financial affairs in privacy, but secrecy laws which facilitate tax evasion are completely unacceptable.

— Dave Hartnett

I was just not thinking when I signed my tax return [omitting twenty-five million dollars in income].

— L. Dennis Kozlowski

Dear Tax Commissioner: Three years ago I cheated on my taxes. Since then I have been unable to sleep at night. Enclosed is $5,000. If I still can't sleep, I'll send you the rest.

— Anonymous

Hell hath no fury. . . . Never cheat on your taxes and your spouse at the same time — exes are a big source of IRS leads.

— *Forbes* Magazine

Avoid falsehoods like the plague except in matters of taxation, which do not count, since here you are not lying to take someone else's goods, but to prevent your own from being unjustly seized.

— Giovanni Morelli

History shows that when the taxes of a nation approach about 20% of the people's income, there begins to be a lack of respect for government . . . . When it reaches 25%, there comes an increase in lawlessness.

— Ronald Reagan

The British government tolerates the offshore financial industry on the assumption that it brings more money into Britain by channeling more expatriate and foreign wealth into London than is taken out by people working tax dodges.

— *The Economist* Magazine

There's no question that it's more fun to do business while relaxing on the beach of some Caribbean paradise than while cooped up in your office back home. But there's more to the offshore world than the sunny climate. There's freedom and privacy beyond your wildest imagination. Off come the shackles of government regulation and the handcuffs of excessive taxation.

— Jerome Schneider

We [marijuana dealers] were the bad guys. Now we are still the bad guys, but we pay taxes.

— Elliot King

Taxpayers who neglect paying tax on offshore income out of ignorance must be educated. Taxpayers who do it on purpose need to be scared.

— Martin A. Sullivan

There is a deep anger against those who use offshore jurisdictions to evade U.S. taxes.

— Carl Levin

Great empires fall because they let their tax bases erode, and tax bases erode because the general interest is always overwhelmed by a narrow spear of special interests. The best we can do is delay the decay.

— Calvin H. Johnson

Due to difficulties in establishing source income, residency has become the standard principle of worldwide taxation of corporations. The residency principle has proved to be a great boon to tax havens, since companies and banks find it beneficial to shift as much of their operations as possible to low- or zero-tax regimes.

— Ronen Palan

As a citizen, you have an obligation to the country's tax system, but you also have an obligation to yourself to know your rights under the law.

— Donald C. Alexander

When a corporate taxpayer selects a competent tax expert, supplies him with all necessary information, and requests him to prepare proper tax returns, we think the taxpayer has done all that ordinary business care and prudence can reasonably demand.

— Thomas Walter Swan

If you are truly serious about preparing your child for the future, don't teach him to subtract — teach him to deduct.

— Fran Lebowitz

What kind of financial shape are you in right now? This scientific quiz will show you. Be honest in your answers: If you lie, you'll only be lying to yourself! The place to lie is on your federal tax return.

— Dave Barry

In the United States we have observed that there are two Internal Revenue Codes — one for Wall Street and one for Main Street. Wall Street can afford and often needs the services of sophisticated tax lawyers. Main Street often can't and doesn't.

— Sheldon I. Banoff

The history of Wall Street and tax accounting rules is that Wall Street always complains about new rules until its denizens figure out how to abuse them.

— Lee A. Sheppard

To collect all the taxes owed — that is, to close the tax gap — is an impossible task.

— Berdji Kenadjian

The avoidance of taxes is the only intellectual pursuit that still carries any reward.

— John Maynard Keynes

Tax avoidance is a natural thing. It's like gravity.

— Jeff VanderWolk

Accounting is no longer a way to provide an accurate and unified view of a company's finances. Instead, it has become a means to an end. For the public books, the goal is to achieve smooth and steady earnings growth that will lift the value of the company's stock . . . . For the IRS, the goal is the exact opposite — keeping income, and thus taxes, to a minimum.

— Alan Murray

[I]n the area of taxation, it is often difficult to determine where business ends and the law begins.

— Ellen Bree Burns

Just as there is an underground economy of gardeners and handy-men and petty merchants who get paid in cash and pay little or no tax, there is also an underground economy among the super rich that lets them understate their true income and overstate their tax deductions.
— David Cay Johnston

Our entire tax system is threatened by the existence of tax avoidance techniques that are only available to the wealthy in our society.
— Barbara Kennelly

The ancient Egyptians built elaborate fortresses and tunnels and even posted guards at tombs to stop grave robbers. In today's America, we call that estate planning.
— Bill Archer

The fairer and lower tax rates are, the less tax evasion, avoidance and noncompliance there will be.
— Arthur B. Laffer

Too many business decisions are made on the basis of tax conse-quences rather than what makes good business sense.
— Harold Igaldoff

[Under the tax laws] a corporation is like a lobster pot: it is easy to enter, difficult to live in, and painful to get out of.
— Boris I. Bittker and James S. Eustice

Never let the tax tail wag the economic dog.
— Laura Peebles

We cannot ignore the reality that the tax laws affect the shape of nearly every business transaction.
— Donald Korb

Employees make the best dates. You don't have to pick them up and they're always tax-deductible.
— Andy Warhol

[T]o base all of your decisions on tax consequences is not necessarily to maintain the proper balance and perspective on what you are doing.
— Barber Conable

The puzzle of tax compliance is why people pay taxes instead of evading them . . . .
— Lars P. Feld and Jean R. Tyran

I do not want you ever to initiate any action for any refunds of taxes without first consulting me and presenting the matter fully to me so that I may judge whether it is an honorable and ethical action to take, not simply legally, but according to my own personal standards.
— Ernest Hemingway

Paying taxes is not a battle aiming at the government's defeat.
— Theodore C. Falk

A tax return is an attested document. It is signed by the taxpayer and the preparer under penalties of perjury. It is not an opening offer.
— Lee A. Sheppard

He [the tax lawyer] is a *citizen* as well as a *tax advisor.*
— Randolph Paul

[A]ny duty the tax bar owes to the tax system is nebulous at best.
— Monte A. Jackel

Tax lawyers spend about a third of their time converting ordinary income into capital gain.
— Walter Blum
(attributed)

As the tax laws get tighter, the tax lawyers get smarter.
— Anonymous

If lawyers were restrained in preparing and filing tax returns on behalf of clients, clients would shop around for lawyers who ignored the restraints.
— Dennis J. Ventry Jr.

[L]awyers of high standing at the bar are advising their clients to utilize devious tax avoidance devices, and they are actively using them themselves.

— Henry E. Morgenthau Jr.

[U]nlike the ordinary tort or contract case, [in tax cases] the other real party in interest is the taxpaying public. If the taxpayer gets off the hook for what he really should be required to pay, the pockets of all have been depleted.

— Theodore Tannenwald Jr.

[T]he [tax] lawyer's passion for technical analysis of the statutory language should always be diluted by distrust of a result that is too good to be true.

— Boris I. Bittker and James S. Eustice

When something sounds too good to be true in the tax law, do it now.

— Philip J. Kavesh

Every day well-trained, well-paid and highly motivated tax professionals have been launching vicious attacks on the tax base and they have had considerable success.

— Calvin H. Johnson

With high taxes, it becomes much more important to save a dollar of taxes than to earn another dollar of income. [High rates] divert attention from production to tax minimization.

— Dan Throop Smith

The tax lawyer need not accept his client's economic and social opinions, but the client is paying for technical attention and undivided concentration upon his affairs. He is equally entitled to performance unfettered by his attorney's economic and social predilections.

— Randolph Paul

A healthy tax base allows the government to collect the same tax at lower rates. A loophole-ridden tax base is the worst of all worlds because it realizes no revenue, but causes economic damage as taxpayers plan around the tax.

— Calvin H. Johnson

Most tax planning adds little or nothing of worth to our society . . . . Tax lawyers perform a legitimate role of interpreting the law, instructing clients in the sometimes bizarre requirements the law imposes to get a given tax treatment, and planning transactions to avoid the occasional warts in the system. It is an honorable profession, and I am a proud member of it. But let's not kid ourselves that most tax planning is productive.

— David A. Weisbach

The less chance you have of successfully defending your income tax return, the greater the chance it will be randomly selected for audit.

— John Peers

It is often not enough for tax advisers to take the current law into account. In many situations, they must also consider their clients' exposure to the risk of change.

— Franklin L. Green

Those who have large estates and watchful lawyers will find ways of minimizing these tax burdens.

— Robert H. Jackson

A tax system of rather high rates gives a multitude of clever individuals in the private sector powerful incentives to game the system. Even the smartest drafters of legislation and regulation cannot be expected to anticipate every device.

— Stephen F. Williams

Antiabuse doctrines are needed . . . because it is impossible for drafters of the tax law to anticipate each and every interaction of the various tax rules. Inevitably, there will be some unforeseen interaction of the tax rules so that, if one arranges one's affairs in just the right manner, magic happens.

— Daniel N. Shaviro and David A. Weisbach

The primary motive behind demands for certainty [in tax laws] is not to assure proper reporting of transactions in the ordinary course of business. The primary motive behind demands for certainty is to know with precision the extent to which the taxpayer can engage in tax-motivating planning — in the vernacular, "How close to the line can I get?"

— Martin J. McMahon Jr.

[W]here the lawyer believes there is a reasonable basis for a position that a particular transaction does not result in taxable income, or that certain expenditures are properly deductible as expenses, the lawyer has no duty to advise that riders be attached to the client's tax return explaining the circumstances surrounding the transactions or the expenditures.

— American Bar Association
Committee on Ethics

Tax evasion often goes hand-in-hand with kick-backs and other crimes motivated by greed.

— Mark Everson

Tax evasion is closely related to money laundering . . . . [T]ax evasion is a natural byproduct of crime, and so criminals are near-automatic tax evaders.

— Martin A. Sullivan

Drug traffickers are also money launderers and tax evaders. It's in their job description. You can't really declare a few million pesos of unexplained income on your tax return and list "drug lord" as your occupation. Besides, the moral threshold that's crossed by falsifying tax returns is nothing for people who regularly bribe police, kidnap judges, and slit the throats of informants.

— Robert Goulder

The difference between tax avoidance and tax evasion is the thickness of a prison wall.

— Denis Healey

You . . . can be a millionaire . . . and never pay taxes! You can be a millionaire . . . and never pay taxes! You say . . . "Steve . . . how can I be a millionaire . . . and never pay taxes?" First . . . get a million dollars. Now . . . you say "Steve . . . what do I say to the tax man when he comes to my door and says, 'You . . . have never paid taxes'?" Two simple words. Two simple words in the English language: "I forgot!" How many times do we let ourselves get into terrible situations because we don't say "I forgot"?

— Steve Martin

If a person is an economic being and figures out the odds, then there is a very high incentive to cheat. That is, of course, putting aside honor, duty and patriotism.

— Jerome Kurtz

Tax avoidance means that you hire a $250,000-fee lawyer, and he changes the word "evasion" into the word "avoidance."

— Franklin D. Roosevelt

[R]elying on the legal and accounting professionals to prescribe appropriate standards of practitioner conduct . . . is an idea whose time has surely passed.

— Michael J. Graetz

Distinguishing tax shelters from real transactions is often a frustrating exercise because tax shelters are usually designed to mimic real transactions. In this respect, tax shelters and real transactions have a relationship analogous to the relationship between money laundering and banking. In both areas, rules designed to curb the abusive activity are a source of complexity in nonabusive cases.

— Peter C. Canellos

Liberals claim to support affirmative action but don't practice it. They support higher taxes but set up complicated tax shelters to avoid paying them. They claim to be ardent environmentalists but abandon their cause when it impinges on their own property rights.

— Peter Schweizer

The argument that "if everyone cheated on their tax returns, we would all suffer," understandably dissuades almost no one from cheating. On the contrary, tax evaders are quite certain that nearly everyone else is cheating, and it is precisely this fact that serves as their justification for doing the same.

— Dennis Prager and Joseph Telushkin

Federal taxation was widely regarded [at Harvard Law School in the 1920s] as a field for accountants rather than for lawyers.

— Erwin N. Griswold

Tax is clearly the quintessential course and the whole law school curriculum should revolve around it.

— Marjorie E. Kornhauser

What advice would I give to a beginning tax professor? I think it would be that the professor should think of teaching some other subject.

— Erwin N. Griswold

This course is *Introduction to Federal Income Taxation*. . . . I hold in my hand what we will explore this semester: *The Internal Revenue Code*. It produces more money than any other law in history, the money necessary to operate the most powerful country that has ever existed on this planet. Simultaneously, it provides economic incentives for a set of favored activities, such as exploring for oil and contributing to religious organizations. It helps people who have lost their jobs, gotten sick or been robbed. It takes more from the rich than from the poor. And it attempts to do all of this without disturbing the free market capitalism that has made this society so successful. In other words, this is the greatest and most ambitious legislation ever enacted!

— Wayne G. Barnett
(paraphrased)

Obviously, we [tax law professors] teach something, but we basically teach a vocabulary, and get people out there so they can learn it on their own. . . . But it's better to know what you don't know than it is to think you know something. If nothing else, I think it's a useful service to scare people. That we easily do. . . . There's an enormous tension between trying to be right, in other words not convey misleading information, and your ability to communicate. Sure I can simplify it to the point where it's comprehensible, but it's also wrong.

— James S. Eustice

The worst aspect of the Internal Revenue Code may be that it channels many very smart students away from productive activities and into tax law, where they are well paid for playing an intellectually challenging game that produces nothing of value to society. Indeed, if given different incentives, some of these very smart students might choose careers that actually help alleviate some of the problems — *e.g.*, poverty, poor education, illness, energy needs — that the Internal Revenue Code deals with so clumsily.

— Jeffery L. Yablon

No child ever grew up wanting to be a tax attorney.

— J. Mark Iwry

[A] tax lawyer is a person who is good with numbers but does not have enough personality to be an accountant.

— James D. Gordon III

Tax lawyers long have been portrayed in the popular culture as something other than normal.

— Paul L. Caron

Those of us in the tax law business know that we are bright, engaging, and athletic; we combine animal magnetism with erudition. However, tax lawyers are lumped with accountants in the public mind, and are burdened with the images of thick spectacles, green eyeshades, cluttered minds, and unlimited capacities for boredom.

— Erik M. Jensen

No one joined a large firm with the goal of becoming a real estate lawyer. There were far more glamorous arenas in which to establish reputations. Litigation was the all-time favorite, and the litigators were still the most revered of all God's lawyers, at least within the firm. A few of the corporate fields attracted top talent — mergers and acquisitions was still hot, securities was an old favorite. My field, antitrust, was highly regarded. Tax law was horribly complex, but its practitioners were greatly admired.

— John Grisham
(*The Street Lawyer*)

[T]here is a great deal of prestige still associated with the practice of . . . tax law.

— Paul J. Sax

Taxation is not the dreary, number-infested subject that many people believe.

— H. David Rosenbloom

Finally, there is even the social notion that tax lawyers are an odd lot. If you don't want to end up being viewed as an oddball, conventional wisdom suggests you may be better off in another area of law.

— Robert W. Wood

People will pay you a lot of money if you pretend to know how the tax code works.

— Adele Valenzuela

My practice is an art . . . . I often deal with the cutting edge of tax law, where guidance is thin and judgment is required. I plan a client's income to minimize taxes and audit risk. I keep up with the latest developments in taxation on a daily basis, which requires hours of reading each week. I had to recruit staff who had or could develop these skills. They are quite rare.

— Jay Starkman

A woman is told by her doctor that she has six months to live. "Is there anything I can do?" she asks.

"Yes, there is," the doctor replies. "You could marry a tax accountant."

"How will that help my illness?" the woman asks.

"Oh, it won't help your illness," says the doctor, "but it will make that six months seem like an eternity!"

— Old Joke

The complexity of the tax law and the opportunities it affords to devise and exploit lucrative special rules and exceptions have spawned armies of tax lawyers, accountants, consultants and lobbyists to serve a select number of affluent individuals and successful businesses. Seldom in the course of human affairs have so few owed so much to so many.

— J. Mark Iwry

Dear Prof. Cox: What I have learned in your course is that federal income tax is extraordinarily complicated; and when I go into business I'll be sure to hire someone who knows what he's doing in this area.

— Unnamed Student at Harvard Business School

Look, we [baseball team owners] play the Star Spangled Banner before every game. You want us to pay income taxes, too?

— Bill Veeck

[T]o a fee-maximizing tax professional, the Internal Revenue Code of 1986, as amended, is merely a platform waiting for energetic entrepreneurs to construct a superstructure of previously unimaginable complexity.

— Boris I. Bittker

Partnerships offer incredible flexibility as building blocks in complex organizations. They can be arranged in tiers and used as substitutes for corporate subsidiaries. Each partnership within an organization requires its own tax return. Multiple partnerships, and thus multiple tax returns, within an organization create the possibility that the details of a given transaction may be distributed across several tax returns. Multiple tax returns within a single economic organization potentially decrease transparency to tax authorities as to the true nature of the economic transactions.

— Charles E. Boynton and Barbara A. Livingston

He [the tax lawyer] must treat his client better than he treats other people.

— Randolph Paul

Just let 'em feel that you can save 'em something on taxes and nobody will keep you out.

— Warren Buffett

It's time we tell the bar associations and the IRS to shove their opinions up their cash cows.

— James Traficant

[T]he worst thing about [the week before tax returns are due] may not be the taxes themselves, but the commiserating rhetoric of the politicians who, having created the present tax system, will spend the next few days deploring it as if it were the handiwork of strangers.

— *The Washington Post*

Congress should know how to levy taxes, and if it doesn't know how to collect them, then a man is a fool to pay the taxes.

— J. Pierpont Morgan

We have a tax code that favors those with the best accountants.

— Shane Keats

[Headline:] Tax Planning May Be Futile

— Albert B. Crenshaw

Nontaxation doesn't help the poor residents of the cash economy. The low tax rate causes employees to migrate to the cash sector; that causes before-tax wages in the sector to fall, and before tax-wages in the noncash sector to rise. At equilibrium, the after-tax return to the employee is the same in either sector.

— Joseph Bankman

[American millionaires] have incredibly low divorce rates. They still clip supermarket coupons, if only to demonstrate the value of thrift to their children. They are far less likely to gamble than other Americans. They shop at price clubs. They spend a significant amount of time with their tax consultants, trying to trim their annual bill.

— David Brooks

Let the tax experts employed by the wealthy work a little harder to figure the proper tax obligation of their clients rather than working hard to enable their clients to avoid their fair burden of tax obligation.

— Walter Reuther

Once he has taken a case, the tax lawyer is obligated to present arguments even though they may contribute to tax avoidance or conflict with his own notions of what the law should be.

— Randolph Paul

Sixty-four percent of women attorneys think that tax lawyers make undesirable dates.

— Daniel Dolan

[It] was like listening to a tax lawyer read the lyrics to a love song. All the words were there, nothing was inaccurate, but all the sizzle was gone.

— Patricia Thomas

[G]enerations of bright people, who could have chosen careers in science, math, engineering or entrepreneurship, were instead lured by lucre into the unproductive but highly paid field of tax law. By now, we have ample proof that a country that pays its most creative lawyers more than its research scientists is a country on the road to ruin.

— Thomas G. Donlan

It seems to me that there must be an ecological limit to the number of paper pushers the earth can sustain, and that human civilization will collapse when the number of, say, tax lawyers exceeds the world's total population of farmers, weavers, fisherpersons, and pediatric nurses.

— Barbara Ehrenreich

Law students who plan to practice in the tax field often take as few advocacy courses as they can get away with. In fact, the persuasive abilities of tax lawyers and tax accountants are probably about the same. Neither group is known for its advocacy skills.

— Joel S. Newman and Michael B. Lang

I always imagined that a client needs at least two tax advisors. One tells him what the law is. The other tells him what he wants the law to be. Then he can choose.

— Terence Floyd Cuff

We think the patenting of tax advice and tax strategies raises a number of difficult policy and practical issues. While the payment of taxes is mandatory, taxpayers are free to arrange their affairs within the bounds of the law in a manner that minimizes their legal liabilities for taxes. We do not believe that it is sound policy to force taxpayers to choose between paying more tax than they are legally obligated to pay and paying royalties to a third party who has patented a tax strategy.

— Tax Section of the New York State
Bar Association

A dog who thinks he is man's best friend is a dog who obviously has never met a tax lawyer.

— Fran Lebowitz

Here's a simple example [of how lawyers can build practices]: An executive at a party asks a fellow guest his profession. When the man says he's a tax lawyer, the executive's eyes involuntarily search the room for more promising conversation. Later he asks another guest, also a tax lawyer, what she does for a living. "I prevent the government from taking my client's money," she replies. The response almost demands the follow-up challenge, "How?" A relationship is born.

— Ed Burke

In contrast with their European counterparts, most American tax lawyers and academics know little about comparative tax law.
— Victor Thuronyi

There are a great many people, I am sorry to say, who go abroad for the very purpose [of avoiding tax], and some of them went abroad during the late [Civil W]ar. They lived in luxury, at the same time at less cost, in a foreign capital; they had none of the voluntary obligations which rest upon citizens, of charity, or contributions, or supporting churches, or anything of that sort, and they escaped taxation.
— George Hoar

It is not in the best interests of any tax practitioner to keep a complicated tax system. We spend too much time interpreting confusing provisions and are often placed in the position of charging our clients so that they can pay more taxes. Often, the person with the more sophisticated adviser will pay more tax on a given transaction than the person who takes a stab at it themselves. This is the exact opposite of what the result should be.
— Ron Hegt

[My law firm] had a rule — at least it seemed to be a rule — that everybody that came had to spend at least a year working on taxes. The general rationale for that rule as far as I could understand it was that taxes were so important to everything that you do, whatever the kind of case you are handling, you have got to know something about the tax consequences of things.
— Charles A. Horsky

When a tax controversy erupts, it is common for clients to blame their tax advisors as well as the IRS for the aggravation they are undergoing; and, if the outcome of the tax controversy is that the taxpayer must write a sizable (as seen by the taxpayer) check to the IRS, it is also common for the client to feel that the tax advisor should somehow share or bear the cost of this disaster.
— Burgess J.W. Raby and William L. Raby

We spent much of the rest of the night in a driving, freezing rain probing the muck and pea soup mud with our bayonets and seeking to dig up and defuse booby-trapped antitank mines . . . . As I spent more time working with landmines and explosives, I learned three important principles:

■ Be careful.

■ Be very careful.

■ Be very, very careful.

I also learned to assume that every weapon is loaded until you check it yourself and prove that it is not. Do not rely on what anyone else tells you. These are not bad principles for practicing tax law today.

— Terence Floyd Cuff

A tax adviser who instills confidence and trust in his or her client or corporate partner becomes highly valued. Indeed, the term guru is generally reserved for two types of individuals — spiritual guides for followers of Eastern religion and tax advisers for adherents of Western capitalism.

— Franklin L. Green

The reality is that most of us practicing tax today have long since compromised our integrity. But if we care about future generations we need to face the fact that tax practice turns our best and brightest into little more than well-paid tax cheats. [I question] whether it is even possible to be a person of integrity and still engage in a lucrative tax practice.

— Paul Streckfus

If a tax system is painted as unfair and immoral, if it is compared to slavery, if its administrators are accused of being abusive, it is only human nature that individuals will be more inclined to evade taxes.

— Martin A. Sullivan

Economic activity [in the late 1970s] was distorted by a witches brew of inflation and high taxes, which meant that speculators and tax lawyers got rich while the rest scrambled.

— Rich Karlgaard

It is seldom given to mortal man to feel superior to a tax lawyer.

— Anthony C. Amsterdam

A good lawyer with a briefcase can steal more than ten men with machine guns.

— Al Capone

[Game Show Host]: You're a genius.
[Contestant]: No, I'm a tax attorney.

— Regis Philbin and Bill MacDonald

The American public enjoys a love/hate relationship with tax laws. On the one hand, tax laws are viewed with some suspicion because they are so technically drafted as to become arcane in their effort at exactitude. On the other hand, the public is wiling to pay a large premium to practitioners who can decipher the arcane and find loopholes.

— Stephen T. Black and Katherine D. Black

[In the aftermath of World War I] this tax business is likely to develop into quite a thing for lawyers.

— Daniel C. Roper

Of course I'm happy. I'm a tax lawyer — money's incredible.

— Alan Bennett
(*The History Boys* screenplay)

The purpose of the attorney-client privilege is expressed almost universally as promoting *compliance* with the law. Yet . . . [t]he larger social interest in facilitating compliance with law in a wide array of disciplines is not so clearly present when it comes to tax. Indeed it is rather difficult to articulate what may be the social interest in tax minimization . . . . While we may despair of the prospect of true tax simplification in our lifetimes, there are meaningful steps that can be taken in that direction. Elimination of the attorney-client privilege in all but criminal tax matters would be one such step.

— Bruce Kayle

With respect to tax advice, the same common law protections of confidentiality which apply to a communication between a taxpayer and an attorney shall also apply to a communication between a taxpayer and any federally authorized tax practitioner to the extent the communication would be considered a privileged communication if it were between a taxpayer and an attorney.

— *Internal Revenue Code*

Tax law is a funny thing. I think it fair to say that most CPAs know something about the federal income tax; many if not most lawyers do not.

— Bernard Wolfman

They rock, they roll, they audit, they do taxes, and they'll even play your next party, business function, wedding, bar mitzvah or IRS audit.

— Website of "The Accounting Crows," a rock band

We have always been fascinated with the mysteries of the tax code and with the people who struggle so mightily to plumb its depths.

— Joel and Ethan Coen

[The accused] doesn't fit the stereotype of a tax lawyer, colleagues say, in part because of his youthful demeanor and affability.

— *The Wall Street Journal*

Who will protect the integrity of the tax law if the tax lawyers won't?

— Christopher Bergin

Then our new CEO backed up a moving van to the building and robbed us. At first we thought he was breaking the law, but he had a written opinion from his tax lawyer saying it was probably okay.

— Scott Adams
("Dilbert")

The First Rule of Practicing Tax Law: If someone has to go to jail, make sure it's the client.

— Fred Drasner

The tax lawyer assists clients solely with their selfish monetary concerns. He helps them in their unchristian endeavor to shift their tax burden to their neighbors. He deprives the government of revenue needed for the common good.
— Frederic G. Corneel

The tax bar is commonly referred to as a "special priesthood," and it is only slightly more tolerant than the Catholic Church in ordaining women tax priests.
— Paul L. Caron

I think there is something desperately wrong with the system when there is only a small subset of people who understand how it works.
— Todd McCracken

There are few greater stimuli to human ingenuity than the prospect of avoiding fiscal liability. Experience shows that under this stimulus human ingenuity outreaches Parliamentary prescience.
— Lord Justice Diplock

If states and localities attempt in a serious way to tax the rich and give to the poor, the rich will depart while the poor will be attracted.
— Paul E. Peterson and Daniel Nadler

If capital can move freely across borders, it will tend to leave high-tax countries to go to low-tax countries.
— Eric Engen and Kevin A. Hassett

Higher tax rates on capital income reduce the incentive to save and invest, which in turn reduces investment and ultimately the capital stock. Capital can easily escape taxation by going abroad, and when that happens, the burden of capital income taxation falls on domestic workers in the form of higher unemployment and lower wages.
— Thomas F. Cooley and Lee E. Ohanian

[T]axes increase smuggling. Whether it's cigarettes or corporate profits, stuff that moves easily over borders is hard to tax.
— Martin A. Sullivan

Like many Americans, I face a patriotic dilemma: how much cheating can I get away with? It's important to pay your taxes but it's just as important to pay as little tax as possible. Think of it as putting big government on a diet.

— Stephen Colbert

They [*i.e.*, welfare cheaters] are no more evil than industrialists using high-powered accountants to avoid taxes.

— Prince Philip,
Duke of Edinburgh

[W]hile I hate all forms of cheating, in my Inferno, tax evaders occupy a circle of their own. I see them not only as backsliders on their own civic responsibility but as stealing from their fellow citizens: The more successfully they escape what they owe, the more the rest of us have to pay. I take great satisfaction, therefore, in the fact that during my tenure as U.S. Attorney for the district of Massachusetts, every tax evader we prosecuted was convicted, and all of them went to jail.

— Elliot L. Richardson

[Making tax evasion a felony] destroys all proportion of punishment, and puts murders upon equal footing with such as are really guilty of no natural, but merely a positive offense.

— William Blackstone

It is sinful to deceive the government regarding taxes and duties.

— *Talmud*

Make sure you pay your taxes; otherwise you can get in a lot of trouble.

— Richard M. Nixon

I've never seen penalties be a deterrent factor in any action taken by a taxpayer.

— N. Jerold Cohen

[P]eople who profess to have high levels of trust in government to do the right thing are significantly less likely to engage in tax noncompliance.

— Joel Slemrod

The only purpose of the [taxpayer] was to escape taxation . . . . The fact that it desired to evade the law, as it is called, is immaterial, because the very meaning of a line in the law is that you may intentionally go as close to it as you can if you do not pass it.

— Oliver Wendell Holmes Jr.

In the interpretation of statutes levying taxes it is the established rule not to . . . enlarge their operations so as to embrace matters not specifically pointed out. In case of doubt they are construed most strongly against the government, and in favor of the citizen.

— James C. McReynolds

We have been mindful that for some businesses there is little, if any, meaningful difference between an improvement in financial performance achieved by cutting operating expenses and one that results from reducing taxes. Both reductions improve the financial statement. The tax law, however, requires that the intended transactions have economic substance separate and distinct from economic benefit achieved solely by tax reduction.

— David Laro

If you cheat [on your corporate taxes], your employees will notice that, and they'll cheat you.

— Anonymous Corporate Executive

Many wealthy people spend substantial time, effort and money to reduce their taxes via aggressive or even illegal means — and then turn around and give the tax savings and more to charity. While some of this seemingly inconsistent behavior is motivated by a desire for the social approval that large charitable contributions often generate, some of it is a function of the fact that, for the wealthy, avoiding taxes is instinctive.

— Jeffery L. Yablon

A number of business owners told us that they or others limited evasion to cash received out of the presence of employees. One business owner told us that when employees were present, he made it a point to immediately enter the payment on the books. Ironically, the anecdotal evidence we received suggests that the biggest fear was not that employees would report them to the government — it was that when employees saw their employer cheat the government they would cheat their employer. Evasion was bad ... because it set a poor moral tone for employees.

— Joseph Bankman

Here's a rule for stock pickers. If the company bilks investors and fools the analysts, it's a sell. If it bilks and fools Uncle Sam, it's a hold or a buy.

— John Rothchild

Higher taxes discourage the "animal spirits" of entrepreneurship. When tax rates are raised, taxpayers are encouraged to shift, hide and underreport income. Taxpayers divert their effort from pro-growth productive investments to seeking tax shelters, tax havens and tax exempt investments. This behavior tends to dampen economic growth and job creation.

— W. Kurt Hauser

A business is nothing more than a conduit for passing along costs to its customers. Taxes are a cost, so tax avoidance is part and parcel of competition to bring consumers better stuff at lower cost.

— Holman W. Jenkins Jr.

Cheating on federal and state income tax is all pervasive in all classes of society; except among the compulsively honest, cheating usually occurs in direct proportion to opportunity.

— Richard Neely

Why is it that few Americans would steal from a local charity, yet a high percentage of taxpayers who have a choice about paying taxes appear to have no compunctions about cheating their fellow citizens?

— Nina E. Olson

Peter Ueberroth, while serving as commissioner of baseball, hired a former IRS agent to give talks to the players on the taxability of autograph income. Apparently, it didn't help enough. Some players walked out on shows if they saw receipts and tax forms. Many others signed only for cash.

— Joel S. Newman

Just because you have a briefcase full of cash doesn't mean that you're out to cheat the government.

— Pete Rose

This year, there are some major changes that you, as a taxpayer, should be aware of, unless — to quote [the Internal Revenue Service Commissioner's] annual Message To Taxpayers — "you wish to become roommates with a federal-prison inmate who weighs 400 pounds and likes to dress you up as Tinkerbell."

— Dave Barry

We still have too many cases of what I might call *moral fraud*, that is, the defeat of taxes through doubtful legal devices which have no real business utility, and to which a downright honest man would not resort to reduce his taxes.

— Henry E. Morgenthau Jr.

Art museums do better [at raising money than animal charities]. And that's not charity. That's tax evasion.

— Gary Michelson

Tax evasion is not a form of conserving investment capital but a brazen abandonment of responsibility to the country.

— Bill Moyers

The world is changing, and standards and mores are changing. Society is coalescing around this idea that hiding your assets from governments to avoid tax is not a good thing.

— Bryan C. Skarlatos

If taxpayers see everyone else getting away with murder, they will ask themselves if they want to be a chump or a cheat.

— Gregory F. Jenner

It is often noted that small businesses are disproportionately large generators of new jobs. Less often, however, is it noted that small businesses are disproportionately large generators of tax fraud.

— Jeffery L. Yablon

In sum, the accepted view is that the taxpayer, or the preparer, may sign a return as "correct" if he believes there is a reasonable possibility the return is not incorrect.

— Frederic G. Corneel

Congress did not intend that a person, by reason of a bona fide misunderstanding as to his liability for the tax, as to his duty to make a return, or as to the adequacy of the records he maintained, should become a criminal by his mere failure to measure up to the prescribed standard of conduct.

— Owen J. Roberts

There is hardly an American citizen above the poverty level whose tax conscience is so completely clear that he isn't scared of being audited.

— "Diogenes"
(nom de plume of an IRS agent)

Lie detector operators in North America often ask subjects if they cheat on their taxes. The reaction to this question is usually intense, which gives the polygraph operator an insight into the emotional responses of the subject. Since most people have cheated on their taxes, a negative answer gives the operator an indication of how the subject reacts when lying. European polygraph operators would not use this question because tax evasion is not a crime in many European countries, and even where it is, people do not consider it a moral wrong.

— Charles Adams

The greatest scourge of mankind, the detestable race of tax informers, must be stopped. We must stifle it in its first efforts and tear out the pernicious tongue of envy. Let not the judges receive . . . information of the informer; let them be given up to punishment as soon as any of them appear.

— Constantine

Individuals who resist taxation on grounds of principle always regard themselves as embattled men under threat, taking a great stand of right against wrong.

— William Brittain-Catlin

One information-reporting requirement added in 1986 required people to include on their tax returns Social Security numbers of all dependents over age two. This caused seven million dependents to disappear from the tax rolls.

— Michael J. Graetz

The tax code makes tax avoidance (which is perfectly legal and proper) easy; and tax evasion (which is a felony), tempting. After all, if the best place to hide a book is in a library, the best place to hide a tax dodge (legal, illegal, or somewhere in between) is in the depths of a tax return the size of one or more phone books.

— John Steele Gordon

Only little people pay taxes.

— Leona Helmsley
(attributed)

Of all the taxes I've paid, 90% of them were after I was 70.

— T. Boone Pickens

In religion as in taxation, the authorities' efforts to enforce compliance have historically been aided by the widely held belief in the severity of the ultimate consequences (hell or audit, as the case may be) but hampered by widely held doubts concerning their probability.

— J. Mark Iwry

For many, tax law is like the Ten Commandments. They pick eight out of the ten rules to follow, decide that they are doing a really commendable job, and just forget about the rest.

— Terence Floyd Cuff

[The tax evader is] in every respect, an excellent citizen, had not the laws of this country made a crime which nature never meant to be so.

— Adam Smith

To the extent that some people are dishonest or careless in their dealings with the government, the majority is forced to carry a heavier tax burden.

— John F. Kennedy

If we can't make sure that everyone pays their fair share, then honest taxpayers get stuck making up the difference.

— Paul H. O'Neill

Familiar bromides such as "taxpayers who cheat raise the burden on the rest of us" or "cheating on taxes is no different than any other form of theft" are either incorrect or don't match our considered moral intuition.

— Joseph Bankman

Everything today is taxes . . . . What better seat on the grandstand of life can I offer you than that of tax counsel . . . . Who is the figure behind every great man, the individual who knows his ultimate secrets? A father confessor? Hell no, the tax expert.

— Louis Auchincloss
(*The Partners*)

We feel the necessity of enjoying ourselves and so we must attempt to do so while we wear this hairshirt. If we go to the opera, it is not for enjoyment, but to be improved. If we visit European cities, it is to be cultured, not to enjoy ourselves . . . . Everything else we do is because it is tax deductible.

— Zero Mostel

In short, it is the ethic of the profession that: The tax practitioner does not regard it as his duty to recommend full and fair disclosure of the facts as to items questionable in law.

— Jerome Hellerstein

At present, a troubling fraction of the finest minds graduating each year devote their talents to financial engineering that changes the timing or characterization of business transaction for tax purposes. What a waste. Let's move to a tax based on real economic activity and channel these minds to a greater social purpose.

— Douglas Holtz-Eakin

[A] society which turns so many of its best and brightest into tax lawyers may be doing something wrong.

— Hoffman F. Fuller

What the low tax rate on capital gains does is spur a huge amount of unproductive tax sheltering. Wealthy individuals invest enormous sums in schemes to convert ordinary income into capital gains, often making investments that would make no sense absent the tax savings. Capital is drawn away from productive investments, hurting the economy. Similarly, the highly talented people who dream up tax shelters could, in a better world, do productive work.

— Leonard E. Burman

It would be sounder taxation policy generally not to recognize either capital gain or capital loss for purposes of income.

— Andrew Mellon

It's a game. We [tax lawyers] teach the rich how to play it so they can stay rich — and the IRS keeps changing the rules so we can keep getting rich teaching them.

— John Grisham
(*The Firm*)

The problem with practicing tax law is that the general rule never seems to apply to anything.

— Brian Blum

Trying to control tax shelters is like stepping on Jell-O. It just squeezes out between your toes and the mess is worse than when you began.

— Anonymous Congressional Staff Member

[Without related-party rules, a taxpayer could] reduce his income tax by transferring his money from one pocket to another even though he uses different trousers. A man with a half-dozen pockets might almost escape liability altogether.

— John Marvin Jones

The tax bar is the repository of the greatest ingenuity in America, and given the chance, those people will do you in.

— Martin D. Ginsburg

So long as we have tax statutes, we will have keen-eyed lawyers and accountants seeking to circumvent them.

— Ferdinand Pecora

Attorneys and accountants should be pillars of our system of taxation, not the architects of circumvention.

— Mark W. Everson

Although new and clever techniques of getting around the tax rules in a legal manner will always be created, the system has evolved to the point that now only experienced tax professionals can play the game. Tax law is now like physics, in that it is no longer the case that smart amateurs can come up with good ideas.

— Jeffery L. Yablon

Every invasion of the plain rights of the citizen has a lawyer behind it. If all lawyers were hanged tomorrow, and their bones sold to a mah jong factory, we'd all be freer and safer, and our taxes would be reduced by almost a half.

— H.L. Mencken

If higher taxes make it more expensive to raise children, people will think more about having another child.

— Nicholas Eberstadt

From a tax point of view you're better off raising horses or cattle than children.

— Patricia R. Schroeder

The taxing act does not require the taxpayer to be an incorrigible optimist [with respect to worthless investments].

— Harlan F. Stone

The way we currently tax capital encourages uneconomical behavior. To the extent that businesses pay tax on income when it is earned, taxing the appreciation and distributions on the intangible assets held by investors (e.g., stock) represents double taxation. To the extent that we insist on imposing this double tax, we should not be surprised that investors enter into contorted financial transactions to lower the after-tax rate of return on their investments.

— Sheldon D. Pollack

[As Justice Potter Stewart said about pornography:] I can't define tax evasion, but I know it when I see it.

— Fred T. Goldberg Jr.

So what can you do to reduce your tax burden? The best way is to keep accurate financial records and thoroughly familiarize yourself with the applicable tax laws, so you can avail yourself of every legal advantage. Like you would ever do *that*. This leaves you with Option B: cheating.

— Dave Barry

Certain acts of tax escaping are clearly evasion; others are clearly avoidance; between the two is a twilight zone in which it is extremely difficult to determine whether a given act falls on one side of the line or the other.

— *National Income Tax* Magazine

The many small stockholders cannot afford professional counsel or evasion devices.

— Robert H. Jackson

The young century wore a merry, untaxed look. People could get rich without cheating the government.

— Ben Hecht

Let's face it, there is no discernable business reason to try to locate a transaction in a place like the Cayman Islands . . . nothing that purports to be resident in the Caymans is managed and controlled there, even if the principals do occasionally visit to conduct scripted board meetings.

— Lee A. Sheppard

Tax solutions that pass muster in New York are no longer adequate; they must also work in New Delhi and Beijing.

— Robert Goulder

If companies and individuals were required to completely relocate to tax havens, or if shipping companies had to relocate to flag of convenience states, then interest in taking advantage of tax havens or flags of convenience would have remained relatively insignificant . . . . What lawyers call "international tax planning" comes down to a plethora of accounting strategies aiming at exploiting legal loopholes that allow individuals and companies to shift residence without actually moving.

— Ronen Palan

Why shouldn't the American people take half my money from me? I took all of it from them.

— Edward A. Filene

The net worth method, it seems, has evolved from the final volley to the first shot in the Government's battle for revenue.

— Tom C. Clark

Today is the first day of the rest of your taxable year.

— Jeffery L. Yablon

I'm against an income tax because all the rich people hire lawyers and accountants to be sure that they don't pay income tax.

— Ann Richards

Business may pass on taxes.

— Stanley F. Reed

True, of course, it is that in a system of taxation so intricate and cast as ours there are many other loopholes unsuspected by the framers of the statute, many other devices whereby burdens can be lowered.

— Benjamin N. Cardozo

[Taxes cannot be escaped] by anticipatory arrangements and contracts however skillfully devised . . . by which the fruits are attributed to a different tree from that on which they grew.

— Oliver Wendell Holmes Jr.

Tax law . . . requires that the intended transactions have economic substance separate and distinct from economic benefit achieved solely by tax reduction.

— David Laro

Needless tax complexity promotes chaos and confusion and gives the taxpayer a ready excuse for inattention to detail merging toward outright noncompliance.

— Gene Steuerle

The fact that the incidences of income taxation may have been taken into account by arranging matters one way rather than another, so long as the way chosen was the way the law allows, does not make a transaction something else than it truly is.

— Felix Frankfurter

Delinquent taxpayers as a class are a poor credit risk; tax default, unless an incident of legitimate tax litigation, is, to the eye sensitive to credit indications, a signal of distress.

— Robert H. Jackson

An economy breathes through its tax loopholes.

— Barry Bracewell-Milnes

I know all those people [*i.e.,* tax evaders]. I have friendly, social, and criminal relations with the whole lot of them.

— Mark Twain

It's a victimless crime, like tax evasion or public indecency.

— Scene from *Will & Grace* television series

Tax evaders under-report the earnings of their legal enterprises, thereby paying less tax than they legally should. Criminals, by contrast, over-report the earnings of any legal enterprises they use for cover, therefore paying more tax than their legitimate front companies would normally be required.

— United Nations Report

That a great reluctance to pay taxes existed in all the colonies, there can be no doubt. It was one of the marked characteristics of the American People long after their separation from England.

— G.S. Callender

From colonial times to the present, the struggle for freedom in the United States has been intertwined with protests against taxation.

— Marjorie E. Kornhauser

The Inland Revenue is not slow — and quite rightly — to take every advantage which is open to it under the taxing statutes for the purpose of depleting the taxpayer's pocket.

— Lord Clyde

If you don't drink, smoke, or drive a car, you're a tax evader.

— Thomas S. Foley

A rate of interest on tax delinquencies which is low in comparison to the taxpayer's borrowing rate — if he can borrow at all — is a temptation to use the state as a convenient, if involuntary, banker by the simple practice of deferring the payment of taxes.

— Robert H. Jackson

An Englishman's home is his tax haven.

— *The Economist* Magazine

There can be no taxation without misrepresentation.

— J.B. Handelsman

[W]hile a taxpayer is free to organize his affairs as he chooses, nevertheless, once having done so, he must accept the tax consequences of his choice, whether contemplated or not, . . . and may not enjoy the benefit of some other route he might have chosen to follow but did not.

— Harry Blackmun

When . . . a taxpayer is presented with what would appear to be a fabulous opportunity to avoid tax obligations, he should recognize that he proceeds at his own peril.

— Morton I. Greenberg

Tax scams are cyclical in nature. An abusive strategy that is discovered and then prohibited by a change in the law will eventually resurface after a few years in a slightly modified form.

— Jay D. Adkisson

It scarcely lies in the mouth of the taxpayer who plays with fire to complain of burnt fingers.

— Lord Greene

The avoidance of tax may be lawful, but it is not yet a virtue.

— Lord Denning

If at first you don't succeed, take the tax loss.

— Kirk Kirkpatrick

ABOUT TAX ANALYSTS

Founded in 1970 as a nonprofit organization to foster free, open, and informed debate about taxation, Tax Analysts is a leading provider of tax news and analysis for the global community.

More than 150,000 tax professionals in law and accounting firms, corporations, and government agencies rely on Tax Analysts' in-depth federal, state, and international content each day.

Tax Analysts has the industry's largest tax-dedicated correspondent staff, with more than 250 domestic and international correspondents.